The Dynamics of Dispute
*The Makings of Machlokess
in Talmudic Times*

By the same author:

Maimonides' Introduction to the Talmud

The Dynamics of Dispute

The Makings of Machlokess in Talmudic Times

by

Zvi Lampel

JUDAICA PRESS, INC.
New York

Library of Congress Cataloging-in-Publication Data

Lampel, Zvi L.
    The dynamics of dispute : the makings of machlokess in Talmudic
times / by Zvi Lampel.
      p. cm.
    Includes bibliographical references and index.
    ISBN 0-910818-96-7 -- ISBN 0-910818-99-1 (pbk.)
    1. Talmud--Hermeneutics. 2. Jewish law--Interpretation and
construction. I. Title II. Title: Machlokess in Talmudic times.
BM503.7.L36 1992
296.1'27406--dc20   90-64381
                                          CIP

For additional information write:
THE JUDAICA PRESS, INC.
123 Ditmas Avenue
Brooklyn, New York 11218

Manufactured in the United States of America

In honor of
my parents
Benjamin and Shirley Lampel
and
my wife's parents
Zoltan and Eva Wieder

RABBI REUVEN FEINSTEIN

ר"מ תפארת ירושלים ד'סטאטען אילאנד

500C GRAND STREET
NEW YORK. N.Y. 10002

(212) 777-7935

Letter of *haskamah* from Rabbi Reuven Feinstein, *rosh hayeshivah* of the Yeshiva of Staten Island.

Contents

דוד קאהן

ביחמ"ד גבול יעבץ
ברוקלין, נוא יארק

בס"ד

כה/ב הכ"ר המאור הגדול ר' בצלאל שי'

ראיתי חבורו על מ... בי"מ ה...
שנתכוונו להוציא לאור וראיתי בה ספר מלוקט
טכתוב כדרך הכתיבה.

קראתי כמה קטעים ... וראיתי איך
שמאריך ומרחיב בעניין ... ...
... ...
...
... ...
...

וכל טוב מני ... קאהן

תכב"ץ ויקר
בג"ג קאהן
יוסף אשר ...

Letter of *haskamah* from Rabbi David Cohen, Congregation
Gvul Yaabetz, Brooklyn, New York.

The Word "Machlokess"

The Hebrew word מַחְלוֹקֶת defies translation. The translation *a difference of opinions* lends an aura of flippancy to the opinions of the Sages involved and detracts from the word's true meaning, one which denotes variant conclusions reached only after intense and thorough research by each side. *Dispute*—a translation we have unhappily resorted to in our title—carries with it connotations of hostility between the Sages which did not exist. Even to call a *machlokess* a *legal dispute*, though it may bring across the sober thought processes and gravity of issues intended, fails to elicit from the Western mind the לשם שמים, the sincere, lofty, indeed holy, nature of the intentions of the Sages in their research and analysis. Torah disputes, *machlokos*, are the result of intense and sincere attempts to fathom the word of G-d, with the strong desire to follow His Will. Nevertheless, for lack of a better term, we are forced in this book to translate *machlokess* as a dispute, disagreement, or the contesting of another's opinions.

Acknowledgments

Novice that I was back in 1971, I wrote the acknowledgments for *Maimonides' Introduction to the Talmud* when the manuscript was ready for the typesetter. I did not realize that the several stages between manuscript and publication (in 1975) would involve still more people to whom I would owe thanks. I would like to take this opportunity to rectify the incurred debts.

Perry Rabinowitz, of Perry Typesetters, introduced me to the world of matrices ("not the kind you sleep on"), galleys, proofs, and linotype, a world designed to give way to computers and cold type.

Jack Goldman, of Judaica Press, rescued my work from financial oblivion, and kept it alive despite problematic circumstances. Avery Gross was kind enough to be an attorney for the contract composition and signing.

I am happy to be able to thank in print my wife, Blima, for years of marital bliss. Her idealism and devotion have enabled me to devote my time to Torah, and inspired me to continue. May Hashem be ממלא משאלות לבנו לטובה, אמן.

The second revised edition of *Introduction* benefited from the editorship of Neva Goldstein Alpern and the skillful typesetting of Simcha Graphic Associates.

This work, which includes explanations of many talmudic passages, required the careful scrutiny of *beki'im b'Shas* whose expertise saved the author from several embarassing mistakes. These experts were Rabbis A. J. Rosenberg (who was responsible for the publisher's acceptance of the original manuscript), Moshe Friedman, Menachem Mendel Goldman, and Meir Goldstein. Equally important was the superb editing of Reva Goldman and Zvi Shapiro, whose questions, observations, and stylistic improvements greatly enhanced the final form of this work. Avrohom B. Walzer of Simcha Graphic Associates guided me through the world of word processing, truly helpful for those who experiment with words, and Rachel Witty oversaw the completion of the work in its final stages.

To Rav Shimon Schwab, *shlita,* and Rabbi Joseph Elias, *shlita,* I express my profound thanks for carefully reading the manuscript and offering valuable suggestions. Most importantly, I thank my parents, Barry and Shirley Lampel, my in-laws, Zoltan and Eva Wieder, and my dear wife Blima, for their support, which made this project possible.

The preparation of this work has been accompanied by major episodes in my life, including my first five years of marriage while a member of the *kollel* of Yeshiva Zichron Mayir of Mountaindale, as a student of Rav Yehuda Davis, *shlita;* the fire that struck my home but that did not destroy this manuscript nor any of my precious possessions; my first five years as a member of the *kollel* of the Yeshiva of Staten Island headed by Rav Reuven Feinstein, *shlita;* and the birth of our precious Chana Fayga, may she grow to emulate her mother, Blima, *shetichyeh* who continues to provide my life with more bliss than can be expressed. For her, and our parents, I offer my thanks to *Hashem Yisborach, Hatov V'hamaytiv.*

Preface

This book builds upon basic information treated quite well in other works.[1] This information includes the nature of the Oral and Written Law, their origins from Sinai, and the general limits and allowances the talmudic Sages were granted in interpreting Biblical Laws and legislating their own. Nevertheless, a brief outline of the basics follows.

1. The *Five Books of Moses* were dictated by G-d to Moses,[2] who wrote them on parchment. The communication was not a private or secret process. G-d made it clear to the entire Jewish nation that Moses was appointed to receive and report G-d's commands and that G-d held him to be reliable in this matter. They themselves, a nation more than 2,000,000 strong, heard G-d speak to Moses and relate to him part of the Torah to be written. It was at their own request that the continuation of that awesome communication was conducted with Moses acting as an intermediary. This historic occurrence is unique in the annals of mankind. No other people, as a group, ever claimed to have witnessed, or reported a tradition of, such

---

[1] Some good books on the fundamentals are *Maimonides' Introduction to the Talmud*, translated by this author (Judaica Press, NY, 1975, 1987), and H. Schimmel's *The Oral Law* (Feldheim 1971, 1978). Rabbi Avigdor Miller's *Rejoice, O Youth!* gives an excellent explanation of these concepts, too.

Books in Hebrew—other than the *Introduction to the Talmud*—which could serve as an introduction to this book, include the works of Rav Zvi Hirsch Hayyos published in כל ספרי מהר"ץ חיות and מעוז הדעת by Rav Yehoshua Heller. But insofar as the particular subject of disputes in the Talmud is concerned, this book treats it more exhaustively than any other I know of.

[2] The Revelation at Mount Sinai took place in the year 2448 from Creation (1212 Before the Common Era).

a public revelation by G-d. The reason is simple: It is impossible to fabricate such a story.

2. G-d purposely omitted many practical details of Torah law observance from Scripture, choosing instead to include them in the Oral Law. It is impossible to observe the Scripture's 613 laws without this *Oral Law.*

3. Though these details and clarifications were not *explicitly* written in the Torah, G-d did plant hints to them, or better, He "encoded" the data, in the text. The Sages were therefore able to find allusions to these clarifications by utilizing special rules of interpretation, which were also given to Moses. But because in many cases Moses did not specify exactly what letter, word or phrase hinted to what clarification, there was room for disagreement in identifying a given clarifications's "clue" in the Written Torah. The law itself, though, remained uncontested.[3] (This idea will be developed further in this book, בע"ה.) This system of interpretation is called דרש, *drash*, hermeneutic methodology. The interpretations it produces are called דרשות, *drashos*, hermeneutic interpretations.

4. Some laws were known to have been provided no Scriptural hints at all. These are called *Halachos L'Moshe MiSinai, Laws Given to Moses (by G-d) at Sinai.* Sometimes, the Talmud says that one or another *Halacha L'Moshe MiSinai* can be "connected" to a Scriptural verse, but this is not meant literally. In such a case, the verse is called a mere *"asmachta,"* a memory aid.

5. In every generation, the Great Sanhedrin[4] decided how the laws applied to new situations. Its Sages drew comparisons between the cases at hand and those in the Torah as described by the Oral Law. The decisions of the Great

---

[3] The stringency of a rabbinical prohibition, however, can be affected by whether it is associated with a Scriptural verse, as in *Shabbos* 34a, *Rashi* ד"ה בעירובי תחומין. Probably, the Sages searched for a forgotten *asmachta* since this rabbinical decree had a history of stringency, indicating that originally there must have been some *asmachta* that helped generate this law in the first place.

[4] *Sanhedrin* is the Greek counterpart for the Hebrew word *zekaynim*, elders or Sages. This body of seventy-one Sages is referred to throughout all the records of Jewish history, beginning with *Exodus* (24:1).

Sanhedrin became mandatory upon all Jewry, by Biblical decree.

6. The Sages also actually extracted details of laws from Scripture by applying the rules of interpretation mentioned above. In such cases, they did not know the law until they "decoded" Scripture.

7. The Sages reached differing conclusions only when the issue depended upon their analysis, as in #3, 5, and 6, above. They never argued against statements they knew came from G-d. Once it would be established that a certain explanation originated with G-d (through Moses), it was immediately adopted by all.

8. The Torah also gave the Sages the responsibility of legislating rules and additional prohibitions to prevent encroachments upon actual Biblical prohibitions. The Torah commands us to obey all the precautionary measures approved by the vote of the Great Sanhedrin. Until such a vote was taken, each district's Sage enacted those decrees which he saw as necessary.

Perspective

The Tablets were six tefachim wide. When G-d gave them to Moses, His grip remained on two tefachim, Moses held two tefachim, and two tefachim remained between them.

Sh'mos Rabbah 47:6

The original plan for this book called for altogether avoiding the theological matters contained in this Perspective. The book was to begin where this discussion ends. For the question addressed by this work is not, "Why did Hashem allow talmudic disputes to develop?" nor, "How can the Sages' opposing opinions all be manifestations of 'The Words of the Living G-d'?" This book was written to answer different, more mundane questions: *How, historically speaking, did the Sages find themselves without unanimously accepted clear and definite answers to some halachic issues; what processes did they use to discover these answers; and why did these processes lead to different conclusions?*

The first break with this plan occurred when it was realized that the reader would be familiar with the expression "These and Those are the Words of the Living G-d," and might use it to contest some of the work's assertions. This necessitated a chapter that reviews, one-by-one, the explanations given to this adage by the major commentaries. This additional chapter was to be appended to the end of the book and the work was to remain at that. However, I then was privileged to a personal meeting with Rav Simon Schwab,[1] *shlita*, who, after reading my manuscript, insisted that the very issue I

---

[1] Rav Simon Schwab is rav of K'Hal Adath Jeshurun in the Washington Heights section of New York City.

1

wished to avoid is a crucial one, and that my book's topic necessarily
evokes questions that must be addressed in a preliminary chapter.
Thus the following presentation of the Rav's teaching.[2]

* * *

We shall explain that the question "How can the Sages' variant
opinions all parallel absolute truth" is groundless, because it is based
upon a false assumption that there is an abstract, Absolute Truth,
independent of G-d's will, to which even He is beholden. This is
false, because the only "Absolute Truth" is G-d Himself, and outside of Him truth is nonexistent. Since there is no abstract Truth to
which G-d is bound, when He decrees that any conclusion drawn by
a Torah-mind (when following His clearly defined limits)[3] is truth—
it is truth.

At Creation, G-d's Will determined what is truth and nontruth,
morality and immorality, good and evil. Moreover, His Will determined the very fact that good and evil, morality and immorality, our
perception of truth and our perception of falsehood, would be pairs
of intrinsically opposite concepts; and His Will could have determined otherwise. In our minds, because of the limits G-d set for the
universe and for man, it is inescapable that a given fact at a given
time or circumstance must be either true or untrue, for only one
thing can exist in the same place and time; but G-d's "mind" and
nature is independent of boundaries of time, space, and causality. He
encompasses all and yet is apart from all, He is at once totally merciful, yet totally just. He grants us free-will, yet has foreknowledge of
our actions. These concepts are paradoxical to our minds only
because of the limited nature of the universe within which we were
created and the boundaries of "reality" imposed upon our thinking
processes. "Better for one not to have come into this world, than for

[2] After the meeting with Rav Schwab, at which the author was presented with
notes, the author composed this chapter. It was carefully read by Rav Schwab, and
considerable time was devoted to correcting and fine-tuning the author's understanding, and the present form is the result. The author expresses his profound
gratitude to Rav Schwab for his attention, time, and fascinating insights, and for
granting permission to use his prestigious name.
[3] These limits, such as the rules of Scriptural interpretation and the concept of Sof
Hora'a, the closing of the Talmud, and others, will be discussed in the course of this
work.

him to direct his mind towards that which is Above and Below, of Before Creation and at the End" (Ḥaggiga 2:1).[4]

* * *

Even after the creation of our world, while it was still solidifying, its contents and concepts were in an amorphous state devoid of logic and sense, a state of *tohu va'vohu*, one that could evoke in the human mind only perplexity and astonishment (cf. *Rashi, B'rayshis* 1:2). An incredulous, baffling, incomprehensible darkness of definitionless, lawless nature hovered over the mysterious depths—until G-d willed that Light and Darkness exist, and exist as opposites. And even then, a crucial issue of reality hung in abeyance: Which was to be considered "Good"—righteous actions of kindness and truth, or dark acts of murder and falseness? *B'rayshis Rabbah* 2:5 refers to G-d's decision:

רבי אבהו אמר מתחילת ברייתו של עולם צפה הקב"ה במעשיהם של צדיקים ומעשיהם של רשעים . . . והארץ היתה תהו ובהו—אלו מעשיהם של רשעים. ויאמר אלקים יהי אור—אלו מעשיהם של צדיקים. אבל איני יודע באיזה מהם חפץ—אם במעשה אלו ואם במעשה אלו. כיון דכתיב וירא אלקים את האור כי טוב—הוי במעשיהן של צדיקים חפץ, ואינו חפץ במעשיהן של רשעים.

Said Rebbi Avahu: At the beginning of the world's creation, The Holy-One Blessed-be-He gazed at the deeds of the righteous and at the deeds of the wicked. . . . "The world was *tohu va'vohu*" (*B'rayshis* 1:2) refers to the deeds of the wicked. "And G-d said, Let there be Light" (*B'rayshis* 1:3) refers to the deeds of the righteous. But I [still] would not know which of them He desires—the deeds of these or the deeds of those. However, once Scripture writes, "And G-d saw the Light that it was Good" (*B'rayshis* 1:4), [we see that] it is the deeds of the righteous that He desires, and that He does not desire the deeds of the wicked.

And so Nature and Morality and Sense were created, and their bylaws, contained in the Torah and its *halachos*, were defined for Man. Good and Evil, Pure and Impure,[5] Kosher and Non-Kosher,

---

[4] We find mind-boggling even the concepts of black holes leading to parallel, inverse universes, which physicists are beginning to explore, although these concepts are conceivably within G-d's present creation, not realms necessarily beyond our conception.

[5] Said Rabban Yoḥonon ben Zakkai, "By your lives! Dead bodies do not [intrinsically] confer *tum'ah*, impurity; and water containing ashes of the Red Cow does not [intrinsically] endow *taharah*, purity. The Holy One, Blessed-be-He, simply deemed it to be so: 'A decree have I declared!'" (*B'rayshis Rabbah* 19:8).

became absolute components of our universe. Murder became for us an absolute evil. Pigs became forbidden food for Jews. Thirty-nine activities became forbidden on Shabbos. Kindness became a virtue. Virtue became a virtue.[6] The Torah's laws, given to us in our world, therefore possess a this-world rationality, even if intellectual limitations prevent some of us from grasping the rationality behind all of them in all situations.

The conclusions of any Sage[7]—even the conclusions that contradict those of other Sages—are intimately connected to G-d's Will and parallel the Absolute Truth, because the author of Absolute Truth is the limitless Creator, and He decreed the Sages' opinions to be Truth. His Absolute Truth is not limited by the kind of "truth" for which our universe is programmed.

* * *

When Moses was given the tablets, *Sh'mos Rabbah* teaches us, G-d's grip remained on the outer two *tefachim* of one side, the two *tefachim* of the *unrevealed* Torah, the unfathomable, undefinable universe preceding even *tohu va'vohu*. Directly grasped by the hand of Moses were the two *tefachim* of the other side, the *revealed* Torah, whose knowledge Moses was permitted to grant to us. The middle two *tefachim*, located at a distance from Moses' grip, consisted of the *inner* Torah, the mysteries meant to be revealed only to Moses and those of special worth.[8] **Our practice is anchored in the halachos Moses told us, and we comprehend them through the universe of logic and sense G-d granted our world. The halacha Moses told us is the halacha which we aspire to follow.** If somehow we find ourselves without knowledge of the *halacha* for a given situation, we were given the tools to decipher it. The Sages of Moses' Great Sanhedrin,

---

[6] Because our ideas of morality and justice are realities only in our world, our forefathers held G-d answerable to their concepts of right and justice only when they sensed that G-d "descended" into the spheres of our universe (see for example *B'rayshis* 11:21, concerning Avraham and Sodom, and *Sh'mos* 2:18, regarding Moses at the burning bush). Only because G-d "descended" onto Mt. Sinai when He revealed His Torah to us (*Sh'mos* 19:18) are we justified in applying to it our system of logic, which includes, for example, the inadmissibility of contradictions and the basing of conclusions through obviating them.

[7] Reached, of course, in accordance with the Torah's directives.

[8] Rav Simon Schwab in the name of the Telzer Rav (Cf. *Y'fay To'ar* on *Sh'mos Rabbah* 47:6).

and all following Great Sanhedrins, were given the power to decide *halacha* for all Jewry based upon the science of Torah interpretation and *halachic* precedent. And if, due to the nature of man, different opinions emerged, we were given the principle of following the majority of Sages.

Considering the above, it is needless to say that we never really מחדש, innovate, explanations of Torah laws. We discover them. *Our* minds are innovated by *them*. Explanations of Scriptural laws do not develop, but are merely uncovered or rediscovered by following the guidelines of analysis revealed by Moses. Certainly, explanations of Scriptural laws are not determined by political or whimsical considerations, but by earnest desire to analyze Scripture's original, unchanging meaning.

* * *

We are now prepared to treat the questions this work was written to address, the questions mentioned in the first paragraph of this chapter and which we shall close with now: *In general, how, historically speaking, did the Sages find themselves without unanimously accepted clear and definite answers to some halachic issues; what processes did they use to discover these answers; and why did these processes lead to different conclusions?*

Introduction

For many, the concept of disputes in the Talmud, and the origins of these disputes, is hazy at best. Among the most basic questions is: Once G-d told Moses the details in performing the laws of the Torah, how perfectly intact did the process of oral transmission keep this information over the centuries?

In answer, one often hears in the name of the Rambam that the laws given to Moses at Sinai were impervious to loss or erroneous transmission.[1] But this leads to a difficulty: If, to know any law details, a student needed only to repeat his teacher's lessons, how does one account for the frequent occurrence of a scholar *disagreeing* with his teacher on such matters? If his teacher is the infallible source of information for G-d's description of the commandments, how could the student offer another opinion? It seems not only blasphemous, but quite irrational, to contest G-d's own report of His Will![2] At any rate, how does one explain the phenomenon, often seen in the Talmud, of two Sages disagreeing over what words their mentor spoke?

The preceding question also makes it difficult to understand another idea one hears in connection with our subject: that all sides of a dispute were somehow right. That is, some *machlokos* may simply be a question of different perceptions of the present situation or circumstances, as some commentators understand the meaning of the adage "These and those are the words of the Living G-d," there-

---

[1] Sources for all assertions will be provided in the appropriate chapters of this book.

[2] The Talmud also contains disagreements voiced by deviant movements such as the Sadducees, Minnim, and Bytoossim, who denied the divine origin of the Torah (see "Epilogue" at the end of this work). This work, however, is concerned only with the disputes among those who remained faithful to Judaism.

by allowing both sides of such "disputes" to stand.[3] But how can one say that all parties of a dispute are right in cases where they are arguing about what one's words were, or, for that matter, in the multitude of *machlokos* about the original law given by G-d at Sinai? Can one assert that Hashem gave Moses several rulings for each case and declared them all valid, though contradictory? Hardly. Besides, the authorities in the Talmud obviously see as their goal the establishment of the *halacha* as it was understood by Moses and they are constantly verifying their opinions by those of their predecessors. Surely Moses, if not G-d, decided upon one way to perform the *mitzvos*.

For example, *Bes Shammai* and *Bes Hillel* disagree whether the Torah requires one to recline while reciting the nighttime *Sh'ma* (*Brachos* 1:3). How could Moses have followed or even advocated both opinions? In his own lifetime, did he and the people recline while reciting *Sh'ma* at night or not? If Moses accepted only one opinion, how could it be said that a different opinion is "correct"?

Similarly, we find that Rebbi Elazar b'Rebbi Shimmon and Rebbi Yehuda HaNassi disagreed (*Yoma* 12b) over the material used to make the belts that the *Kohanim* were obligated to wear (*Sh'mos* 29:9). One maintains they were made of linen; the other insists that they were made of linen and wool. But which material did Moses have the *Kohanim* wear?

Again, does the Torah say that people convicted for execution are also given lashes? This was an issue debated by Rebbi Akiva and Rebbi Yishmael (*Makkos* 17:1). But surely, the worshippers of the Golden Calf were either lashed or they weren't. How could both opinions be correct? Can we say that they were correct in the sense that though they were contradictory, they were all logically valid? Why, then, would each Sage insist that his opponent was wrong? And given the same data to work with, how did the Sages arrive at different conclusions?

Those who begin study of the Talmud with mature minds often have these questions quite immediately; usually, however, without receiving satisfactory answers. They learn to suppress their questions, anticipating that they will be enlightened through years of study. But years later, more often than not, they are dismayed to find that the haze never lifted: When asked the same questions by their students, they remain no less befuddled than before.

---

[3] A chapter of this work is devoted to the various understandings of this adage.

G-d forbid that we reproach anyone. The Talmud treats a vast array of subjects, each with its own numerous problems. (And there are certainly several other vital areas of Torah study that demand concentrated effort.) It is normal, and sometimes even necessary, to leave a problem unsolved for a long while. One must gather and arrange facts before arriving at conclusions. Yet the phenomenon of *machlokess* occurs in, and is basic to, virtually every passage in the Talmud. As long as its nature remains unclear, the meaning of most of the Talmud must remain unclear as well. All would agree that one's study of the Talmud would be unsound were he unaware of the principle that the Torah and Oral Law are G-d-given. An inadequate understanding of *machlokess*, specifically regarding how it exists in face of the Oral Law's divine origin, must rank second to such an unawareness.

This book will explore and—I pray to Hashem—clearly and correctly answer the issues outlined above.[4] To some, my answers—backed by, or rather, reached through, authoritative sources—may seem surprising or even radical. To others, seasoned Torah scholars, I trust, they may seem *"pashut"*—obvious. At any rate, my goal is to provide comprehensive answers that are factual, clear, cohesive, unsimplistic and unevasive.

Machlokess Occurs Relatively Infrequently

To avoid any misconceptions, we must temper our remarks. It is true that *machlokos* appear frequently in the Talmud. But taken within the perspective of the entire body of the Oral Law, any *machlokess* is really an aberration—an exception to the rule. This fact tends to fall into eclipse because the Talmud often passes over or merely implies

---

[4] Among many other questions that will be addressed as well are: Did Moses really receive and teach the text of the Babylonian and Jerusalem Talmuds to the people? Did the Sages in the Talmud, who lived centuries after Moses, merely follow a script which told them what opinions to hold, when to disagree with each other, which arguments to use, what facts to use in refuting a challenge? Did they actually know how their positions were destined to be defended by future Sages, the names of these men, and the words they were to use?

How did the Sages determine *halachos* when they did not have them by tradition? Did they actually extract information by *darshonning*, interpreting Scriptural passages, or were *drashos* used only to give a Biblical "stamp of approval" to laws arrived at through other means? And in either case, why did the *halachic* method produce variant results when used by different Sages? Did the Sages of the Talmud ever make mistakes? Were they ever vague in their teachings?

the huge numbers of points agreed upon by all discussants, consign-
ing to the scholar the task of reconstructing them. The issues in
dispute usually concern technical points of law that rarely affect
day-to-day life; details that relate to hypothetical, borderline,
remote or rare cases. Maximum and minimum measurements
(—*May a sukka's height be less than 10 tefachim—about 30 inches
high? May it be over 20 ahmos—about 40 feet tall?—*) are relevant to
emergency situations, not to normal ones. It must also be remembered that in countless cases all scholars were in *agreement* even
about such "academic" details. *(Suppose two people enter court,
each gingerly holding the edge of the same garment, neither having
pulled it away from the other, each sincerely claiming, and willing to
swear, that he had picked it up from the ground before the other
had, neither offering any evidence to back his claim:* Even in such a
case there is no *halachic* dispute. No one declares that the court
should excuse itself from the case; no one holds that the judges
arbitrarily decide who the rightful owner is. All agree that the garment is sold and that the money for it is divided between the two
litigants [*Bava Metsia* 1:1]). Certainly, countless fundamental rules
normally called upon suffered no disputes. One can verify our point
simply by perusing the Rambam's *Sefer Hamitzvos* and *Mishneh
Torah*, with their commentaries. (The Rambam explains each mitzva
starting with its most basic concept, and the commentaries pinpoint
the talmudic opinion upon which he based his decisions.) One may
be quite surprised at the relatively small number of issues that had
been subject to debate and at how deeply "buried" these are within
the entire rubric of laws. Famous and complex issues, subject to
volumes of profound writings and hours upon hours of incisive lectures, seemingly lose their sense of urgency when viewed in the
context of daily living.

Nevertheless, disputes there are aplenty.

Disputes Over Enacting Gezayros (Precautionary Measures) and Takkonos (Rectifying Enactments)

The least understood disputes are those regarding *Biblical*, as
opposed to "*rabbinical*," laws. The way in which disputes arose over
enacting non-Biblical laws is fairly obvious. These were matters of
judgement. For example, in the case of a *gezayra* (precautionary
measure), judgement is called for to determine questions such as:
When people perform one permitted action, are they drawn by habit

to committing a serious prohibition?[5] Or, by their permitting one truly acceptable activity, would the Sages be encouraging the mis-impression that the Torah condones another similar but strictly for-bidden one? Are such fears legitimate, plausible, and strong enough to warrant a universal decree forbidding the heretofore permitted action? As situations arose that suggested the need for a decree, different Sages naturally had different opinions as to whether it was indeed helpful or necessary to enact one.

On a local level, a Sage's decision to enact a decree involved sensing his community's perceptions and habits. For example, the Rambam explains[6] that eating poultry together with milk originally was not prohibited. However, as time went on, some people con-fused poultry with meat[7] and this led to a laxity with regard to actual meat and milk mixtures. Perceiving this violation of Jewish law, most rabbis decreed upon their cities that poultry be treated as meat, that is, that it not be eaten together with milk. This prohibition was eventually accepted by all authorities and recorded as universal law in the Talmud. However, before the closing of the Talmud took place (actually, long before) there was a Sage who continued to permit the mixture of poultry and milk: Rebbi Yosay of Galilee did not think this prohibition necessary, and the people of his city ate freely of the combination (*Shabbos* 130a).[8]

---

[5] To illustrate, doing business on Shabbos is technically permitted by the Torah as long as one avoids performing any of the 39 forbidden activities (ל"ט מלאכות). However, since doing business often entails writing—a forbidden activity—it was officially decreed (already in Biblical times—see *Jeremiah* 17:21-22) that all business activity on Shabbos be suspended. One doing business is likely to find himself writ-ing out of habit.

[6] *Introduction to the Talmud*, p. 91: שהרי בשר עוף בחלב הוא גזירה מדרבנן כדי להרחיק מן העבירה, ולא נאסר בתורה אלא בשר בהמה וחיה. אבל אסרו חכמים בשר עוף כדי להרחיק מן האיסור. ויש מהם מי שלא יגזור גזירה זו. שרבי יוסי [הגלילי] היה מתיר בשר עוף בחלב, וכל אנשי עירו היו אוכלים אותו, כמו שנתפרסם בתלמוד (שבת דף קל.).

[7] Conventionally speaking, poultry and meat are related: Both are sold in butcher shops, as opposed to say, fish. Perhaps this is because both poultry and meat are prepared through slaughter, whereas fish, like dairy products, are not.

[8] Rebbi Yosay of Galilee lived in the second century of the Common Era, circa 3880. (This was between the destruction of the Second Temple in 3828 and the Bar Kochba Rebellion of 3895.) Rebbi Yosay's ruling remained in effect at least until the Mishna was closed, c. 3965 (the beginning of the third century C.E.), and perhaps until the Talmud (Gemora) was closed, c. 4220 (fifth century, c. 460 C.E.).

When the *Great Sanhedrin* was confronted with the monumental decision as to whether to enact a *gezayra* or *takkonna* binding on all Jewry for all time, different Sages had different opinions on the matter. They would discuss the issues and then come to a vote. The opinions about rabbinical decrees reported in the *mishnayos* consist of the major ones considered.

This simple explanation suffices to explain *machlokos* only at the stage of the original decision. Once we go beyond this stage, to later *machlokos* arising about these past decisions, the same puzzles emerge as those regarding *machlokos* over Scriptural laws: How did disputes arise over the details of decrees enacted by the Sages in the past? For that matter, how could it be that Sages disagreed about whether a certain decree was indeed ever made at all? The answers, too, will be similar to those regarding *machlokos* about biblical laws.

Chapter 1

Precedents, Drashos, And Logic

Whatever the reasons that the Sages lacked details of G-d's original Will—these reasons will be discussed in later chapters—why did conclusions differ when the Sages sought to determine those details? Answering this requires that we first understand the process used by the Sages to determine any *halacha*—disputed or not.

The Groundwork for P'sak

This process consisted of "reconstructing" or "deducing" the *halacha* by piecing together the facts that *were* available, fitting them into a harmonious whole, and observing the laws that then emerged. Though of infinitely more profound importance than assembling a jigsaw puzzle, the process involved is similar. A jigsaw puzzle is a picture broken up into irregularly shaped pieces. Even without being told how the pieces are supposed to be arranged or without having seen the original picture, any skilled expert will ably arrange the pieces to reproduce it. So too with determining the original Will of G-d.

Proceeding with this metaphor, we can discern why *machlokos*, differences of opinion, were possible:

Imagine that several experts, besides not having seen the original picture, are given pieces which, by being arranged in various ways, are capable of producing variant, though all fairly coherent, images. Complicate this further with the suggestions that some pieces may be missing and that some pieces, regardless of their arrangement, may interlock only with difficulty. The assemblers of the diagram-less puzzle may be forced to create some new pieces to complete the picture, and even then may be forced to settle for some less-than-perfect fits.—Some edges may have to overlap, some pieces may need to be slightly bent, some cracks may have to remain. The experts' only guide is the knowledge that the picture with the least objectionable faults would probably be the closest to the original one. Now, even in such circumstances, all the experts may finally assemble the same picture. But then again, they may not. In the latter case, each expert will feel that all in all, the total picture that he has assembled, despite any forced structuring, is the most coherent one that can be produced and most accurately reflects the original intent of the puzzle's designer.

Applying this concept to reconstructing the Sinaitic Will of G-d, we can say that the missing instructions are the keys that would explicitly reveal how the extant pieces of information[1] are meant to fit together and what *halachic* picture is meant to be formed.[2] The missing pieces are the *halachic* details the Sages did not have, further hindering their task to reconstruct the original picture. The difficult fittings, overlappings, and remaining cracks that result after the best attempts are the קושיות, *kushyos*, the objections the *Gemora* raises against the final picture an authority proposed or the objections that one opponent raises against another's conclusion. Each Sage rendered a symmetrical structure of *halacha* by collating all his pieces of information, adjusting the facts to each other in an attempt to keep the sum total as plausible as possible. And each felt that he most closely duplicated G-d's intent at Sinai. This, in essence, was the Talmudic method.

The Early Commentators Follow Suit

The talmudic method was continued by the *Rishonim*, the early commentators such as *Rashi* and *Tosefos*. Despite apparent difficulties with any one interpretation of a Talmudic passage, a *Rishon* may decide that when all factors are taken into account, that difficulty

---

[1] Later in this chapter we shall describe in detail the nature of these pieces of information.

[2] See Additional Notes at the end of this chapter for a hypothetical illustration of this.

must be accepted as part of the original intent. Take, as an example, the occasional need to "bend" the meaning of a word. Overwhelming evidence may demand that in a particular instance, a word must tolerate a definition other than the one it usually has. In such a case, a *Rishon* may resort to saying that there the word must be taken "לאו דווקא," loosely. An illustration of this is seen in the *Rosh*:

ונראה לי דלאו פירכא היא (עד) לסתור דין זה מכל אלו הראיות שהבאנו עליו. ואיכא
למימר שלא דקדק התנא בלשונו לשנות "עדים" ולאשמעינן דעד אחד לא מהני,
אלא אגב ריהטא נקט, דאורחיה בכל דוכתא למיתני "עדים" ופירושו "עדות"
המועלת לו (רא"ש בבא מציעא דף ב' אות ג'.)

Considering all the proofs I have brought, it seems to me that the Talmud's use of the plural "עדים," *witnesses*, does not conclusively contradict my conclusion [that even *one* witness is sufficient in this case]. One can safely say that the *Tanna's* use of the word in the plural was not deliberate, intended to indicate that one witness is insufficient. The *Tanna* simply said "witnesses" in the plural spontaneously, because that is how the concept of *effective testimony* is usually expressed (*Rosh, Bava Metsia* page 2, heading #3).

The Ramban on Analysis

Since pieces are missing, no one theory can be totally proven or disproven. As long as the strict methodology of *halachic* determination is being followed, the faults that one expert sees in another's final picture cannot be so severe as to totally do away with it. The Ramban[3] expresses this concept in words that should be seriously studied by every student of the Talmud:

ואע"ג דלישנא בתרא סלקא בקשיא—מ"מ אפשר לדחויי הכי. דהכי נקטינן משמיה
דרבוותא קמאי ז"ל: דכל קשיא לא לגמרי איתותב, אלא למקשה בעלמא הוא דקשיא.

Although the *Gemora* [in this passage] remains with a difficulty raised against the second opinion, it is possible to ward off that problem as we have done. For we have an accepted principle from the ancient rabbis, may their memory be blessed, that no objection raised in the *Gemora* [against an authority's position] totally disproves [that position]. It is only an objection [strong

---

[3] *Ḥiddushay HaRamban* p. 2 on *Bava Bassra* 2b ד"ה שם וליעבד לגו.

enough to discredit the theory] in the eyes of the opponent raising it.

This is not only true for those quoted in the Talmud, it is also
true for those who interpret it. The Ramban explains this position in
the introduction to his *Sefer Milchomos Hashem, Battles [For the
Sake] of Hashem*, his defense of the *Ryf* (Rav Yitzchak al Fasi) in
face of the attacks of Rav Zeraḥia (the *Baal Ha'Ma'ohr*). The work
concerns *poskening*, deciding the *halacha* through analyzing the
Gemora and explaining the *Gemora's* statements):

ואתה המסתכל בספרי, אל תאמר בלבבך כי כל תשובותי על הרב רבי זרחיה ז"ל כולן
בעיני תשובות נצחות, ומכריחות אותך להודות בהם על פני עקשותך, ותתפאר
בהיותך מספק אחת מהן על לומדיה, או תטריח על דעתך להכנס בנקב המחט לדחות
מעליך הכרח ראיותי. אין הדבר כן. כי יודע כל לומד תלמודֵנו שאין בחלוקת
מפרשיו ראיות גמורות. ולא ברוב קושיות חלוטות. שאין בחכמה הזאת מופת בדור
כגון חשבוני התשבורות ונסיוני התכונה. אבל נשים כל מאדֵנו ודיֵינו בכל מחלוקת:
בהרחיק אחת מן הדעות בסברות מכריעות, ונדחוק עליה השמועות, ונשים יתרון
הכשר לבעל דינה מפשטי ההלכות והוגן הסוגיות עם הסכמת השכל הנכון. וזאת
תכלית יכלתנו, וכוונת כל חכם וירא האלקים בחכמת הגמרא.

Do not imagine that I consider all my arguments against Rabbi
Zeraḥia—may he rest in peace—to be the last words on the subject, or to be so strong that, despite all resistance, you will be
compelled to agree to my stand. . . . For everyone who studies
our Talmud knows that when our commentators disagree over
something, no one of them has any absolute proofs for his side,
no matter how many difficulties he can raise against his
opponent. Our subject is not simple mathematics, in which only
one conclusion can possibly be reached. In every talmudic dispute, all our strength and might is devoted to laying aside one
opinion in preference to another by means of logical evidence.
We then interpret all [related] statements in that light, sometimes in a forced way. We give the seal of approval to that total
picture which seems easiest to accept, considering all the data
involved. This is our goal and the goal of every G-d-fearing
scholar of talmudic science.

And so when two *Amoraim* argue over the meaning of a *mishna*,
we must not imagine it to be obviously clear that one is right and the
other is wrong. The men of the Talmud were sincere people. If a new

piece of information—say an authoritative *braissa*[4] or a persuasive
line of argument—was introduced, which closed the case definitively, then of course the other side would retract,[5] though it was unusual for these experts to form opinions before uncovering all pertinent information. Neither should we jump to the other extreme and
conclude that the opinions expressed in the Talmud, or about it by
the *Rishonim*, are in any degree whimsical or capricious. The intense
conviction with which we see each opponent defending his position
shows that he sincerely believes that he is *right*. Each will admit that
he cannot demolish his opponent's stand with an indisputable,
black-and-white statement that says he is right and the other
wrong. Nevertheless, given all the available data, each speaker in the
Talmud holds that the totality points more towards his own conclusion, and each *Rishon* maintains that his conclusion is the one that
the Talmud intended everyone to reach—despite the occasional need
to force an interpretation on datum whose plain sense contradicts
the desired impression. As the Rambam states (*Introduction to the
Talmud*) matters of judgement are by nature subject to debate.

The Subliminal Forces Behind Judgement

Why, however, is this so? Why do authorities differ in their judgement on which "picture" is the most likely? Why does each one feel
that the objections brought against him are, all-in-all, weaker than
those he has against his opponent, and that his proofs are stronger?
The answer to this fundamental question is provided by *Ohr Yisroel*
(p. 44-46):

ובכ"ז, האדם באשר הוא אדם, אם כי בידו וכחו להפשיט שכלו מהתפעלות כחות
נפשו—עד אשר יהיו כחות נפשו הוזים הוזים שוכבים (בלי התעוררות, למען לא יפרצו
בכח השכלי להטותו)—בכ"ז אדם הוא, וכחות נפשו בקרבו המה, אין בידו להפרישם

---

[4] A *braissa* (lit. outside [source]) is a documented teaching by a pre-*Amoraic*
authority that was not included in the collection of teachings contained in the
Mishna, often for reasons of brevity.

[5] The *Tannaim* of *Bes Hillel* are reported to have retracted their opinion in favor of
Bes Shammai's in no less than nine *mishnayos* of the (Babylonian) Talmud (*Yevomos* 15:2,3; *Gittin* 4:5; *Aid'yos* 1:12, 13, 14; *Kaylim* 9:20; *Oholos* 2:2,4) and twice
in the Jerusalem Talmud (*Beytsa* 1:3, *Sota* end of *perek* 4). As the Mishna in
Aid'yos (1:12) declares, the original opinion and record of retraction is recorded to
teach us the integrity and sincerity of the Sages.

משכלו. לזאת אין ביד האדם לבא אל שכל אמתי המפורש ומובדל לגמרי מכחות
הנפשיות, והתורה נתונה לבני אדם לשפוט בה ע"פ שכל אנושי (בטהרתו
האפשרית—עי' בכורות י"ז ב'—דרחמנא אמר עביד ובכל היכי דמצית למעביד
ניחא ליה) וע"פ רבוי הראיות ומשקלם יתבררו הדברים, ולאיזה צד אשר יפול ערך
הראיות, אם מצד הרבוי או מצד המשקל, שם תהיה ההכרעה וכן יקום הדבר.

מצד רבוי הראיות שוים כל בני אדם בשכלם, אם רק מבין למו להבין הראיות
במתכונתם. אכן מצד המשקל שונים רוח בני אדם זה מזה, הוא הוא שיקול הדעת,
אשר דעתם של בני אדם נפרדת למרבה.

. . . סיבת מחלוקתם היתה משנוי מזג כחות נפשם, אשר אין ביד האדם להפירישם
משכלו (כנ"ל), ואין לכל חוקר בתורת ה', אלא מה שעיניו רואות, לאחר היכולת,
ושמירת ערכו לבל יפרץ גבולו, ובטהרת שכלו לפי כח האנושי.

Even with all this in mind [namely that Torah-learning requires
totally unbiased application of purely objective intellect], man,
by virtue of being man, though he has the power and ability to
flay his intellect so as not to be influenced by his *kochos ha-
neffesh* [his subliminal dispositions], to the extent that they
become sleeping dreamers (dormant and inactivated so as not to
break into his intellect and cause it to err)—with all this in mind,
he is but a human, and his subliminal dispositions lie within
him. He is unable to separate them from his intellect. For this
reason man does not have the power to arrive at [a form of] the
true [absolute] intellect, totally severed and separated from the
subliminal powers of the psyche. Yet the Torah was given to
man to judge through following human intellect (in the purest
form possible—see *Bechoros* 17b, which states that the Merciful
One says "do," and he is pleased by whatever results one's
efforts produce) and matters are to be clarified through amass-
ing pieces of evidence and weighing them, and to whichever side
the weight of the proofs fall, whether due to their quantity or
quality, that is how the matter will stand.

[Now,] all human beings are of the same mind regarding [their
appreciation of] the quantity of proofs [that may be brought for
a position on an issue] as long as they understand the proofs as
they were intended. But regarding the process of weighing the
facts, each human being's spirit differs one from another, and
this very process is the one referred to as "*shikkul ha-dahs*," the
weighing [of facts] by the mind, in which the intellects of
human beings differ greatly.

. . . [T]he cause for their disputes was in the different composi-
tions of each one's *kochos ha-neffesh*, the subliminal disposi-
tional forces of one's psyche [that compels his particular evaluation of things], which no human has the power to sever from his
intellect (as mentioned above); and any investigator into the

Torah of Hashem can only depend upon his own perspective
once he makes all attempts to avoid subjectivism and to excer-
cise his process of assessment while carefully restraining it from
exceeding its limits, and applying as pure and unbiased an
intellect as is humanly possible.

Hashem created all men with variant subliminal forces that
compel each one to strongly feel one way and not another when
judging the quality and proper arrangment of evidence. The Torah
scholar, especially, has the task to rid himself as much as possible of
any such interference with pure and unbiased excercises of his intellect. (It is for this reason, incidentally, that we subject ourselves to
the judgement of Torah greats of each generation, who work upon
themselves to be uninfluenced by forces either external or internal to
them and thereby create the most precision-tuned instruments of
intellect by which to know the will of Hashem.)

Interaction of Drashos and Kabballos

The pieces of the *halachic* puzzles the Sages had to work with were
of two types: (1) the set of י״ג מדות שהתורה נדרשת בהן, the Thirteen
Rules of Torah Interpretation[6] (and all other methods of *drash*,
Torah interpretation) including their basic rules of operation, and (2)
קבלות, *kabballos*, the collection of information that was *not* lost:
explanations declared by G-d that remained extant, decisions that
previous generations were known to have made and practices they
were known to have followed.

Interpretation Rules Interacting with Kabballos

These two types of sources also interacted with each other and their
own natures and workings were thereby defined ever more tightly,
as can be seen in the passage from *Bava Metsia* 54b in *Addendum I*.
The passage clearly demonstrates how the extant *halachos* (such as

---

[6] These rules are listed near the beginning of our prayer books, in the morning services, beginning with "Rabbi Yishmael says, 'The Torah is analyzed with thirteen
rules.'" Some of these rules are cited further in the text, and more will be explained
in the chapter "Loss of Halachos," footnotes 23-27. By the time of the *Rishonim*
(see *Kuzari* 3:73) and even as far back as Rabbeynu Nissim Gaon (c. 800 CE; see his
commentary in our editions of *Brachos* 20a) the science of *drash* was lost. *Malbim*
(*Ahyelless HaShachar*, Introduction to *Vayikra*) attempts to reconstruct the many
other rules of interpretation.

those recorded in the Mishna) and interpretation rules (such as קרא
יתירא, extra verbiage, and גזירה שוה, cloning laws from one area of law
to another, based upon similar phraseology) were used to shed light
on each other.

Drashos That Do Not Affect Practice

Drash actually has two somewhat distinct uses: the use as a tool by
which to discover Biblical references to known oral laws and the use
as a tool by which to generate details of *halachos*. The Rambam
elaborates[7] on the kind of *drash* which demonstrates the Scriptural
indication for a known oral law, stating that though the *drash* may
be in dispute, the law itself is not. The Rambam emphasizes that
such *drashic* disputes are essentially academic. The law's description
is virtually unaffected by the verses which are *"darshonned"* to indicate it. After all, the law was known before the *drash* was discovered. So, even if we find Sages arguing over what verse is meant
to "note" a certain law, all the Sages agree on what the law itself is.

Why did the Sages search for the correct indications for laws
which were already known to be true? And why did each Sage
adamantly argue that *his drash* was the hint planted for a law in the
Torah—and not his opponent's *drash*? The Rambam explains[8] that
discovering the רמזים, *remazim*, the Torah's indications for the oral
laws, was originally a basic activity of Torah study and research; for
by showing how intimations to the Oral Law were "planted" in the
Written Law, the Sages were succeeding "להראות חכמת הכתוב," to
demonstrate the profundity of the Written Law.[9] This was their purpose in life: to discover and teach the true and precise intentions of
each and every letter of Scripture.

Seeking Drashos as Sources for Observable Facts

Therefore the Sages even search for Scriptural references to natural
phenomena, such as the ability of rain to cause plant growth!

(כתובות י:) ואמר רב חנה בגדתאה: מטר משקה, מרוה, ומזבל, ומעדן, וממשיך. אמר
רבא בר רבי ישמעאל, ואיתימא, רב יימר בר שלמיא, מאי קרא?—,,תלמיה רוה נחת
גדודיה ברביבים תמוגגנה צמחה תברך (תהלים ס"ה:י"א)."

---

[7] *Maimonides' Introduction to the Talmud*, pp. 82ff.

[8] *Sefer HaMitzvos, Shoresh Shayni*.

[9] See Additional Notes at the end of this chapter.

Said Rav Ḥanna Bagdassa'a: "Rain waters [the ground], slakes the thirst [of the produce], fertilizes, imparts luster [to the fruits] and draws [them] forth.[10]" Rava bar Rebbi Yishmael, or Rav Yaymar bar Shalmia said, "What is the Scriptural verse for this? [—*T'hillim* 65:11]" (*Kesubos* 10b).

Similarly, we find verses presented as sources for the facts that Babylonia is to the north of Israel (*Bava Bassra* 25b, *Gittin* 6a) and that the Atlantic Ocean nourishes the entire earth (*Taanis* 9b).[11]

Such endeavors may seem strange—if we fail to recognize the importance of correctly identifying the references in the Torah to all things in existence, whether they are laws for man or laws and facts of nature. For the Torah is the blueprint of all existence, and to perceive all existence from this blueprint is the ultimate service of Hashem.

Drashos Generated Laws, As Well

There are many examples of disputes in identifying hints to well-known *halachos*. (Two of the Rambam's own examples[12] are the disputes over the source in the Written Law for the identification of "פרי עץ הדר, the fruit of the glorious tree" (*Vayikra* 23:40) as the esrog, and the explanation that "עין תחת עין, eye replaces eye" (*D'varim* 19:21), refers only to monetary compensation.)[13] The Babylonian Talmud itself calls attention to this phenomenon in four places, stating that certain disputes—over which verse we are to use to support certain Biblical laws—were only academic: "משמעות דורשין איכא בינייהו" (*Bava Metsia* 22a, *Sanhedrin* 75a, *Avoda Zorra* 76b, *Shavuos* 19a).

However, some of these passages (*Bava Metsia* 22a, *Shavuos* 19a) feature another Sage who maintains that to choose one *drash* over the other *will* change some details of practice. These passages demonstrate that sometimes a supportive *drash* may influence law

---

[10] Translation by Rav Avigdor Miller, in *Sing, You Righteous*, p. 246 (*Rugby Young Israel*, 5733 [1983]). He comments, "Today we do not fully understand the exact meaning of all five [words]."

[11] See also *Hullin* 77a with Rashi's commentary on שליא של בהמה שיצאה מקצתה.

[12] *Maimonides' Introduction to the Talmud*, pp. 82, 83.

[13] *Succa* 35a and *Bava Kamma* 84a, respectively.

details. Indeed, the Talmud *often* points out details that are in dispute based upon the *drash* one accepts. Such expressions as "מאן דדריש מהאי קרא, למה לא דריש מאידך, Why did the one authority not *darshon* the same verse as the other authority?" followed by answers involving opposing opinions of law, are familiar to all who study the Talmud. Apparently, *drashos* did generate nuances to the law.

Questioning the Ability of Drash to Generate Halachos

Of course, one may place such passages in a different perspective and insist that the differing *drashos* did not really *generate* the opposing opinions of law. One may maintain that since different *Amoraim* had different ideas about details of the *mitzvos*, perhaps they were forced to find Scriptural indications that would support *their* versions of the details. According to this view, the *drashos* would remain merely as backup-devices for independently reached conclusions.

Indeed, some recent Torah-scholars, notably Rav Yitzchak Isaac Rabinowitz in his *sefer, Doros Harishonim,*[14] have proposed that *as a rule* this is how we must understand the function of *drashos.* These scholars maintain that the Sages of the Talmud based their conclusions solely upon their analyses of statements and of precedents made and set by former authorities. Only after they arrived at their conclusions through such means did they "attach" a *drash* to "support" themselves.[15]

However, as we have indicated, the simple understanding of the Talmud and the approach of the *Rishonim* do not seem to bear out this opinion. Besides the constant debates among the Sages of the Talmud over the validity of their opponent's *drashos* and the insistence that their opponents "do something" with the *posuk* if their thesis is to be accepted, we find passages in the Talmud which seem to leave no way out of the conclusion that the *drashos* were seriously treated as tools for generating *halachos.* The reader's attention is

---

[14] חלק רביעי, פרק ז, דף רל"ה (הוצאת דפוס גאלדע, תרס"ו): שאין בישראל מפרשי המצוות אשר הוציאו מצוות מדרשות וחידשו דברים . . . כי כל דברי התנאים כולם הנם רק בגדר דברי המשנה ביסודה, ולמדה ונלמדה משם כל אחד על פי דרכו וסגנון קבלתו מרבו בביאור דברי המשנה ובפירושה. ועל כן הנא גם רמזי דקרא אשר סמכו גם בהם את דבריהם אינם כי אם בדרך „ליכא מידי דלא רמיזי באורייתא." וע" עוד חלק א' כרך שלישי פרק כ"ט דף קמ"ח ולהלן.

[15] See Additional Notes at the end of this chapter.

again called to the passage from *Bava Metsia* 54a quoted in *Addendum I.* Another example is the following passage in *Bava Metsia* 5a:

מתניתא קא רמית עליה דרבי חייא?! רבי חייא תנא הוא ופליג!

והא קרא קאמר!!

You are citing a contradicting *braissa* to prove Rebbi Ḥiyya
incorrect? Rebbi Ḥiyya is himself a *Tanna* and has a right to his
own opinion against another *Tanna*!

[Yes,] but the *braissa* cites [a *drash* of a] Scriptural verse [as its
source]!

As a *Tanna*, Rebbi Ḥeeya had the authority to differ with a *halacha* recorded in a *braissa*. Yet we see that since the *braissa* had a
drash as its source, he was constrained from contesting that *halacha
unless he could provide an alternate drash for the verse cited!* He
does, indeed, proceed to do so. All this would be incomprehensible
were *drashos* not intended seriously as actual *sources* for the opinions, sources which had to be reckoned with.[16]

To bring a more complex example of a *drash* considered to be a
significant generator of a law, we cite a passage in *Gittin* 39a which
can be abridged and paraphrased as follows:

גר שמת ובזבזו ישראל נכסיו והיו בהן עבדים . . . אבא שאול אומר . . . קטנים—כל
המחזיק בהן זכה בהן (דאין להן יד לקנות את עצמן מידי הפקר).

אמר רבי יעקב בר אידי א"ר יהושע בן לוי, הלכה כאבא שאול.

בפירוש שמיע לך או מכללא איתמר לך?

מאי בללא?

מדרבי גמר לה לה מאשה—מה אשה בשטר אף עבד נמי בשטר, ואמרת, א"כ מה
אשה איסורא ולא ממונא אף עבד נמי.

ואי מכללא, מאי? א"ל אדרבה. דוק מיניה לאידך גיסא: מה אשה בין גדולה בין
קטנה, אף עבד בין גדול בין קטן.

א"ל: בפירוש שמיע לי.

---

[16] See also *Rashi's* comment on *Gittin* 38b: קשיא לרב (בברייתא) וכיון דיליף טעמא מקרא
(אע"פ שתנא הוא ופליג). "The fact that the Tanna [of the *braissa*] derived [his opinion]
from [a *drash* of] a verse discredits Rav['s] opinion, despite the former defense of
Rav that he is qualified to contest the opinion of *Tannaim*]."

Abba Shaul says that if a convert [who, by *halachic* definition, has no heirs] dies, [his slaves are not inherited by his former relatives, since upon his conversion they were no longer *halachically* related to him. Therefore, if his slaves are adults, they take possession of themselves and become free. But] anyone may claim possession of his non-adult slaves, since, as minors, they lack the legal power to claim ownership of property [including themselves].

Rebbi Yaakov bar-Idi said in the name of Rebbi Y'hoshua ben Levy: The *halacha* follows Abba Shaul.

[How do you know Rebbi Y'hoshua ben Levy said that?] Did you hear him say so explicitly, or is it merely your own inference [based on something else he had said]?

What would the inference be based on?

[The inference would be] Rebbi Y'hoshua ben Levy's citation of a ruling by Rebbi concerning a servant, coupled with Rebbi Yohonon's declaration that Rebbi's source was a *gezayra shavva drash* equating the laws of releasing a servant to those of divorcing a wife. That is, did you reason that [based on the *drash*] only an *adult* servant can be compared to a wife insofar as automatically becoming free through the master's death, as opposed to a *non*-adult servant? (The reasoning would be based upon the fact that only an adult servant has the same laws as a wife regarding the [legally inadequate] attempts by the husband/master to sever the relationship by merely declaring verbally that he is no longer their's.) If so, it can be shown that the *gezeyra shavva* should not be applied in this aspect.

Rebbi Yaakov ben Idi: No, I heard it from Rebbi Y'hoshua ben Levy explicitly.

Here we see a *drash* taken quite seriously as a source for law. If it were merely a "back-up" for a law arrived at independently of the *drash*, the *Gemora* would not have entertained the notion that the *gezeyra shavva* was R'Yaakov bar Idi's source. Any technical distinction that existed between applications of the *drash* would have been irrelevant. Rebbi Yohonon's declaration that his mentor's (Rebbi's) source was a *gezeyra shavva* would not have been noteworthy. Another clear example of a *machlokess* based upon *drash* rather than s'vara, from *Temura* 6b, is cited in *Addendum II.*[17]

---

[17] See Additional Notes at the end of this chapter.

At any rate, the Rambam[18] certainly maintains that *drash* was used to discover new laws:

דברים שנתחדשו בכל דור ודור בדיניהם שלא למדו מפי השמועה אלא במדה . . .
מי"ג מדות שהתורה נדרשת בהן והסכימו עליהן בית דין הגדול.

[There were] matters that were newly discovered in each generation which were not learned through oral transmission but through applying, with the consensus of the Great Sanhedrin, one or more of the Thirteen Rules of Torah Interpretation.

Again, he states:[19]

משפטים ודינים מופלאים שלא קיבלום ממשה ודנו בהם ב"ד של אותו הדור במדות
שהתורה נדרשת בהן, ופסקו אותם הזקנים וגמרו שהדין כך הוא.

[There were] profound laws that they did not receive from Moses, which the Sanhedrin of each generation determined through using the interpretation rules by which the Torah is searchedut.

And, in *Sefer HaMitzvos*, *Shoresh Shayni*, he writes,

הנא לא כל מה שנמצא לחכמים שהוציאו בהיקש משלש עשרה מדות נאמר שהוא
נאמר למשה בסיני.

[We] cannot say that every [detail] that we find extracted by the Sages through applying the logic of the *Thirteen Rules* was said to Moses at Sinai.

Most Law-Details Were Generated by Drashos

To quote the above citation in full, we see that the Rambam tells us that *most halachic* details—numbering in the thousands—came through the method of *drash*:

כבר בארנו בפתיחת חבורינו בפירוש המשנה שרוב דיני התורה יצאו בשלש עשרה
מדות שהתורה נדרשת בהן . . . וכשהיה כן הנא לא כל מה שנמצא לחכמים
שהוציאו בהיקש משלש עשרה מדות נאמר שהוא נאמר למשה בסיני . . . ואילו מנה
. . . כל דבר שנלמד בתורה במדה משלש עשרה מדות שהתורה נדרשת בהן היה עולה

---

[18] *Introduction to Mishneh Torah*, page 4, top of column 1, in our editions.
[19] *Ibid.*, column 2.

מנין המצות לאלפים רבות. . . . אמרם בגמרא בתמורה (דף ט"ז) אלף ושבע מאות
קלין וחמורין וגזרות שוות ודקדוקי סופרים שנשתכחו בימי אבלו של משה ואעפ"כ
החזירן עתניאל בן קנז מפלפולו . . . וכשהיו כך הנשכחות כמה היה הכלל שנשכח
ממנו זה המספר . . . ונאמר עליהם דקדוקי סופרים כי . . . לא שמעו בסיני.

We have already mentioned in the introduction to our commentary on the Mishna[20] that *most* of the Torah's law details eman-
ated through application of the Thirteen Rules of Torah
Interpretation. . . . This being so, we cannot say that every
[detail] that we find extracted by the Sages through applying the
logic of the Thirteen Rules was said to Moses at Sinai. Were one
to count . . . everything that the Torah teaches through the
Thirteen Rules of Interpretation, the sum would reach many
thousands. . . . *Temura* 16a states, "The [laws derived through]
kal v'homers, gezayros shavvos, and *dikdukay soferim* that
were forgotten during the days of mourning for Moses numbered 1,700; nevertheless, Osniel ben K'naz reinstated them
through his analysis." . . . How large must have been the original total [of *unforgotten* laws derived by Torah analysis] of which
this number was certainly only a fraction! . . . And they [the
laws] are called *dikdukay soferim,* exactitudes of the Scribes,
because . . . the people did not hear [them] at Sinai.

Such a statement makes it difficult to accept the position of the
Doros Harishonim[21] that the Rambam, too, asserts that very *few*
drashos were of the kind that actually *generated* the laws.

Interpreting and Discovering the Rules of Interpretation

Not only did disputes arise over the proper meshing of facts and

[20] דע כי כל מצוה שנתן הקב"ה למשה רבינו ע"ה נתנה לו בפירושה . . . ומי שלא שמע בו פירוש מפי הנביא
מן העניינים המשתרגים מהם, הוציא דינים בסברות במדות השלש עשרה הנתונות על הר סיני שהתורה נדרשת
בהם.
It should be understood that with every *mitzva* that The Holy-One-Blessed-be-
He gave to Moses, He gave him its clarification . . . Whoever did not hear from that
prophet a clarification concerning the matters that branch out from them (*sic*)
would extract the law-details by applying the logic of the Thirteen Rules of Torah
Interpretation, which were given at Mount Sinai.
[21] E.g., Part IV, Ch. 9, p. 497. (See his qualification *ibid.* Ch. 14, p. 514 ff.) Moreover, despite his assertion that never in the Talmud are *drashos* used to solve doubts
over which *s'vara,* sequence of logic, to use (*ibid.* Ch. 11, p. 486 ff.), at least one
exception to that rule can be found in *Shabbos* 13a, regarding marital behavior.

interpretation rules, there was even room to interpret,[22] and therefore dispute over, the operation of the interpretation rules themselves. Such disputes are listed in the כללי י"ג מדות כו', *The Principles of the Thirteen Methods of Torah Interpretation* in the back of our editions of Tractate *Brachos*.

Moreover, there was room to discover heretofore unknown rules of Torah interpretation. An interesting example of this is presented to us in *Bava Kamma* 41b. Shimmon HaAmsuni had developed a system of finding a *remez*, written indication, in the Torah for many extant oral laws. The system involved using the word "את" (in certain circumstances),[23] which appears before the object of a verb. He used this occurrence to indicate that not only is the predicate, or law, of the verse assigned to the object named there, but it is also assigned to something else closely related conceptually to that object.

For example, we know through the Oral Law that we are forbidden to eat not only unkosher animals, but their milk as well. Though the Written Torah states nothing about their milk, it uses the wording "את הגמל" in its list of forbidden animals. Shimmon HaAmsuni determined that the word "את" was planted in front of the word "גמל," camel, to serve as a *remez*, hint, to the oral law: Not only the animal, but the closest edible associated to it—its milk—is included in the prohibition, too. Thus was created a new formula by which to discover unresolved answers about law details.

The acid test for the validity of such a formula was to use it consistently and see if it would produce any laws that were known to be *untrue*. If it did, the formula would have to be discarded, together with the answers it provided.

Indeed, this is what happened. The method worked perfectly throughout the Torah, except for one verse: "את ד' אלקיך תירא, You must fear Hashem, your G-d." At this point, Shimmon HaAmsuni stopped. According to the teachings he had received, as he understood them, the obligation of awe applied to the object of the sentence, *Hashem*, is totally inapplicable to anything or anyone else. There is no other object that even comes close to G-d in this respect. In no way can the fear due Hashem be required towards any other

---

[22] I use the word "interpret" reluctantly. Unfortunately, some unscrupulous people take license to distort statements, ignore facts, and misrepresent quotations with the excuse that they are "interpreting" them. In this book, "interpretations" means the findings of Sages who accept the Torah, sincerely desire to know what it means, and delve into it with that purpose in mind.

[23] See *Malbim's Ayelless HaShachar*, rule 612.

being. On this basis, he deemed false his method of *darshonning*
"את," and he felt compelled to discredit that word as a valid indication for known oral laws and, apparently, all details that were generated on the basis of this system.

This was, of course, a major move. His disciples, who naturally
had attended many lectures of his and had been deciding *halachos*
based upon his teachings, were dumbfounded at his retraction. "But
what will be of all your *drashos?*" they cried. "Just as I would have
received reward for correctly *darshonning*," he replied, "so will I
receive reward for desisting." (כשם שאני מקבל שכר על הדרישה, כך אני,,
מקבל שכר על הפרישה.")

What makes this account all the more amazing, and a tribute to
Shimmon HaAmsuni's integrity, is that he held fast to his retraction
despite the fact that Rabbi Akiva continued to accept this method.
Rabbi Akiva taught that, indeed, Torah scholars are due the same
awe that we must give Hashem, and so the use of "את" in this way is
valid. Shimmon HaAmsuni could not accept such an equation, and
so he abandoned his formula for *darshonning* the word "את."[24]

The fact that *halachic* and *drashic* principles can be understood
to shape each other in conflicting ways is responsible for a familiar
kind of שקלא וטריא, verbal exchange, found in the Talmud: One sage
darshons a Scriptural phrase as the source for a *halacha*; another
Sage, who denies that *halacha*, is shown to use the phrase for
another *halacha*, which is universally accepted, whereupon the first
Sage is expected to show his source for that other *halacha*, and so on.
Both Sages possessed the knowledge of certain known *halachos* and
were aware of certain verses that called for *drashos*. Each one put
these pieces of data together in the way he felt formed the most
symmetrical whole picture. The conclusions could vary as long as
some pieces of information were missing, particularly the data on
how to arrange all the known facts.

Drashos Were Not Independent of Other Factors

As was explained earlier, *drashos* were not independent of other
tools for understanding the Torah's details. They interacted with
surviving laws and precedents, resulting in an interlaced structure
which revealed the final "picture" of the law. Indeed, a decision

---

[24] No doubt, Shimmon HaAmsuni's rejection was a result of collating, differently
from Rabbi Akiva, principles expressed by past authorities.

based upon a דרש alone is not highly regarded. The *Yerushalmi Tal-mud* states the principle, "כל תורה שאין לו בית אב אינו תורה, Any Torah [decision] that lacks a *bace ahv* is no Torah" (ירושלמי פאה עמוד 78 [לט:] שורה ט'). What is meant by something that lacks a *bace ahv?* The *Meiri* explains that it means "כל תורה שאינה מקובלת מפי הראוי לסמוך עליו", anything which was not received from someone fit to rely upon.[25] The *Introduction* to the *Ohr Zarua* (section 34) explains the same statement similarly:

> כלומר, כל התורה שאין לה קבלה אינה תורה לסמוך עליה למעשה; אלא הקבלה היא העיקר למעשה ולא סברא וכו'.

All Torah-teachings which are not based on something handed down are not fit to be relied upon for practical [as opposed to merely academic] purposes. The *tradition (kabballa)* is the major factor, and not *s'vara* [i.e., *drash*].[26]

Drashos Only Supplied Details of Laws Already Present

It should also be mentioned that according to Rambam, the new facts that were influenced by *drashos* are nevertheless mere פירושים, clari-fications, of Scriptural laws. They are not altogether new laws. They merely pinpoint which one of several ways of understanding and applying a verse is correct. The *drashos* function to define strictly the terms the Torah uses:

> שכל מה שנלמד [בי"ג מדות] הם ענפים מן השרשים שנאמרו לו למשה בסיני בבאור והם תרי"ג מצוות.

Everything derived [through application of the *Thirteen Interpretation Rules*] are branches of the main laws—i.e., the

---

[25] Perhaps a *drash* with a בית אב, *bace ahv*, is one that has the consensus of the Great Sanhedrin, led by the בית דין (אב), *Ahv Bace Din*. An individual's *drash* simply does not carry the weight held by a *drash* agreed upon by all the members of the Great Sanhedrin.

[26] It is true that *s'vara* generally refers to the analysis of a previous authority's state-ments. But in this context, it does seem to mean a *drasha*. For the Jerusalem Tal-mud's passage immediately follows a famous account of Hillel and the B'nay B'sayra. Hillel presented *drashos* to prove his position on a certain issue, and the B'nay [Sons of] B'sayra accepted his decision only after he revealed that it came from his teachers. The principle is then stated that *s'vara* alone is not good enough to decide a law. Evidently, *s'vara* here does mean *drashos*.

613 commandments—that were explicitly told to Moses at Sinai.[27]

Ever Since Moses

We have already cited the Rambam's statement[28] that this kind of analysis took place ever since the days Moses received the Torah. This included the generation of Joshua:

וכאשר מת משה ע"ה אחר שהנחיל ליהושע מה שנאצל עליו מן הפירוש, והחכים והתבונן בו יהושע ואנשי דורו . . . ומי שלא שמע בו פירוש מפי הנביא, ע"ה—מן העניינים המשתרגים מהם—הוציא דינים בסברות, במדות השלוש עשרה הנתונות על הר סיני שהתורה נדרשת בהם. ובאותם הדינים שהוציאום, יש דברים . . . מה שנפלה בו מחלוקת. . . . כי מדות ההיקש שעל דרך התווכחת יקרה בסברותיהם המקרה הזה. . . . וכאשר מת יהושע בן נון ע"ה למד לזקנים מה שקיבל מן הפירוש, ומה שהוציאו בזמנו מן הדינים. . . . ואין זמן שלא היה בו התבוננות וחידוש העניינים.[29]

> When Moses died, after bequeathing to Joshua the entire explanation that he had been granted, Joshua and the men of his generation grew in wisdom through it and analyzed it. . . . And whatever laws they did not hear from the lips of the Prophet—consisting of corollaries of what *was* said by Moses—they extracted by means of the Thirteen Rules of Interpretation given by Hashem at Mt. Sinai. The results of these extractions differed, though, with different people . . . as is natural with conclusions reached through human analysis. . . . And when Joshua died, he taught The Elders whatever he had received of the Explanation from Moses, and whatever laws had been extracted in his time. . . . And there was no time in which the analysis of the *p'sukim* and the making of original discoveries was absent.[30]

And so wherever there were no specific, previous rulings by which to abide, the Sages had to determine those details by means of *drashos*, coupled with careful analysis of past teachings. As explained by the *Rishonim*, this principle clearly operates through-

[27] *Sefer HaMitzvos, Shoresh Shayni*, p. 50 in our editions.

[28] Beginning of *Shoresh Shayni* of *Sefer HaMitzvos* (citing *Temura* 16a), p. 29 in our editions.

[29] *Introduction to the Talmud, (Hakdama L'Payrush HaMishnayos)* Hebrew section, p. 10.

[30] *Ibid.*, English section, p. 73.

out the *Gemora*. Different minds reached different conclusions as to
the correct *halacha*.

Four Modes of Halachic Decision

Despite this chapter's concentration upon primary analysis of Scriptural verses, an important fact must be kept in mind. Whenever we
speak of Rabbis determining the *halacha*, we must differentiate
between the different levels on which they are operating. The
mechanics of *p'sak* used by the later authorities must not be confused with the methods of earlier ones, who still mastered the science
of directly interpreting the Torah's verses. Scholars attempting to
define the original intent of earlier authorities—concerning either
Torah laws or rabbinical decrees—work on a different level from
those who had the power to enact the original decrees. Wherever
analysis was needed to determine the *halacha*, five operations may
be isolated:

1. One operation of *p'sak* was direct analysis of the Torah's
    p'sukim,[31] using the authoritative methods of interpreta-
    tion.[32]

2. Another level of *p'sak* refrains from such direct analysis
    of Scripture. Instead, scholars accept that the intent and
    concept of *p'sukim* are as they had been determined to be
    by earlier authorities. The scholars merely seek to apply
    those renderings of the *p'sukim* and the precedents based
    upon them to present situations. Judgement is called for
    in deciding which precedents are comparable to given
    situations.

3. Another level simply attempts to determine the accurate
    version of the words of previous authorities. The present
    case is known to be dealt with by those authorities, and
    the current decisors are interested solely in determining

[31] The method of direct interpretation of Scripture to generate *halachic* details began
in the time of Moses (c. 2448) but ended by the time the Talmud was completed,
1800 years later. All other modes of *p'sak* listed are operative today.
[32] Analogous to this—regarding rabbinical decrees—are original decisions, based
upon assessing the needs of the Jewish nation. This analogy to rabbinical decrees
will follow through with all the following operations of *p'sak* as well.

those authorities' opinions. Here, direct judgments about the merits of the factors in the case—let alone about the intent of Scripture—do not play a role. These are accepted to be as portrayed by the previous authorities.

4. Another step involves deciding which former authority we shall follow. This decision is often based upon the status of an authority or the way in which the Talmud presents his opinion. (For instance, his opinion may be shown to bear many difficulties, or it may be supported by later authorities.) Decisions are made using rules of p'sak and are not based on the decisor's own philosophy or his evaluation of the spokesmen's judgments.

5. Different authorities may naturally reach different conclusions using any of the above-described levels of analysis. The final mode of p'sak involves deciding between them.

One is often confronted by the confusion over these different levels of p'sak. For example, statements made by the Rambam are often touted as representative of "his original insight," or "his lenient attitude." But those who understand halachic procedure recognize that he is actually citing a talmudic opinion which is to be followed based upon a relatively mechanical application of the rules of p'sak.

More Behind the Opinions than Appears

It is also important to realize that when the Talmud tells us the Sages' reasons for their conclusions, we are not necessarily getting the whole story. If we were attending the Sages' yeshivos, we undoubtedly would have heard many more explanations and proofs supporting their opinions. The Gemora Eruvin 22a tells us that Shlomo HaMelech (King Solomon) could cite 1,005 reasons for anything that came from the סופרים:[33]

וידבר שלשת אלפים משל ויהי שירו חמשה וֹאלף (מלכים א' ה:י"ב) מלמד שאמר שלמה . . . על כל דבר ודבר של סופרים חמשׁה ואלף טעמים.

[33] The Scholars, an early title for the Rabbis or Sages. (See Divray Hayomim I, 2:55 and Kiddushin 30a.)

"And he said three thousand parables and his song was one thousand and five" (*Melachim I* 5:12). This teaches us that Shlomo said . . . one thousand and five reasons for each matter of the *Soferim*.

A fascinating passage in *Yevomos* 16a illustrates this point. Under discussion is the matter of *yibbum*. The Torah (*D'varim* 25:5-10) teaches us that if one's paternal brother had married but died childless, one is obligated to perform either *yibbum* or *halitsa*. That is, he must either marry the widow—even though she is his sister-in-law, a relative otherwise forbidden to him as an *erva*[34]—or he must perform *halitsa* to allow the widow to marry another man.[35] However, if she happens to be an *erva* to him on additional grounds, *yibbum* is forbidden and *halitsa* is unnecessary for allowing her to marry someone else. For example, if she happens to be his daughter, he may not perform *yibbum* with her. (His late brother was perfectly able to marry her, his niece. Such a union is even considered meritorious.)[36]

Introducing an additional factor into the case leads to a controversial issue. It is possible, in a given instance, that the late brother had *two* wives (which was long permitted until the 10th century C.E., when it was forbidden by the *Bes Din* of Rabbeynu Gershom), one wife being the daughter (בת) of the surviving brother, and so forbidden to him, and the other, her *co-wife* (צרה) not related to him at all (other than having been his sister-in-law). Should the surviving brother marry this latter צרת הבת, [brother's] daughter's co-wife, through *yibbum*? Or does the fact that *one* of the wives was forbidden prohibit *all* of his late brother's wives to him, making *yibbum* unlawful and *halitsa* unnecessary?

This is disputed in a *mishna* in *Yevomos* 13a (also *Aid'yos* 4:8). *Bes Hillel* forbids *yibbum* in such a situation and *Bes Shammai* encourages it. *Bes Hillel's* reason, given in a *braissa* (*Yevomos* 3b), is based on a *drash* of the word לצרור[37] in *Vayikra* 18:18. Upon this

---

[34] An *erva* is a relative with whom sexual union is gravely forbidden. The relatives so prohibited are referrred to in *Vayikra* 18.

[35] Among *Ashkenazim*, *yibbum* is no longer practiced, making *halitsa* an imperative for the widow who desires to remarry.

[36] *Ramah*, following *Rashbam*, *Evven Ha'ezzer* 2:5.

[37] The Rambam (*Hilchos Yibbum V'Halitsa* 6:9) gives another source. See Rabbi Baruch Epstein's note 6 on *Vayikra* 10:6 in his *Torah Temima*.

law, *Bes Hillel* bases a huge and complex body of teachings about
צרת הבת, as illustrated in the first *mishna* in *Yevomos*. *Bes Shammai's*
reason to reject this *drash* is another *drash*, of the verse (*D'varim*
25:5) "לא תהיה אשת המת החוצה לאיש זר, The deceased's wife shall not go
outside to an unrelated man." This and a *s'vara* offered by Rava
(*Yevomos* 13b)[38] are the only reasons given for *Bes Shammai's*
opinion (*Yevomos* 13b; see *Tosefos*).

Now, in *Yevomos* 16a, we have our fascinating passage:

ת"ש: בימי רבי דוסא בן הרכינס הותרה צרת הבת לאחין, והיה הדבר קשה לחכמים
מפני שחכם גדול היה ... התחילו מסבבים אותו בהלכות עד שהגיעו לצרת הבת.
אמרו ליה צרת הבת מהו ... אמר להן הלכה כבית הלל ... אמרו ליה והלא משמך
אמרו הלכה כבית שמאי ... אמר להם אח קטן יש לי בכור שטן הוא (פרש"י: חריף
ועומד על שמועתו ועושה מעשה ואינו שב משמועתו לעשות כרבים) ... והוא
מתלמידי שמאי. והזהירו שלא יקפח אתכם בהלכות לפי שיש עמו שלש מאות
תשובות בצרת הבת שהיא מותרת.

In the days of Rebbi Dosa the son of Horkinus, צרת הבת was
declared [in his name] to be permitted to a surviving brother.
This troubled the Sages [who forbade such a union on Biblical
grounds], because Rebbi Dosa the son of Horkinus was an
authoritative figure [and some people would understandably
follow his decision] ... They involved him in halachic discussion, finally touching upon the subject of צרת הבת. They asked
him, "What is the *halacha* concerning צרת הבת?" He replied that
the *halacha* follows *Bes Hillel's* opinion [that it is forbidden].
They said, "But don't people quote you as saying that here we
follow *Bes Shammai's* opinion [that it is permitted]?" He
answered, "I have a younger brother [also a 'son of Horkinus']
who is extremely sharp, stands firmly by the way he was taught
and acts on it; and he is a disciple of Shammai. [It was this
brother, and not I, who declared it permissible.] Now, beware
getting involved with him in *halachic* discussion, for he has
three hundred proofs that צרת הבת is permitted!"

"Three hundred proofs!" And yet, before this passage, we only
knew of one or two. We have no idea what the other many proofs
were. What great and complex debates must have been carried on
over that issue; yet we are ignorant of most of the arguments each
side presented!

---

[38] The *s'vara*, logical halachic principle, is "אין איסור חל על איסור, an object already off-
limits does not accept additional prohibitions."

Obviously, the Mishna and Gemora present to us only selected explanations for why each Sage held as he did. But there may have been, in any given case, hundreds of pieces of evidence behind a decision which remain unknown to us.

Tracing the Links

This same passage illustrates another important principle: From reading the *mishna* in *Yevomos* one would think that the issue of צרת הבת was introduced by *Bes Hillel*, who, based on a *drash*, forbade such a union. But the story goes on to tell us that after Rebbi Dosa ben-Horkinus warned the Sages of his brother's skills in proving that צרת הבת is permitted, he went on to say,

אבל מעיד אני עלי שמים וארץ שעל מדוכה זו ישב חגי הנביא ואמר . . . צרת הבת
אסורה.

But I call to witness upon myself the Heavens and the Earth that the Prophet Ḥaggai sat on this seat and said that צרת הבת is forbidden!

We now discover that the matter had already been taken up in the days of the Prophets,[39] though it would seem from the *mishna* to be an issue first discussed by *Bes Hillel* and *Bes Shammai* several centuries later.[40]

This is not an unusual occurrence. Frequently, statements did not originate with the authorities we see making them.[41] In a system where preservation of previous information was so important, much of what we find in the Talmud consists of reports and interpretations of previously made statements. The Sages quoted in the Talmud are reasserting and reaffirming what their teachers taught them and are involved in proving and defending these teachings against challenges from opponents doing the same with *their* mentors' teachings. Even the proofs and disproofs may be repetitions of arguments

---

[39] See Additional Notes at the end of this chapter.

[40] See Additional Notes at the end of this chapter.

[41] The *Gemora* regularly *assumes* that a teaching by an *Amora* does not originate with him, but with a received teaching going at least as far back as the *Tannaim*. See Additional Notes to Chapter 1, note 41.

that had been around for generations.[42] This brings us to an observation and a problem.

Where to Start, Where to End?

Sometimes the *Gemora* traces a statement of an *Amora* through a chain of teachers and says, for example, "אמר רבה אמר רב יהודה אמר שמואל, Rabba said Rav Yehuda said Shmuel said . . . " but sometimes it attributes the statement only to the earliest of the authorities in the chain and simply says, "אמר שמואל, Shmuel said." Now, it was through Shmuel's disciples' disciples that Ravina and Rav Ashi, who canonized the words of the *Gemora*, always received their information about what Shmuel, who lived long before them, said. Why in some instances did Ravina and Rav Ashi give us the most recent link in the chain of tradition and in other instances only the original propounder of the statement?[43] Moreover, sometimes the *Gemora* begins its reverse-order list with a more recent authority and sometimes with an earlier, but not the earliest, one. For example, sometimes it will state, "אמר רב יהודה אמר שמואל, Rav Yehuda said Shmuel said," sometimes, " אמר רבה אמר רב יהודה אמר שמואל, Rabba said Rav Yehuda said Shmuel said," and sometimes, "אמר רבא אמר רבה אמר רב יהודה, Rava said Rabba said Rav Yehuda said." When Rav Ashi and Ravina reported a statement, tracing it to its earliest source, on what basis did they decide whether to begin with their own source of information (e.g., their teacher Rava), or to skip one or two steps away from their source and begin from there (with Rabba or Rav Yehuda), or to simply cite the statement in the name of Shmuel? What determined with whom to start the list and with whom to terminate it? Furthermore, since even the earliest link named is often not the actual *original* author of the statement, why do they not

---

[42] Consequently, it is often unclear when a *machlokess* actually arose for the first time. But sometimes we can tell exactly when one began, such as when we see two disciples disagreeing over the intention of their mentor's statement. Examples of such arguments will be seen in chapter 7.

[43] At times another style is used: A recent authority is listed, and then a much earlier authority, skipping intermediary links. This phenomenon is discussed in *Nazir* 56b and *Yerushalmi Shabbos* 1:2 and *Shekallim* 2:5, end of *Gemora*. The conclusion is simply that it is not necessary, when listing one's sources, to cite more than the most recent and the most ancient links known (see Rashi on *Nazir*, *loc. cit.*) But we are raising other problems.

always trace the statement all the way back to its original propounder?

A Possible Explanation

The question could be answered by saying that certain statements or
maxims were recorded in the name of the authority who first popu-
larized them. Let's say Shmuel declared, "דינא דמלכותא דינא, The law
of the land is the law [when it does not contradict Jewish law]" and
everybody heard about it. When later generations cited that maxim,
they would preface it with "אמר שמואל, Shmuel said." Thus, Ravina
and Rav Ashi, too, reported the maxim in the name of Shmuel alone.

But other statements did not gain such publicity until later, when
they were reported by their author's disciple or by the disciple's disciple, and so forth. Then, the statement became known by the words
in which that disciple reported it: "א'רב יהודה א'שמואל, Rav Yehuda
said Shmuel said" or "אמר רבה א'רב יהודה א'שמואל Rabba said Rav
Yehuda said that Shmuel said."

Finally, if the statement only became known to Ravina and Rav
Ashi through a report of a third- or fourth-generation disciple who
listed all the links up to a point and then stopped, then Ravina and
Rav Ashi reported all those links, starting with their source and
going all the way back to the earliest author that source reported.

The Strata of the Talmud

This fits in well with the approach developed by Rav Y.I. Halevy in
his *Doros Harishonim*.[44] He maintains that at periodic junctions the
discussions of the Sages were put down into formulated wording.
That wording then became the "text" which the following generations of Sages analyzed and discussed. Eventually, the same thing
occurred with the discussions of *those* Sages: *Their* discussions
became formally worded, and later Sages analyzed *them*.

The *Doros Harishonim* further demonstrates that a major wording formulation was canonized (orally, not in writing) during the
time of the Academy of Abbaye and Rava (4100, 340 C.E.), when
every single Jewish Sage was an active participant of that one
academy. Ravina and Rav Ashi primarily were involved in analyz-

---

[44] Rav Halevy's approach is followed by Rabbi Avigdor Miller, שליט"א, in his
English works, *Torah Nation* and *Exalted People*.

ing the ''Gemora'' formulated by Abbaye and Rava.[45] That is why the discussions of the Sages are referred to (*Succa* 28a) as ''הוויות דאביי ורבא, the discussions of Abbaye and Rava,'' even though Abbaye and Rava lived more than a century before the חתימת הש״ס, the final ''Closing of the Gemora,'' by Ravina and Rav Ashi and their disciples. The *Doros Harishonim* maintains that the narrative of the Gemora, the ''סתמא דגמרא,'' is the work of Abbaye and Rava.

Ravina and Rav Ashi (c. 4200) therefore contributed to the Talmud an analysis of the earlier ''text'' established by Abbaye and Rava (c. 4100) just as *that* ''text'' is an analysis of the *Mishna* completed by Rebbi Yehuda HaNassi (c. 4000) as an analysis of the ''text'' established by the Academy of Yavneh (c. 3800), which was an analysis of the ''text'' set by the Academy of Hillel and Shammai (c. 3700), which had analyzed the ''text'' set by the *Men of the Great Assembly* of Biblical times (c. 3400).[46]

This explains why some *Gemora* passages begin their reversed-order list of authorities not with Ravina and Rav Ashi's teachers, but with the teachers of Abbaye and Rava, the earlier Sages. Those passages are themselves the preserved texts already canonized as the סתמא דגמרא, the *anonymous narrative*, by Abbaye and Rava, a century before the time of Ravina and Rav Ashi's canonization of the *Gemora*. We can therefore find the Gemora quoting Rabba directly—''אמר רבה כה וכה, Rabba (the teacher of Abbaye and Rava) said such-and-such''—even though he lived long before Ravina and Rav Ashi.

This approach makes clear otherwise perplexing sequences of discussion in the Talmud. Consider the following passage from *Gittin* 38b:

גופא אמר רב יהודה אמר שמואל, כל המשחרר עבדו עובר בעשה שנאמר לעולם בהם תעבודו.

מיתיבי: מעשה ברבי אליעזר שנכנס בבית הכנסת ולא מצא עשרה, ושחרר עבדו והשלימו לעשרה.

---

[45] Cf. *Kiddushin* 53a: ''Said Rav Aḥa son of Rava in the name of the *Gemora* . . .'' and Rashi's comment: ''כך נקבעה בגמרא ושגורה בפי בני בית המדרש, (The text) was formalized that way in the *Gemora*, (memorized) and readily on the lips of the scholars.''

[46] The Jerusalem Talmud itself (*Shekallim 5:1*) indicates that The Men of the Great Assembly, a thousand years after the Oral Law was revealed at Sinai, were the first to categorize and standardize its wording. Rabbeynu Saadia Gaon (*Sefer Hagaluy*) also writes that this Sanhedrin was responsible for the original phraseology of the Mishna.

מצוה שאני.:

ת"ר: לעולם בהם תעבדו—רשות, דברי רבי ישמעאל. ר"ע אומר חובה.

ודלמא ר"א סבר לה כמאן דאמר רשות (פרש"י: כר' ישמעאל ומאי דוחקיה לשנויי
לעיל מצוה שאני).

Rav Yehuda [the *Amora*] said in the name of Shmuel: Anyone who frees his Canaanite servant transgresses the command, "You shall work them forever" (*Vayikra* 25:46).

Objection: Rebbi Eliezer [the *Tanna*] once entered the synagogue and did not find ten men there [for a *minyan*], and he freed his servant [which makes him a Jew] to make up the number.

For a *mitzva*, it's different.

* * *

[But] the *Tannaim* taught: Rebbi Yishmael stated, "The *posuk* translates, 'You are *permitted* to work them forever.'" Rabbi Akiva stated, "It translates, 'You *must* work them forever.'"

[—So what forced them to answer, above, "For a *mitzva*, it's different"?—*Rashi*] Perhaps Rebbi Eliezer simply held as the one who permitted it!

Apparently, the final two paragraphs are an analysis of the passage before them, just as the *Gemora* is an analysis of the *Mishna*.[47] Perhaps the original statement, "אמר רב יהודה אמר שמואל, Rav Yehuda said that Shmuel said" was what Rav Yehuda's student, Rabba, reported to his own students, Rava and Abbaye. They, in turn, drafted this information into the anonymously stated *Gemora* passage together with the difficulty raised against it and their answer, "מצוה שאני." A century later, Ravina and Rav Ashi had this text before them. They then preserved it and added comments of their own:[48] "Perhaps Rebbi Eliezer simply held as the one who permitted it!"

We will further develop the by-ways of *halachic* analysis and *machlokess*. But the next several chapters will explore how it came to pass that the Sages did not possess from Moses ready *halachic* responses to all situations.

---

[47] This would also account for "two vertical dots" (three asterisks in the translation) interrupting the passage, without resorting to the claim of a printing error.
[48] Or of predecessors.

Additional Notes to Chapter 1

2. As a hypothetical example of this process, let us imagine two statements. One says: *It is forbidden to build on Shabbos.* The other says:
   Build a synagogue every day.

   Left unqualified, the statements are in conflict regarding building a
   synagogue on Shabbos. Without a tradition telling us which command
   overrides the other, we would have several possibilities to consider:
   The rule is to refrain from building on Shabbos, but building synagogues is an exception. Or the rule is to build synagogues every day, but
   the Shabbos prohibition overrides it. Or perhaps both statements were
   not made by the same author; one author held that there was no daily
   imperative to build a synagogue at all, whereas the other maintained
   that anything—not to mention a synagogue—may be built on Shabbos.
   Other laws, too, besides the ones about building synagogues on Shabbos, may be influenced by how we choose to modify and relate these
   statements to each other, just as in our metaphor of the multi-
   possibility jigsaw puzzle, wherever we place one piece will determine
   where and how we will place others and, accordingly, a different "picture" of *halachos* will emerge. These decisions were made by the
   authorities quoted in the Talmud.

9. The last words of *Shoresh Shayni* in *Sefer HaMitzvos*. It is interesting
   to trace the "מלאכת ה'" of each era. In the *Introduction* to his *Mishneh
   Torah*, the Rambam states that at the close of the Talmud, scrutinizing
   the Gemora and applying it to everyday life became the מלאכת ה', Divine Task, of the Sages (*Gaonim*). He describes the work of the previous Sages, the *Amoraim*, as doing the same with the words of the
   Mishna. Rashi (*Sota* 20a ד"ה והדר אתא לקמיה דר"ע למסבר סברא) describes
   the *Tannaim's* own studies ("תלמוד שהיה בימי התנאים") to have been the
   analysis of the earlier *mishnayos*. And finally, the direct analysis of the
   Torah's words, "להראות חכמת הכתוב, to demonstrate the profundity of the
   Written Law," by showing how it really contains the Oral Law as well,
   was the preceding Sages' מלאכת ה', Divine Task.

15. The *Maharal of Prague*, in *Sefer Be'er HaGola*, end of *Be'er HaShlishi*,
    may support this approach. He writes:
    ועוד יש לך לדעת ולהבין, כי כל מה שדרשו חכמים מן הכתוב, לא היה עיקר שלמדו זה מן
    הכתוב, רק כי בלא זה הדבר הוא כך לפי דעת ושכל חכמים. והדבר הוא אמת בעצמו, רק שאי
    אפשר שלא יהיה נרמז הדבר בכתוב, כי התורה היא תמימה ויש בה הכל, ולפיכך אי אפשר
    שלא יהיה הדבר נרמז במדרש, אף שהוא רחוק מאד סוף סוף נמצא בתורה הכל כמו שראוי
    לתורה.

    Translation is difficult. It *might* be as follows:
    "[Concerning] all that the Sages *darshonned* from Scripture, the main

thing is not that they derived it from that source. The law, according to the Sages' knowledge, is as they saw [it to be] without benefit of that derivation. The fact is independently so. Only, it is impossible for it not to be hinted at in Scripture, since the Torah is perfect and contains everything that is true. It is therefore impossible for the fact not to be hinted at through the vehicle of *drash*. As is proper for the Torah, everything is ultimately to be found within it, even if through an indication that is remote.''

Nevertheless, in the entire section preceding this statement, the *Maharal* maintained and demonstrated that the "חכמה", was closely connected to the verse cited and that ''והם עיקר פשט הכתוב''—it is not merely a "poetic device.''

Rabbi Joseph Elias, in personal conversation, has pointed out that another support for the *Doros Harishonim's* approach may be the *Ohr HaḤayyim's* commentary on *Vayikra* 13:34:

ואין הכרח לדרשת הלל עד שעלה לא״י וידע שכן באה ההלכה. מעתה נחזור לקבוע ההלכה בכתוב. . . . ולא תקשה דלמא נתכוון הכתוב באומר טהור אפילו ידע הוא שהוא טהור, כי אין זה אלא דחיה, ותצדק קודם בירור האמת שכך באה הלכה. אבל אחר שהדין שאנו קובעים ביתור הוא הלכה, יותר נבחר לומר לזה נתכוון מלדחות דחיות. וזה כלל נכון בפירוש התורה.

The law that Hillel reached through *drash* was inconclusive until he went up to Israel and [thereby] knew that the *halacha* came [from previous generations] as he had determined. As of then we can go back to establish that the intent of Scripture is to state that this is the true *halacha*. . . . And [so] do not raise the objection that the verse may [tolerate another meaning] . . . for this is merely an alternate suggestion, acceptable only before the truth—that the *halacha* is such-and-such—has come down. But once a meaning that conforms to the *halacha* can be assigned to the verse, it is preferable to say that this was its intent, rather than to engage in raising other possibilities.

17. Have these facts completely disproven the approach of the *Doros Harishonim*? Actually, the only iron-clad proof against it would be passages in which—solely on the basis of a *drash*—an *Amora* conceded to his opponent about a *halacha*. But the *Doros Harishonim* would probably dismiss even that as a proof against him by saying that the concession was actually based on a logic-related reconsideration upon which the *Gemora* did not wish to elaborate. That is his approach, and to support it, he cites many passages which clearly seem to present a *posuk* as an *Amora's* source and then shows other passages in which the same *Amora* presented, as proof for the same thing, a quotation from a past mentor. This proves, he maintains, that the real source of the *Amora's* opinion was not the *drash* but his understanding of his mentor's teachings. Of course, it is possible to reply that the *posuk* was the source used by that mentor, as well, and so was part of the disciple's *kabballa*.

39. Nevertheless, we needn't say that *Bes Shammai* was rejecting a *drash* made by ancient generations (although, technically, it may have had the right to do so, as will be explained in the chapter entitled "Disputes Over Drashos Previously Accepted by Sanhedrin"). And certainly we needn't say that *Bes Shammai* was disagreeing with the prophet's report of a קבלה from Moses. Rav Moshe Feinstein, *z"l*, writes in *Dibros Moshe, Shabbos,* p. 130:

וחגי הנביא אמרה זה מצד חכמתו וקבלתו מרבותיו שאם יש קושיא מוכרחין לחזור, ואף שאפשר שאיכא תירוץ שלא הבינו לתרץ—לא שייך זה כשהיו כולם יחד. שמוכרחין להחליט חכמי דור זה—שהיו בעלי הוראה ומסנהדרין ובכחם גם לחלוק על דורות הראשונים.

Ḥaggai the Prophet said this based on his own wisdom and his *kabballa* from his teachers, which means that if there would be a difficulty found with accepting it as true, the later Sages would be obliged to retract. And although there is possibly some unknown answer, this is not grounds [to ignore the difficulty] since the Sanhedrin sat together, compelling the Sages of that generation to reach a decision based on their own judgment—being that they were qualified to promulgate *halacha* and that they were of the Sanhedrin, having the power to contest the decisions of the ancient generations.

The עיון יעקב suggests a way in which *Bes Shammai* merely may have been disagreeing with *Bes Hillel* in *interpreting* the words of the prophet: True, Ḥaggai is known to have said, "צרת הבת אסורה, the co-wife of one's daughter is prohibited," but he did not necessarily mean that she is prohibited to *him*, as Rebbi Dosa ben-Horkinus took it. It may mean that she is prohibited to marry anyone else without dissolving her relationship with her late husband's brother through *ḥalitsa*, and *yibbum* with him is encouraged.

40. צרת הבת is the first known long-standing *machlokess* that had a practical difference on a purely *Biblical* level. Actually, there were even earlier *machlokos*, such as one in the days of King Shaul and David (*Sanhedrin* 19b). But the *Maharatz Ḥayyos* (*Mishpaht HaHora'a*, 9, see also *Gra* 'א אות on *Temura* 16a) explains that these were settled immediately. (See *Tosefos, Ḥaggiga* 16a ד"ה יוסי בן יועזר כו'.) The classically cited first long-standing *machlokess* was about "סמיכה" (*Yerushalmi, Ḥaggiga* 2:2). This involved the requirement regarding some sacrifices (see *Menachos* 16a) that one place his hands upon the animal to be offered, leaning upon it with his full body's weight (see *Vayikra* 1:4, 3:2). Under dispute was whether this סמיכה, leaning, must be done when the procedure of the offering begins (i.e., immediately preceding the *shechita*) or whether it may be done some time in advance. This became a practical issue once there was a rabbinical prohibition against supporting oneself upon animals on *Shabbos* and *Yom Tov*: If it is Biblically permissible to perform *semicha* sometime before the sacrifice is

offered, then it *must* be done *before* the arrival of *Yom Tov*, and not *on* the *Yom Tov*.

41. In footnote 41 proper, we have noted that the *Gemora* regularly *assumes* that a teaching by an *Amora* does not originate with him, but with a received teaching going at least as far back as the *Tannaim*. This explains passages such as one in *Bava Metsia* 95a, which records a dispute between *Amoraim* over a *halacha* (אם יש פטור של "אם בעליו עמו" בשומר חנם, כמו שיש גבי שואל)—based upon a *machlokess* over how to *darshon p'sukim* (היינו, אם מקרא נדרש ע"י וי"ו מוסיף רק לפניו—לפסוק של שומר שכר—או אפילו ללפני פניו—לפסוק של שומר חנם)—yet objections are raised against one of the Amoraim on the grounds that "his" proposed *halacha* is not mentioned in Tannaitic sources. Evidently, despite the original presentation of the *machlokess* as being one of *Amoraim* over a *drash*, it is assumed that their stands were meant to represent what they thought the *Tannaim* held.

Chapter 2

The Problem

I t should be obvious that the need to correctly perform *mitzvos* began the moment Moses brought the Torah to the people. When the Torah forbade *m'lacha*, "work," once a week, the need to define the term was urgent. We are told[1] that the Sages derived, from the activities involved in erecting the *Mishkan* (the portable Tabernacle of the Israelites' forty-year stay in the Wilderness) the identities of thirty-nine forbidden activities. One is left with the impression that this analysis first took place years after Moses' time. But did not Moses and his own generation desire to keep the Sabbath—whose desecration was a capital crime? Surely the specific activities that were forbidden must have been clear to that generation no less than they are to ours. Indeed, we know that an individual of Moses' time was recognized as being guilty of Sabbath desecration because he gathered wood on that day (*Bamidbar* 15:32-36). The gathering of wood was forbidden as one of the thirty-nine *m'lachos* and everyone was expected to know the fact.

It is self-evident, then, that the need to know the definitions of forbidden activity did not suddenly materialize generations after Moses and that they were clear to Moses and the people. Moreover, Moses' own generation may have needed to analyze the work done on the *Mishkan* in order to draw parallels to learn what activities

---

[1] *Shabbos* 49b.

were forbidden on Shabbos, if these were not explicitly told to them by G-d. Quite likely, this study was immediately begun in preparation for encountering questionable situations as well as future kinds of society and technologies, and at any rate it certainly was considered to be of academic value as pure Torah-study. Thus, the Sages of whom the *Gemora* speaks as deriving the thirty-nine *m'lachos* from the *m'lachos* involved in erecting the *Mishkan* may well have included those Sages of Moses' own days.

And so it is with all the *mitzvos*. Their practical details were necessarily revealed in Moses' own lifetime and this is how later generations knew how to perform them. Thus, in observance of the commands whose Scriptural instructions are inexplicit, King Solomon of the First Temple era, just as we, waved the "four species" on *Succos*, and Joshua, just as we, placed *tefillin* on his arms and head. Except for a small number of *halachic* parameters and definitions that were formally given over to the Sages to create,[2] the particulars for fulfilling the commandments were necessarily known in a specific, unambiguous manner from the time of Sinai. The *mitzvos* were not given to us in the form of vague principles which future generations were to expand upon. The specifics for performing the *mitzvos* existed the moment the basic commandments were given and the people of Moses' and Joshua's time obeyed the *mitzvos* in a specific way. It is precisely for this reason that the question of this book becomes manifest: Since the *mitzvos* were already understood and practiced in the time of Moses and Joshua, how did it occur that *machlokos*, different opinions, later arose regarding their correct fulfillment? One may reply that G-d left it to later generations to determine, through following the set guidelines in analysis of the Torah, details first relevant to them—and *machlokess* was a natural outcome. The documentation for this possibility will be presented later. But how do we explain the existence of *machlokos* among the Sages of the Talmud, who lived centuries after Moses, over issues already relevant to Moses' own generation? Such issues either had been treated explicitly by the *Oral Law* or had to have been decided upon by the Sanhedrin of Moses' time. Certainly, Moses' generation had to carry out the *mitzvos*, too. And presumably the later Sages wished to practice them the same way.

---

[2] Such as the *m'lachos* to be forbidden on *Chol HaMoed*, the intermediate days of the Three Festivals (*Ḥaggiga* 18a). Again, the first Sages to pass decisions on these definitions must have been those of Moses' own time.

No Original Practice to Duplicate?

Some may simply attempt to deny that any matters subject to *mach-lokos* were relevant in Moses' time—the few examples cited in our Introduction being the only exceptions to the rule, and therefore insignificant. They may assert that any *halachos* we find under dispute in the Talmud were not practiced in any form whatsoever in Moses' days. The argument would be made that *kashrus, shechita*[3] and crime were hardly topical for those sustained by *manna* and whose conduct was constantly supervised by officers. After all, as pointed out in the Introduction itself, many *machlokos* involve remote and hypothetical situations and borderline cases. One may argue that they were never of immediate concern to Moses' generation. One may theorize that no questions concerning transgressions were raised in any of the early generations of piety and strict precautions. We cannot prove that any of the 207 prohibitions entailing lashing (*Hilchos Sanhedrin* 19:1-4) were committed in Moses' time, and considering the people's caliber and their system of policing, it is unlikely that any were. Again, of the 36 transgressions that entail capital punishment (*Hilchos Sanhedrin* 15:10-12), we know of only four that were committed.[4]

It may even be claimed that questions about the correct way to punish wrongdoers went unasked in Moses' time since even concerning sins that were committed, we cannot prove that the standard punishments were meted out. For example, in the case of שתוי יין שמשש, a *Kohane* who illegally performs the Temple service after drinking wine (*Vayikra* 10:9, *Sanhedrin* 22b, 83b), there is a *mach-lokess* if his punishment includes lashings (*Makkos* 13a-b). Now, according to one opinion, this prohibition was transgressed in Moses' time (*Vayikra Rabba* 12:1, cited by Rashi on *Vayikra* 10:2). Yet we cannot look back to that incident to see whether the standard punishment should include lashings, because a Heavenly punishment was immediately meted out, too swiftly for Moses' Sanhedrin to mete out any of its own. Similarly, there is a dispute (*Sanhedrin* 80b) about the warning that must be given a would-be perpetrator

---

[3] In *Hilchos Shechita* 4:17, the Rambam writes that while in the desert, the Jews were not commanded to follow the standard laws of kosher slaughter.

[4] Two involving idolatry (*Sh'mos* 32 regarding the Golden Calf affair, and *Bamidbar* 25, regarding the *Baal Peor*), one involving blasphemy (*Vayikra* 24:10), and one involving Shabbos desecration (*Bamidbar* 15:32).

of a capital crime to make him culpable: Must the warning include naming the precise form of execution for which the criminal would be liable? Apparently, to solve the problem we need only cite the case in the Torah (*Bamidbar* 15:32 *ff.*) in which someone had committed a sin necessitating capital punishment, but was kept imprisoned until G-d Himself revealed that he was to be stoned, because even Moses was unsure of the form of capital punishment due. Obviously, then, no precise warning was given and yet he was executed, proving that such precise warning is unnecessary. How did the Sage who held that the form of execution must be an integral part of the warning reconcile his tradition with this obvious fact? The answer is supplied by the Talmud itself (*Makkos* 13a-b): According to this Sage's learning, the punishment meted out was simply an instance of *hora'as sha'a*, an exceptional measure that G-d ordered taken, from which we cannot learn standard procedure.

The Laws Were Known

However, this argument—that such details of *halacha* were unknown to later disputants because they were not topical in Moses' time and therefore had never been determined before—disregards the consideration that the Jews of the Wilderness, having no other pursuits, spent their lives intensely studying the Torah's laws for the sake of posterity. The laws may not have all been practiced, but they were known. The Talmud and the *Rishonim* clearly emphasize that the basic details of all the *mitzvos* were taught to the people. And although punishments for crimes may have been for them an academic study, the avoidance of the slightest scintilla of misbehavior was a vital concern. Besides, many commandments of commission were of practical concern even to them. At any rate, even if details were not relevant to Moses' generation, they were to Joshua's, or the Judges.' Surely the Sages would settle for practicing the laws as they were performed by any of those earlier generations, and surely these generations practiced them.

And so we remain with our original problem: Why did the Sages have to determine the correct performance of the Torah's precepts, concerning laws that were relevant in the past? The precepts presumably should be performed as they were then.

The following chapters will present and discuss some solutions to this problem.

Chapter 3

Loss of Halachos

An obvious solution to why the Sages needed to determine details of Torah-law is that as generations passed, the transmitted data on a given point of law—either that given by G-d or determined by Moses' Sanhedrin—was simply lost.[1] The scholars of later generations were therefore charged with reconstructing the forgotten details of the law by utilizing whatever pertinent information they still had.

The Objection

There is, of course, a ready objection to this suggestion. How *could* any law become lost? The *mitzva* was practiced by Moses' generation, the next generation duplicated the practice, and each following generation repeated the practice of its predecessors. When could any practice have possibly slipped away?

The answer is that the knowledge of some details was not continuously relevant. The situations demanding clarification were rare, or the mitzva somehow fell into disuse for a substantial length of time.[2]

The Talmud readily acknowledges that there were laws forgotten

---

[1] See Additional Notes to this chapter.

[2] See Additional Notes at the end of this chapter.

during periods of disuse. The Talmud delineates how this occurred with a rabbinical decree (*Brachos* 33a):

מזכירין . . . הבדלה [במוצאי שבת] בחונן הדעת.

ר"ע אומר אומרה ברכה רביעית בפני עצמה.

רבי אליעזר אומר בהודאה.

א"ל רב שמן בר אבא לר"יוחנן: מכדי. אנשי כנה"ג תקנו להם לישראל ברכות ותפילות קדושות והבדלות. נחזי היכן תקון.

א"ל: בתחילה קבעוה בתפילה. העשירו [לקנות יין] קבעוה על הכוס. (פרש"י: ואז נשתכח תקנת עזרא, וכשחזרו ו)העני—חזרו וקבעוה בתפילה [ונחלקו היאך יאמרוה].

[In the Saturday night *Sh'moneh Essray*] the *havdala* recitation is inserted in the חונן הדעת *bracha*. Rabbi Akiva says that the recitation forms a fourth, independent *bracha*. And Rebbi Eliezer says that the recitation is inserted in the *bracha* that begins מודים אנחנו לך.

[The *Amora*] Rav Shimmon bar Abba asked Rav Yoḥonon: "[Why are there three positions on the matter?] The *Anshay Knessess HaG'dola*, The Men of the Great Assembly, are the ones who instituted the blessings, *Sh'moneh Essray* prayers, words of the *kiddush* over wine, and *havdala* [four centuries before the proponents named]! Why not just see how they prescribed saying the *havdala*?"

He replied: "Although they originally decreed that it should be said within the *Sh'moneh Essray*, when the nation's wealth grew the Sages decreed that it should be said outside the *Sh'moneh Essray*, over a cup of wine [Rashi: and the nation then forgot the original practice (of exactly where in the *Sh'moneh Essray* it used to be recited); When again] they became poor, the Sages reestablished the law to say it in the *Sh'moneh Essray* [but disagreed over exactly where it should be inserted].

Similarly, a *Tosefos* in *Brachos* 22b connects remembrance of laws to their frequency of practice. The *Gemora* states:

מכדי: כולהו אמוראי ותנאי בדעזרא קמיפלגי; ונחזי עזרא היכי תיקן!

Let's see: The *Amoraim* and *Tannaim* are all arguing over a decree of Ezra. Why not just see how Ezra decreed it should be done!

Tosefos remarks:

בהרבה מקומות גבי שאר תקנות לא פריך גמ' הכי. אלא שאני הכא דדבר הרגיל בכל
יום הוא, על כן אנו זכורים.

In many other places, regarding other *takkonos*, the *Gemora*
does not raise this problem [that no argument should exist].
However, this case [concerning the method of purification needed by a man who had a seminal emission while ill] is unique,
since it concerns a constant occurrence. Therefore, we ought to
remember how it was done.[3]

And so we see that details of laws previously practiced were lost
due to interruptions of their practice. These interruptions were of
such duration that even the Sages became unfamiliar with the previously known details of law. The *Gemora* raises no objection at all
to the idea that these laws were forgotten.

Naturally, the solutions to issues reached by generations following Moses' were likewise forgettable, as is indicated by the *Gemora*
in *Succa* 25a:

אמרו על רבן יוחנן בן זכאי שלא הניח . . . הויות דאביי ורבא.

It was said of Rabban Yoḥonon ben Zakkai that he left nothing
[unmastered, including . . .] the issues analyzed by Abbaye and
Rava.

Rabban Yoḥonon ben Zakkai was a *Tanna*, yet he dealt with the
issues taken up by Abbaye and Rava, *Amoraim* who lived three centuries later. The purpose of this statement is to show the greatness of
Rabban Yoḥonon ben Zakkai. But the question presents itself: if he
already had solved the issues, why weren't Abbaye and Rava aware
of the solutions? Rashi explains:

ובימי אמוראים נשתכחו.

In the days of the *Amoraim*, these solutions were forgotten [and
the issues had to be reinvestigated].

[3] The *Gemora's* answer is that Ezra, when he made the decree, did not specify provisions for the detail in question, and it had never yet been tackled.

Even Moses Forgot

There is no reason to restrict the phenomenon of forgetting to rabbinical decrees. *Midrash Sh'mos Rabba* (41:6, see also *Nedarim* 38a) reports how Moses himself, while on Mount Sinai, found it impossible to remember the Torah laws that he was being taught. He endured this grueling and frustrating experience for a full forty days until finally he cried out, *"Ribbono Shel Olom!* (Master of the World!) Here I was for forty days and nights, and I have nothing to show for it!" Thereupon Hashem granted Moses the knowledge of the Torah as a gift.[4]

If *Moses* forgot what he was being taught by Hashem, certainly those of lesser caliber, including the Sages of the following generation, could forget, too.

Admittedly, one totally opposed to the idea that oral laws could be forgotten may insist that this Midrash is speaking of an extraordinary exception to the rule. The Talmud *Yerushalmi* (*Horios* 3:5) which also reports that Moses could not remember the information, proceeds to explain why Hashem allowed this to happen: to teach those slow in learning to be persistent. Moses went through forty days of frustrated attempts to retain his facts, yet each day he persevered and started anew his attempt to remember the information. Hashem finally "put" it into his mind. Likewise, the *Yerushalmi* teaches, persistence on our part will eventually result in retention. One might perhaps insist that Moses' forgetfulness was especially contrived by Hashem to teach this lesson, but that it was not "natural" for him or anyone else to forget oral laws. Therefore, once the people and their leaders *were* taught by Moses, they ("naturally") retained the information and relayed it intact to the next generation, and so on. However, this position is untenable, for we are told that even after Moses' return from Mount Sinai an unhappy incident caused the forgetting of oral laws (*Temura* 16a):

אמר רב יהודה אמר רב: בשעה שנפטר משה רבינו . . . אמר ליה ליהושע, שאל ממני
כל ספיקות שיש לך. אמר לו, רבי, כלום הנחתיך שעה אחת? . . . מיד תשש כחו של
יהושע [משה] ונשתכחו ממנו שלש מאות הלכות, ונולדו לו שבע מאות ספיקות

---

[4] This is the *Midrashic* explanation for the use of the word ״ויתן״ in the verse (*Sh'mos* 31:18) ״בהר סיני שני לוחות העדות וגו׳ ויתן אל משה ככלותו לדבר אתו״ "And He gave to Moses, when he had finished speaking to him upon Mt. Sinai, two tablets of testimony." The word used for *gave* can also connote the verb, *gifted.*

ועמדו כל ישראל להורגו. אמר לו הקב״ה, לומר לָךְ—אי אפשר; לֵךְ וטורדן
במלחמה.

Rav Yehuda said in the name of Rav: "When Moses was about
to leave this world . . . he told Joshua, 'Ask me about any [*halachic*] uncertainties you have.' Joshua replied, '[Do you think I
lack anything from you?] Have I ever left your presence for a
moment? . . . ' Immediately, Joshua grew weak; he forgot 300
halachos, and 700 uncertainties arose in his mind, and all Israel
arose to kill him.[5] The Holy One told him: 'For Me to tell you
the *halachos* is impossible. Go and preoccupy them in warfare!'"

Many other *halachos* were also lost almost as soon as they
became known—probably before they were called into practice—due
to the shock over Moses' death. These numbered in the thousands
(*Temura* 15b):

אמר רב יהודה אמר שמואל: [אע״פ שבהלכות שקבלו ממשה שזכרו, היו גמירין
(בדיוק—רש״י, תוס׳, רבינו גרשום) כמשה רבינו, מ״מ] שלש אלפים הלכות
נשתכחו בימי אבלו של משה.

Rav Yehuda said in the name of Shmuel: "[Even after Moses'
death, the people mastered as well as Moses whatever *halachos*
they received from him that they still remembered. Neverthe-
less] 3,000 *halachos* were forgotten during the period they
mourned his death."

Even analysis provided no unanimous conclusion as to their
original form. To create a standard *halachic* practice, the Sanhedrin
had to resort to following majority opinion (*Temura* 15b):

תניא: (פרש״י: [ובאלו ששכחו] דלא היו יודעין להחזיר אותן. . .—מתוך פלפול—
הלכה היאך, והיו חלוקין בהן) אם רבו מטמאין—טמאו; אם רבו טהורין— טיהרו.

A *Braissa* states: ([And of those that were forgotten] which they
couldn't restore through *pilpul,* analysis, and which resulted in
machlokess—Rashi) if the majority [of Sanhedrin] decided that

---

[5] Other *halachos* temporarily slipped the minds of Moses ((*Bamidbar* 27:5 and
31:21, see Rashi there, and *Z'vahim* 101a) and David (*Bamidbar Rabba* 4:21, 21:12.

something was טמא, then it was declared so; if the majority felt it was טהור, then it was declared so.[6]

But our protagonist may only slightly retreat from his former position and argue that laws given to Moses were still impervious to loss, and attribute the forgetability of the above-cited *halachos* to the claim that they were originally *drash*-generated, not Sinaitic, as is the case of the *halachos* mentioned in a similar passage (*Temura* 16a):

אלף ושבע מאות קלין וחמורין וגזירות שוות ודקדוקי סופרים נשתכחו בימי אבלו
של משה. אמר רבי אבהו, אף על פי כן, החזירן עתניאל בן קנז מתוך פלפולו . . .

1,700 *halachos* arrived at through *kal v'homers* and *gezeyra shavvas* were forgotten during the mourning period over Moses' death.[7] Said Rebbi Avahu: "Nevertheless, they were reconstructed through the *pilpul*, analysis, of Osniel ben Kenaz."[8]

Our protagonist may also claim that no originally Sinaitic *halacha* was ever permanently forgotten, for a prophet (in his capacity as a Sage) restored it[9] or a Sage or Sanhedrin succeeded in rescuing it

---

[6] As one may imagine, the people were quite agitated over the sudden loss of Torah rules so soon after they were revealed [*Temura* 16a]:

אמר רב יהודה אמר שמואל . . . אמרו לו ליהושע, שאל! אמר להם, לא בשמים היא. אמרו לו לשמואל, שאל!
אמר להם, „אלה המצות"—שאין הנביא רשאי לחדש דבר מעתה.

(Rav Yehuda said in the name of Shmuel: " . . . They told Joshua, 'Ask!' He replied, '[G-d has already said (*D'varim* 30:12)]: *It is not [any longer] in Heaven!*' They told Shmuel the Prophet, 'Ask!' He replied, '[G-d has already said (*Vayikra*, last verse)] *These [alone] are the mitzvos,* meaning that no prophet is permitted to declare any more [Torah commandments].'" See Additional Notes at the end of this chapter.

[7] In the *Sefer HaMitzvos, Shoresh Shayni* (p. 50 in our editions), the Rambam understands that these 1,700 *halachos* had originated, before Moses' death, through *drashos*. He cites this passage to prove that laws derived through *drash* generally cannot be individually counted under the label of the "613 Laws told to Moses at Sinai," but must be considered as details of Scripturally recorded laws.

[8] Osniel ben Kenaz was the Judge and leader after Joshua's death (*Judges* 3:9). He was the brother (*ibid.*) of Calev (the spy who, together with Joshua, refused to report negatively about Canaan to Moses [*Bamidbar* 13:30]) and became Calev's son-in-law (Joshua 15:17).

[9] *Shabbos* 104a and *Megilla* 3a (quoted in next chapter) regarding מנצפ״ך, the forms of the Hebrew letters when they occur at the ends of words, and *Succah* 44a regard-

from only near oblivion.[10] In other words, he may grant that loss
could occur regarding rabbinical ordinances, past applications of the
oral law to new situations, or regarding laws generated through *drashos*, but will deny that *halachos* explicitly told to Moses at Sinai[11]
could have been forgotten.[12] However, this distinction is simply
untrue. At least one *Halacha L'Moshe MiSinai* was among the forgotten *halachos* spoken of above and its form clearly remained a
matter of dispute (*Temura* 16a):

אמר רבי יצחק נפחא: אף חטאת שמתו [ס"א: שנתכפרו—ש"מ] בעליה נשתכחו
בימי אבלו של משה.

["If after someone consecrated an animal as a sin-offering it
wandered away and he therefore designated and used a new
animal for the offering and then the original animal was found,
what shall be done with it? That is, since it was once designated
for holy purposes, it can no longer simply be used mundanely
but neither can it be used for its designated purpose since the sin
was already atoned for.] Said Rebbi Yitzchak Nafḥa: [The solution to the issue surrounding the *Halacha L'Moshe MiSinai*[13]
that] a sin-offering whose owner already received atonement[14]
[became a matter of dispute because it] was [one of those laws]
'forgotten during the period of mourning for Moses.'"

ing three *Halachos L'Moshe MiSinai* concerning practices of Temple times (see
Tosefos). These matters were forgotten during the Babylonian Exile.

[10] *Succah* 20a in reference to Ezra, Hillel, and Rebbi Ḥeeya with his sons. *Yerushalmi, Payah* 1:1 (ג' דף), *Yerushalmi, Shabbos* 1:4 (דף א"י), and *Yerushalmi Kesubos*
11:1 (נ: דף).

[11] We are referring both to technical *Halachos L'Moshe MiSinai* and all other *peru-
shim m'kuballim miSinai*, details received from G-d. The only difference between
the two is whether they have indications in Scripture, a distinction that has no bearing on our subject. The Rambam states his principle that "there is no machlokess
with them" in reference to both types of Sinaitic *halachos* (*Maimonides' Introduction to the Talmud*, p. 84).

[12] As will be seen in the following chapter, the Rambam seems to argue very forcefully against suggesting that any Sinaitic law could be forgotten. We will deal with
his position there.

[13] *Temura* 18b, *B'choros* 16a.

[14] As per the alternate reading cited in *Sheeta Mikubetzes* in the *Gemora's* margin.
Our text reads: "[the issue surrounding] a sin-offering whose owner [e.g., designa-
tor] died [before actually using it to attain atonement]." From the *Gemora* it
becomes clear that the basic issue is the same in either case.

In *Temura* 15a-16a we see the dynamics of the attempt to reconstruct the original law.

משנה: חטאת היחיד שכפרו בעליה מתה, ושל צבור אינה מתה.

רבי יהודה אומר, תמות.

ת״ר: רבי שמעון אומר, . . . ילמד סתום מן המפורש: מה מפורש ביחיד ולא בצבור,
אף בשכיפרו בעליה . . . ביחיד דברים אמורים ולא בצבור. . . .

אמר ריש לקיש, ארבעה נתנו להן והעמידום על חמש. . . .

רבי נתן אומר, אחת נתנה להן והעמידוה על חמש. . . .

Mishna: [What is done with a previously lost animal consecrated as] a sin offering which [was found again after] its owner already used another one to gain forgiveness? It is allowed to die.

[This is speaking of an *individual's* sin offering.] But [such an animal] of a *national* sin offering is not let to die. [Instead, it is allowed to graze until it blemishes itself, whereupon one is allowed to sell it and use the money towards other sacrificial needs].

Rebbi Yehuda [disagrees and says that] it [the national sin offering, too] is allowed to die.

Rebbi Shimmon says [the *Halacha L'moshe MiSinai*[15] is that altogether] there are five types of sin offering that are let to die. [One is our case.] Just as three of them can only be those of an individual,[16] our case must also be speaking only of an individual's. That is the one left to die, but not a national sin offering!

Resh Lakish said: "They were given [as *Halacha L'Moshe MiSinai*] that four [of the five we let to die, and the fifth is left to graze. But during the people's mourning over Moses' death, they forgot which cases were the rule and which was the exception. So to be safe] they established the rule that all five be let to die. . . . "

Rebbi Nosson said: "[The *Halacha L'Moshe MiSinai* was that] only one [of the five is to be let to die.] But [to be safe] they established the rule for all five (*Rashi*: because they forgot which case got that *halacha* . . . actually two things were forgotten . . .)."

---

[15] *Temura* 18b, *B'choros* 16a.

[16] The *Gemora* explains why.

And so it is clear that laws given by G-d to Moses were susceptible to the people's loss, and that this can account for the need to
redetermine what the law was through analysis, which allows for
machlokos.

Another Proof: The Thirteen Principles of Torah Interpretation

Another proof that Sinaitic Oral Laws were no less susceptible to
loss than other laws: The Thirteen Principles of Torah Interpretation
were of course part of the Oral Law of Sinai.[17] Yet details of these
very guidelines are subject to *machlokos.* A look in the back of our
Gemora Brachos in the work, קיצור כללים מי"ג מדות שהתורה נדרשת בהן,
Abridged Guidelines to the Thirteen Interpretation Rules, shows
that there are *machlokos* over details of their mechanics.[18] What
further proof is necessary to show that *oral laws* given at Sinai and
conveyed to us by Moses must have been partially lost!

All Types of Oral Laws Forgotten

And so it is not surprising that the classic talmudic commentators
find no trouble with the idea that oral laws suffered loss. On the
contrary, in *Eruvin* 21b, for example, Rashi (ד"ה ויותר מהמה) plainly
comments:

אלו דברי תורה שנמסרו למשה על פה שנחלקו בהן חכמי ישראל לאחר שנתמעט
הלב ושכחו. . .

[Kohelless 12:11 refers to] the words of Torah that were given
[by Hashem] to Moses [orally, concerning] which the Sages of
Israel held disputes, since intellectual abilities decreased and the
Sages forgot [their learning].

---

[17] *Maimonides' Introduction to the Talmud*, p. 38; Hebrew Section, p. 4: '' . . . מדות
השלש עשרה הנתונות על הר סיני שהתורה נדרשת בהם.'' As mentioned in Chapter 1, these rules
of interpretation were utilized by Moses himself to produce thousands of law details
(*Sefer HaMitzvos, Shoresh Shayni*, p. 50 in our editions).
[18] Such as whether, concerning the mechanics of למדין ומשיבין ג"ש; אין עונשין מן הדין if
כללי דון מינה ואוקי באתריה או דון מינה ומינה, over בדמופנה מצד אחד; over whether to *darshon*
ריבויי ומיעוטי or ופרטי; and concerning the מדה of יצא לדון בדבר חדש there is a מחלוקת
whether דאיהו בלבד הוא דלא גמר מכלליה אבל כלליה גמר מיניה. See Additional Notes at
the end of this chapter.

Here we have a clear pronouncement that (1) parts of the *Oral Law* given to us by Hashem were eventually forgotten and (2) that this was a cause for *machlokos*.

We will see in the next chapter more examples of *Halachos L'Moshe MiSinai* that fell victim to loss and *machlokess*. It is only logical that the *origin* of a law does not affect its remembrance. Why should telling the people that a certain law-detail had been explicated by Hashem make them less liable to forget it than had the law come through a *gezayra shavva*? Likewise, there is no reason a technical *Halacha L'Moshe MiSinai* should be less susceptible to loss than any other type of oral law. The Rambam's objections to saying that *machlokos* stem from forgetting oral laws—to be dealt with in the next chapter—were stated regarding all oral laws, not only *Halachos L'Moshe MiSinai*. *Halachos L'Moshe MiSinai* are unique among oral laws only in that they are not even hinted at in Scripture.[19]

Machlokos Concerning Halachos L'Moshe MiSinai

Is it reasonable to construct a scenario where one Sage did not learn of a particular oral explanation and developed an interpretation of the law on his own, in the process disputing a law that Moses received at Sinai? Might it also be possible that even though a law is remembered, its origin could have become obscure, none knowing for certain if it had originated as a law told to Moses at Sinai, or as a rabbinical law, or as the result of a *drash*? Indeed, there are such *machlokos*. However, as soon as a Sage declared that the source for a ruling was a *Halacha L'Moshe MiSinai*, he would be interrogated to determine the truth of the claim. If it checked out, then any opposing views would of course be retracted.[20] As the saying among the Sages went (*Yevomos* 76b), "אם הלכה—נקבל; ואם לדין—יש תשובה!", If it *is* truly a *Halacha*, then I'll accept it, but if it's only a דין, a conclusion based upon analysis, there's a rejoinder (I can make)!" Obviously, the one who made this statement considered the possibility real, though unlikely, that he was unwittingly disputing a *Sinaitic Halacha*.

---

[19] *Maimonides' Introduction to the Talmud*, p. 84.

[20] *Cf. Tosefos, Yevomos* 77b, and מהרש"א מהדורא בתרא on it.

No Refusal to Accept Facts

Normally, as soon as a Sage is given *any* data of which he was previously unaware, he will accept it (assuming, of course, that he considers the information reliable).[21]

The following *Mishna* and *Gemora* (*Needa* 7b) show this attitude in action:

משנה: רבי אליעזר אומר ד' נשים דיין שעתן: בתולה, מעוברת, מניקה, וזקינה (משום גזירה).

א'רבי יהושע: אני לא שמעתי אלא בתולה. אבל הלכה כר"א.

גמ': תניא אמר לו רבי אליעזר לרבי יהושע: אתה לא שמעת [אלא אחת ו]אני שמעתי הרבה. אין אומרים למי שלא ראה את החדש, יבא ויעיד, אלא למי שראהו.

כל ימיו של רבי אליעזר היו עושין כרבי יהושע. לאחר פטירתו של ר"א החזיר רבי יהושע את הדבר ליושנו כר"א. בחייו מ"ט לא? משום דר"א שמותי הוא, וסבר [רבי יהושע] אי עבדינן כוותיה בחדא, עבדינן כוותיה באחרנייתא, ומשום כבודו דר"א לא מצינן מחינן בהו. לאחר פטירתו של ר"א דמצינו מחינן בהו—החזיר את הדבר ליושנו.

MISHNA: Rebbi Eliezer says: "[The law is] דיין שעתן[22] concerning *four* kinds of women: a virgin, a pregnant woman, a nursing woman, and an elderly woman."

Rebbi Yehoshua says: "I only heard this about a virgin. But the law is as Rebbi Eliezer said."

GEMORA: A *braissa* states: "Rebbi Eliezer had replied to Rebbi Yehoshua : 'You only heard it about one, and I heard it about several! We don't ask someone who has *not* seen the new moon to testify that it appeared; we ask the one who *did* see it [since he obviously has more complete information]!'"

The *Gemora* continues:

[Actually, since Rebbi Eliezer's information was more complete, Rebbi Yehoshua (the *Av Bes Din* of the Sanhedrin) privately admitted that it was correct. Nevertheless,] as long as Rebbi

---

[21] See Additional Notes at the end of this chapter.
[22] That is, "[the law is] satisfied [to begin considering objects they touched as unfit for holy purposes with] the time [they actually noticed their menstrual bleeding, and does not consider the objects unfit as of the time the bleeding must have started]."

Eliezer [the Ḥacham, the Sage acknowledged as the greatest *halachic* expert] was still alive, the Sanhedrin followed Rebbi Yehoshua. After Rebbi Eliezer died, though, Rebbi Yehoshua himself instituted Rebbi Eliezer's [more lenient] account of the law, which was [admittedly] the original version! [Why then didn't Rebbi Yehoshua proclaim during Rebbi Eliezer's lifetime that the latter was correct? Because] Rebbi Eliezer was a follower of Shammai, and Rebbi Yehoshua was afraid that if we would approve of Rebbi Eliezer's opinion in even one controversial matter, people would be prone to accept his rulings in other controversies [where the law does not follow *Bes Shammai's* opinion] as well. But to inform the people of their error [on the side of severity] during Rebbi Eliezer's lifetime would have encroached upon his honor. After his death, the law could be reinstated in its original [more lenient] form, and [if the people would follow Rebbi Eliezer's other rulings] we could correct them [without creating a confrontation encroaching upon Rebbi Eliezer's honor].

Here was an unusual case in which—because of special circumstances[23]—Rebbi Yehoshua refused to accept the obviously more complete information possessed by Rebbi Eliezer. We see that normally he should and would have. Usually, those with less information admitted that the truth lay with those who possessed more information. Still, until it was confirmed that someone's opinion was based upon complete and compelling data, another opinion could exist due to a lack or loss of original data. When just some parties had lost the data, apprising them of the lost data could solve the issue immediately. When the data had become lost to all parties, the issue would remain in dispute until a vote was taken.

---

[23] This was at the time of Yavneh, when the decision to follow *Bes Hillel* and not *Bes Shammai* was still fresh. Special efforts were required to reinforce this attitude among all the people. See chapter "The Control and Proliferation of Machlokess" under subtitle *When it was Forbidden to be Stringent.*

Additional Notes to Chapter 3

1. *Rav Nissim Gaon* states in his *Introduction to the Talmud* (usually printed along with the tractate *Brachos*):

לא סרה הקבלה והמסורה משומרת בין האומה וכאשר היה האדם קורא ועשו להם ציצית היה
אומר כי זו הציצית היא ציצית נשים אותה בכנף הטלית מספר חוטיה ח' ויש בה ה' קשרים
וידע כל פתרוני הציצית וענייניה היה שמור אצלו הכל בקבלה ובמסורת וכן כל המצות כולן
כאשר היו קוראין אותו היו יודעין לכמה ענינים מתחלקת כל מצוה ומצוה ומה תחתיה
מהפתרון. אבל דבר שהיו עושין כל עת ועת כמו המלאכות וחיוב המועדים ואכילת הטמון
והאליה לא נעלם אפי' מהנשים ואפי' מהעבדים כי כל יום הן רואין אותו הענין והיו עושין
אותו. ולא סרה האומה מזה המנהג מימות משה ועד אחר חורבן בית שני בק"נ שנה בימי ר'
יהודה הנשיא . . . וכאשר ראה העתקת האומה בדלדול ובחסרון . . . עלה בלבו שיקבץ כל מה
שיש בידם מהקבלה . . . וחברה חיבור . . . וקראה משנה.

Among the people, the teachings, transmitted by Moses, never turned to depart. When a person read the verse, "And you shall make for yourselves *tsitsis*" he knew that this word was referring to *tsitsis* that we place on each corner of our four-cornered garments—the number of its threads is eight and each thread has five knots. He would know all the correct interpretation behind the *tsitsis* and its facts would be preserved by him, all through the process of the Receiving and Transmitting [of the Torah]. And so it was with each one of all the *mitzvos*. When the people would see it written in the Torah, they would know how many parts there were to each and every mitzva and its underlying interpretation. Indeed, any matters that came up all the time—such as *melachos* (the activities forbidden on Shabbos and Yom Tov) or the obligations on the *mo'addim* (the holydays) or the eating of forbidden animal parts—were never forgotten even by the women and servants. For the people faced such matters every day and reacted to them in practice. The people never veered from this practice from the days of Moses until after the destruction of the Second Temple . . . in the days of Rebbi Yehuda HaNassi. . . . And when he saw the nation's poor and lacking situation . . . it occured to him that he should gather together all that they possessed of the Received Tradition . . . and he [together with all the Sages of his day] composed a work . . . and called it the *Mishna*.

Rav Nissim Gaon's words clearly contradict our thesis that over time some details of *mitzva* obvservance may have fallen into disuse and become forgotten. At face value they read that until the time of Rebbi Yehuda HaNassi everything about all the *mitzvos* remained crystal clear and that *mitzvos* that occurred daily were different only in that they remained clear even to women and slaves. However, his words "that he should gather together *all that they possessed* of the Received Tradition" imply that there *was* some loss of information, as is evident from the disputes found in the *Mishna*. Indeed, unless we resort to the possibility that some corruptions found themselves into this text, we must find perplexing the example chosen to illustrate a fact that was never forgotten. The number of threads required for *tsitsis* is indeed a matter of dispute between *Bes Hillel* and *Bes Shammai* (*Menachos* 41b). There is even a *machlokess* over whether women are obligated to wear *tsitsis* on their garments, and Rav Yehuda had his wife do so (*Menachos* 43a). (The issue was whether the Torah's mitzva of *tsitsis* is restricted to the day-time. As a rule, women are not obligated in time-bound commandments of commission.) Once we accept the possibility of loss, the existence of a dispute over the number of threads required in *tsitsis* can be explained as a result of long periods of time over which four-cornered garments of wool or linen were out of style. According to the Rambam, at least, such were the only kind of garments Biblically required to have *tsitsis* attached (*Hilchos Tsitsis* 3:1-2).

2. A similar possibility exists for basically academic issues. Rav Yechiel Dov Weissberger, quoted in the *Artscroll Divray HaYamim* by Rabbis Eisenman and Danziger (*Mesora*, 1987), speculates upon the reason that the *Targum*, the Aramaic translation of Scriptures given at Sinai, was eventually "forgotten until *Onkelos* restored it" (*Megilla* 3a): We know that *Targumim* were originally Aramaic translations and commentaries recited simultaneously with the Scriptural readings in the synagogue since the time of Ezra (*Rav Hai Gaon, Sefer Halttim*, 187; Rambam, *Hilchos T'filla*, 12:10. The practice continued into the time of the *Gaonim* [500-1038 C.E.] but died out where and when Aramaic ceased as the vernacular—E. Levy, *Y'sodos HaT'filla, S'farim Avraham Tzioni*, Tel Aviv, 1967, p. 328). But those who recited the translations, *Meturgamim*, later began to embellish them—sometimes erroneously. The original commentary of the *p'sukim* (and of the *mitzvos* they contain) was buried within the embellishments and had to be weeded of false additions. In other words, excessive commentary led to the same result as direct forgetfulness.

6. Though the Torah itself (*Sh'mos* 23:2) declares majority rule decisive, academically there is a recognized inferiority to a *halacha* reached by such recourse rather than unanimous opinion. The *Mishna Berurah, Biur Haytave, Biur HaGra* and *Bes Yosef* (*Orach Ḥayyim* 50) cite the *Ra'ah*, who maintains that *Perek Ayzehu M'Ko'mon* was chosen in the morning prayers as a representative *mishna* because "שבפרק זה אין בו מחלוקת, והיא משנה ברורה למשה מסיני, it contains no *machlokess*, and is [therefore] a *clear mishna* delivered to Moses at Sinai." (Nevertheless there are apparently at least two *machlokos* in this *perek*, one concerning פסח עד חצות and one concerning שירי הדם אינן מעכבין).

18. The workings of the 13 Rules of Torah Interpretation are complicated
and cannot be made very simple within the confines of footnotes. But
the following is an attempt:

בקל וחומר—מחלוקת באם אין עונשין מן הדין

The rule of *kal v'ḥomer, lenient and stringent*, works with the logic that if
the Torah assigns to a subject a leniency or stringency because it (the subject) has a certain property, things with a higher degree of that property
should certainly be assigned that leniency or stringency. In the realm of
punishments assigned to criminal acts, there is a disagreement over
whether that logic is *halachically* valid for determining physical punishments, or only for determining monetary penalties.

בגזירה שוה—מחלוקת באם למידין ומשיבין בדמופנה מצד אחד

Where two cases are similarly worded in the Torah, the laws stated in each
case are shared by both—if the similar wording is superfluous in at least one
case. This method of hermeneutics is called *gezayra shavva, equal decree*. If
the superfluous wording is present in only one of the two passages, there is
a *machlokess* whether a logical objection (פירכא) will then nullify the equation. Different laws will thereby result.

דון מינה ומינה, או דון מינה ואוקי באתריה

Another detail of *gezayra shavva* operation is under dispute: When the
laws of one subject are carried over to a second, do they operate exactly as
they had in the original subject, or do they adopt the modifications common to the second subject's other laws.

כלל ופרט ורבוי ומיעוט

In a sentence such as "When a man shall offer a sacrifice—[one consisting]
of an animal, of cattle, or of sheep shall he offer" (*Vayikra* 1:2), the word
"animal" represents a *set* (כלל) within which the *elements* (פרטים) "sheep"
and "cattle" had already been included. The Torah's purpose in specifying
the elements is to limit the set. Some understood the limitation to be to
those things most similar to elements named. Others understood it to be
solely to the specific elements named. (Had an element alone been specified,
without an accompanying set, then the element would be understood as a
בנין אב, a mere *prototype*, that represents all possible subjects, as long as
they share its most basic properties.) The first rendering is called רבוי ומיעוט,
expansion and limitation; the second rendering is called כלל ופרט, *set and
element*.

ביצא לדון בדבר חדש, מחלוקת אם איהו בלבד דלא גמר מכלליה, אבל כלליה גמר מיניה

When an entire *set* (כלל) is given some laws, and then an individual *element* of that set (פרט) is given an additional law, that law is assigned to the entire set (כלל), as well. But if any laws later assigned to any individual element (פרט) of a set (כלל) contradict any laws previously assigned to the whole set, that individual element (פרט) is thereupon treated apart from the set (כלל) in all ways and loses all the laws the set had been given (unless the Torah specifically reinstates those laws to that individual element [פרט]). There is a *machlokess* whether the entire set (כלל) also loses the *non*-contradictory laws it had gained from the element (פרט).

21. See *Needa* 72b, where Rabbi Akiva produces a *drash* to support the *Halacha L'Moshe MiSinai* that the oil used in the *Todah (Thanksgiving)* Offering must measure one half *log* (the first *halacha* in the Rambam's list of *Halachos L'Moshe MiSinai*) and is told by Rabbi Elazar ben Azaria, "Akiva, even if you *darshon* all day, I will not listen; . . . the law . . . is a *Halacha L'Moshe MiSinai!*" We suggest that the Rambam's decision for following Rebbi Elazar ben Azaria's position on this issue (*Maaseh Hakorbonos* 9:20) despite the general rule that we follow Rabbi Akiva's opinions was made precisely because Rabbi Akiva was clearly lacking information.

Chapter 4

The Rambam's Attack on Attributing Machlokess to Forgetfulness

Representative of the Rambam's statements about *machlokess* is this one in *Hilchos Mahmrim* (1:3):

דברי קבלה אין בהן מחלוקת לעולם. וכל דבר שתמצא בו מחלוקת, בידוע שאינו קבלה ממשה רבינו.

There is never a *machlokess* concerning matters that were received [by way of the chain of Torah transmission through the generations]. In anything that you find a *machlokess*—it is known that it is not something received from Moses.

The Rambam, it would appear, maintains that there were never *machlokos* concerning laws that Moses revealed to us, for the reason that any Sinaitic information revealed to us by Moses was forever to remain clear and never to be lost or forgotten. This impression is reinforced by passages from the Rambam's introduction to his commentary on the Mishna:

The First Passages[1]

וזה עיקר יש לך לעמוד על סודו. והוא שהפירושים המקובלים מפי משה אין מחלוקת
בהם בשום פנים, שהרי מאז ועד עתה לא מצאנו מחלוקת נפלה בזמן מן הזמנים
מימות משה ועד רב אשי בין החכמים כדי שיאמר אחד המוציא עין חבירו יוציאו את
עינו שני' עין בעין ויאמר השני אינו אלא כופר בלבד שחייב לתת וכו' וכיוצא בזה
בכלל המצות אין מחלוקת בהן שכולן פירושים מקובלים מפי משה. ועליהם ועל
דומיהם אמרו כל התורה נאמרה כללותיה ופרטותיה ודקדוקיה מסיני.

אבל אע"פ שהן מקובלין ואין מחלוקת בהם, מחכמת התורה הנתונה לנו נוכל להוציא
ממנה אלו הפירושים בדרכי מדרכי הסברות והאסמכתות והראיות והרמזים המצואים
במקרא. וכשתראה אותם בתלמוד מעיינים וחולקין זה על זה במערכת העיון ומביאין
ראיות על אחד מאלו הפירושים. .אלו הראיות לא הביאום מפני שנשתבש עליהם
הענין עד שנודע להם מהראיות האלה. . .אבל חקרו על הרמז הנמצא בכתוב לזה
הפירוש המקובל.

This is a fundamental principle which you must master: The
explanations received from Moses' lips have no *machlokess* in
any way whatsoever. We have never, at any time in history,
found a *machlokess* in which, because of the verse "an eye for
an eye" (D'varim 19:21) one scholar would suggest that a man
who pokes out someone's eye should have his eye removed, and
another scholar would argue that the verse means monetary
compensation [the actual *halacha*]. Likewise with all the mitzvos. They are subject to no *machlokess* [Hebrew: אין מחלוקת בהן]
because they all are explanations we received from Moses.

But although they had been handed down and they are not subject to *machlokess*, these explanations can, in addition, be
extracted from the verses of the Written Torah through our
[Sinaitically-revealed] science of Torah-interpretation. [This is
the area in which we find disputes about these divinely-revealed
details.] Wherever in the Talmud you find the Sages analyzing
and debating each other through constructing logical sequences,
bringing Scriptural proofs for their elucidations—the proofs
were not brought because the matter was so unclear that they
needed these proofs to solve it . . . Rather, [these "proofs" were
brought because] the Sages were searching for the precise indication planted in the verse for the [well-known] original Sinaitic
details which were received from Moses.

---

[1] *Introduction to the Talmud,* Hebrew pp. 11-12, English pp. 81-84.

חלקי הדינין . . . החלק הראשון פירושים מקובלים מפי משה ויש להם רמז בכתיב
. . . אין בו מחלוקת. אבל כשיאמר האחד כך קבלתי, אין לדבר עליו [קפח: ומסתלק
הויכוח].

החלק השני הם הדינים שנאמר בהן הלכה למשה מסיני ואין ראיות עליהם כמו
שזכרנו וזה כמו כן אין חולק עליו.

החלק השלישי הדינין שהוציאו על דרכי הסברה. ונפלה בה מחלוקת . . . ומפני כך
אומרים [יבמות דף ע"ו:] "אם הלכה נקבל ואם לדין יש תשובה". . . . אבל נפלה
המחלוקת והעיון בדבר שלא נשמע בו ההלכה.

The Oral Laws . . . can be divided into . . . :

1. Explanations received from the lips of Moses and which are
   hinted to in the Scriptures: . . . There is absolutely no *machlokess* about any such *halacha* (Hebrew: אין בו מחלוקת). Once
   one says, "So have I received," all debate dissipates.

2. Laws called *Halachos L'Moshe MiSinai*: These, as we mentioned, have no Scriptural indications, and concerning these,
   too, no one differs (Hebrew: אין חולק בו).

3. Laws derived through logic: Such were subject to *machlokess* . . . Thus they say, "If it is a *halacha* we will accept it,
   but if it is a logical inference, we have a retort" (*Yevomos*
   76b) . . . *Machlokess* and analysis arose [only] over things
   concerning which no *halacha* was heard.

The Second Passage[2]

Thus far concerning *machlokess* and Sinaitic laws.[3] The Rambam
continues, regarding the issue of the Oral Law's being forgotten:

. . . אבל מי שיחשוב שהדינין שנחלקין בהם כמו כן מקובלים מפי משה, וחושבים
שנפלה המחלוקת . . . מפני שאחד מהם קבל קבלה אמת והשני . . . שכח . . . זה
דבר מגונה מאד. והוא דברי מי שאין לו שכל ואין בידו עיקרים. ופוגם באנשים אשר
נתקבלו מהם המצוות. וכל זה שוא ובטל.

[2] *Ibid.* Hebrew pp. 14-15, English pp. 88-90.
[3] We are using the phrase "Sinaitic laws" in its broad sense. As can be seen from the
above quotations, the Rambam's objection to associating *machlokess* to oral laws is
with any laws that originated at Sinai, whether they are technical *Halachos L'Moshe
MiSinai* (i.e., lacking Scriptural indication—see below under subheading *The
Second Passage*) or not.

Some may think that the laws that were disputed [Hebrew: שנחלקין בהם] were also received from Moses' lips. They may conjecture that disagreements arose . . . [because] one of the disputants received the teaching (*kabballa*) correctly, whereas the other . . . forgot [what he was taught]. . . . [T]his is a very repugnant thing to say and these are words of senseless people who do not understand matters of basic principle, and such words besmirch the people from whom we received the commandments. The entire conjecture is less than worthless.

It becomes obvious why some conclude that according to the Rambam explanations which originated with Moses were never forgotten and thus never subjected to analysis and dispute, and that any disputes which *did* occur were only over identifying the exact hint in the Torah for the known laws.

Difficulties in This Interpretation

But we cannot possibly interpret the Rambam this way. Such an understanding is replete with difficulties. In the previous chapter, we have shown that the Talmud clearly accepts the idea that oral laws had been lost, and that in trying to rediscover them, the Sages fell into dispute. Indeed, the classic *Responsa Ḥavvos Ya'ir*[4] lists eight *Halachos L'Moshe MiSinai* (out of the Rambam's own list of thirty) which were clearly lost and/or argued about.[5] He also shows that there are more than fifty *Halachos L'Moshe MiSinai*, which the Rambam did not list, also subject to dispute. On this basis he makes an almost scathing attack on the Rambam's position as he understands it. He goes so far as to suggest that the Rambam wrote these words in the ignorance of his youth, reluctantly rejecting this possibility only because the Rambam maintained this position in his later works as well.

Furthermore, anyone acquainted with *Gemora* study knows that there certainly are *machlokos* over how to properly fulfill Scriptural laws. Certainly, the *p'sukim*, verses of the Torah, themselves came from Sinai and there are innumerable instances of *machlokos* over what they mean. Also, as we noted in the previous chapter, the *Thirteen Interpretation Rules*, revealed at Sinai, are subject to *machlo-*

---

[4] *Responsa of Rav Ya'ir Chaim ben Rav Moshe Shimshon* (17th century), #192.
[5] See Additional Notes at the end of this chapter.

kess. Clearly the Rambam, or anyone, cannot seriously maintain that merely because a law originated at Sinai there could be no loss of it and no *machlokess* over it.

The Rambam Allows for Forgetfulness

In fact, in his *Mishneh Torah* (*Hilchos Shofar* 3:2) the Rambam unhesitatingly states that an oral Sinaitic explanation *had* been lost, namely the oral instructions for correctly sounding the *shofar* on *Rosh HaShonna.* There he explains a talmudic passage in which three different opinions are given on how the shofar-blasts should sound on *Rosh HaShonna.* The talmud proceeds to say that a certain authority ultimately decreed that we should blow all three ways, and it tells us why.

The Rambam explains the passage as follows:

תרועה זו האמורה בתורה נסתפק לנו בה ספק לפי אורך השנים ורוב הגלות ואין אנו יודעים היאך היא. אם היא היללה . . . או האנחה . . . או שניהם כאחד . . . לכך אנו עושין הכל.

It had become unclear to us how the *teruah* [the middle blast of the triple-blasts we must sound on *Rosh Hashonna*] was supposed to sound. This happened because of the many years [that passed] and terrible exiles we've gone through. Thus we do not know whether [the weeping sound called for is] supposed to sound like a chain of short, staccato clucks . . . or like repeated moans of distress . . . or like both of those sounds, one after the other. [Each of the three Sages of the Talmud offered one of these possibilities.] . . . Therefore [in order to make sure that we do it correctly], we blow each triple-blast all three ways.

In this passage, the Rambam accounted for a three-way *machlokess* in the *Gemora* by explaining that the precise Torah-law had indeed been *forgotten.* Clearly, we cannot attribute to the Rambam any assertion that oral laws given to Moses at Sinai were invulnerable to universal loss and *machlokess.*[6] How then do we account for his statements that gave rise to this assertion?

---

[6] See Additional Notes at the end of this chapter.

The Usual Solution

The usual solution offered[7] is that the Rambam's denial of loss of
Sinaitic laws and *machlokess* about them refers only to matters of
"fundamental importance" or those that "go to the root of the law,"
affecting the basic validity or invalidity of an object or action. Some
Rishonim, as well, such as the *Raavad*,[8] seem to make a point of this.
However, there are difficulties with this explanation.

First of all, this differentiation between *machlokos* over the basic
and *machlokos* over its details should logically apply to rabbinical
laws as well: Their basics should be immune, and details subject, to
loss and *machlokess*.[9] But the Rambam emphatically restricted his
principle to laws received at Sinai.

Secondly, what constitutes the foundation and what the detail,
which in advance will determine whether a given law will be susceptible to loss and *machlokess*? *All* the oral laws are detailed instructions for practicing the laws of the Written Torah. And among the
oral laws themselves, virtually any law can be categorized as a detail
of some other "umbrella" *halacha*. Is the *machlokess* over the
number of fringes required for the *tsitsis* of a garment a *machlokess*
about a basic law or a detail? What about the kind of sounds one
must blow on a *shofar* on *Rosh Hashonna*? Or whether one may
perform *yibbum* with his daughter's co-wife? By its very nature,
every argument is about some agreed upon fact. To say that arguments arise only about accepted basics is a redundancy, and it would
be illogical to restrict this rule to only some matters (Sinaitic laws as
opposed to rabbinical laws).

What the Rambam Meant Re: Machlokess and Sinaitic Laws[10]

We shall propose a different understanding of the Rambam's and

[7] See Additional Notes at the end of this chapter.
[8] See Additional Notes at the end of this chapter.
[9] Indeed, one modern work does apply the principle to rabbinical laws as well:
"There were many students who knew only the explicit Halacha as revealed to
Moshe *Rabbeynu* ... However, intricate details of the law and of the Rabbinic
enactments that are mastered only through long and steady personal association
with great teachers were not learned thoroughly enough and some were forgotten."—*History of the Jewish People*, *The Second Temple Era*, Rabbi Hersh
Goldwurm, *et al*, Artscroll/Mesorah/Hillel, 1982, p. 142.
[10] The explanation that follows will also be found in *Torahs Nevi'im* by Rav Z. H.
Hayyos, pages 116-117 (כתבי מהר"ץ חיות, הוצאת ספרים "דברי חכמים," ירושלים, תשי"ח).

Raavad's statements contrasting basic laws with their details. They mean not that Sinaitic laws remained extant and clear because they were basic, but the reverse: Simply that those Sinaitic teachings that happened to remain extant, precisely because they were known to be extant Sinaitic teachings, stood as the uncontested prime material to be subject only to analysis and analytical debate and not challenge. This is why in all his works the Rambam compares the issues under debate to ענפים, branches of the received information. The *machlokos* are not against any principles received but concerning issues that branch out of them.

Let us isolate and deal with the Rambam's statements about *machlokos* involving laws revealed at Sinai (to return to his stand on their forgetability later).[11] A convincing case can be made that the Rambam's point is simply that there were no *machlokos with,* i.e., *against* extant information that came from G-d *because* it was recognized as originating with G-d.

A Matter of Translation: "Arguing About" Vs. "Contesting"

We contend that correctly understanding the Rambam is a matter of proper translation and that the correct translation of "אין בו מחלוקת" is: there is no *machlokess with,* not "there is no *machlokess about.*" And the Rambam simply means that no Sage contested any laws that were known to have originated with Moses, not that no Sage disagreed *about* such laws.[12] He fully agrees that the Sages may have had different interpretations of laws regardless of their source.[13]

The Rambam's own remarks on the last *mishna* in *Aid'yos* (8:7) demonstrate that this is his position. The *mishna* reads:

א"ר יהושע: מקובל אני מרבן יוחנן בן זכאי, ששמע מרבו, ורבו מרבו, הלמ"ס, שאין אליהו בא . . . אלא לרחק המקורבין בזרוע, ולקבל המרוחקין בזרוע. . . .

ר' יהודה אומר: לקרב, אבל לא לרחק.

ר"ש אומר: להשוות המחלוקת.

[11] I.e., the "First" and "Second Passages" of this chapter's beginning, respectively.
[12] See Additional Notes at the end of this chapter.
[13] We will soon explain why the Rambam felt compelled to make this apparently obvious point.

וחכמים אומרים: לא לרחק, ולא לקרב, אלא לעשות שלום בעולם.

Rebbi Yehoshua said: "I have a קבלה, a piece of transmitted information, from [my teacher] Rabban Yoḥonon ben Zakkai, who heard from his mentor, who heard from *his* mentor, in a chain of tradition going all the way back to Moses, that Elijah [the prophet] is coming solely to thrust away those who [regarding their lineages] are [wrongly considered] close [in relationship to those who are pure] and to bring in those who are far away. . . ."

Rebbi Yehuda [his *talmid's talmid*] said: "To bring in but not to thrust away."

Rebbi Shimmon [a colleague of Rebbi Yehuda] said: "To straighten out disputes."

And the [majority of] Sages say: "Not to thrust away, and not to bring near, but to produce harmony in the world."

Here we have a *Halacha L'Moshe MiSinai* about a most basic matter, over which there definitely is a *machlokos*, and in his commentary on this *mishna* the Rambam makes the point we propounded: There certainly can be *machlokos* **about** *Halachos L'Moshe MiSinai*. There just cannot be any *with*, i.e., *against* them.

The Rambam states:

לא נשמע ממשה רבנו ע״ה זה הלשון. אבל שמע ממנו זה הענין. לפי שמשה ספר בביאת המשיח. ולשון התורה: ״אם יהיה נדחך בקצה השמים וגו׳ ושב אלקיך את שבותך וגו׳ ומל ה׳ אלקיך וגו׳,״ וזולת זה. והגיד להם ג״כ מפי הגבורה בהקדמותיו וסבותיו, ושיקדים אותו האיש לישר לו הארץ, והוא אליהו, והודע להם שהאיש ההוא לא יוסיף ולא יגרע בתורה, אבל יסלק ויסיר החמסים בלבד. ואין בזה מחלוקת ולא הכחשה. אבל נפלה המחלוקת ברעות שיסיר—מה הם. . . .

This wording was not heard from Moshe *Rabbeynu*, may his memory be blessed. But the subject was heard from him, since Moses described the coming of the Messiah, the fact that he shall remove evil from the world, and that Elijah will proceed him to straighten the world for him. . . . With this there is no *machlokess* or denial. But *machlokess* did arise over precisely what evils [Elijah] is going to eliminate.

Here, then, is the Rambam's point. There can never be a dispute against "wording . . . heard from Moshe *Rabbeynu*." If ever it seems that a reported *Halacha L'Moshe MiSinai* is being challenged, it must be understood that the "report" was *not* something actually heard from Moses but an interpretation of something that was. For the Sinaitic teaching whose meaning the disputants are analyzing is not contestable.

I originally reached this conclusion through an internal, contextual analysis of the Rambam's writings cited above. We will explain this in detail later. But for the sake of clarity we will first present external, historical evidence, bringing to light the issues confronting the Rambam when he wrote his words.[14]

The Rambam's Target: The Karaites

The days of the Rambam were marked by intense intellectual warfare with the Karaites. When the Rambam arrived in Alexandria, Egypt, the *majority* of its Jews were under the influence of that heretical sect. The Karaites' point of dissension was that Judaism did not truly possess any Sinaitically-revealed oral explanations of Scripture. They accused the Sages of inventing, willfully or not, false renderings of the Torah's intentions—specifically regarding their teachings attributing non-literal meanings to Scripture's words. They claimed, for example, that the Sages had no basis for declaring that "an eye for an eye" was meant as an expression for monetary compensation to the victim. They ridiculed the Sages' insistence that their renderings were explicitly taught by G-d to Moses and preserved as the Oral Law. The Karaites declared that the meanings attributed by the Sages to Scripture's words were man-made interpretations or conventions. This, they argued, was manifest by the fact that the Sages themselves did not agree on many points of *mitzva* observance. *According to the Karaites, the existence of* machlokess *belied the claim of an extant divine explanation of Scripture's instructions.*

In this vein, the tenth-century Karaite historian Yosef Yaakov Kirkasanni in his work, *Sefer HaMe'oros*, compiled a list of the *halachic* disputes between the rabbis of Babylonia and those of Eretz Yisrael and wrote, "This demolishes their claim to possession of a Sinaitically-revealed explanation of the Torah." He continues:

> They [the Orthodox Jews] believe that their laws and regulations have been transmitted by the prophets. If that were the case, there ought not to exist any differences of opinion among

---

[14] See Philip Birnbaum's introduction to *Maimonides' Mishneh Torah (Yahd ha-Ḥazakah)*, Hebrew Publishing Co., N.Y., 1944.

them; and the fact that such differences of opinion do exist refutes their presumptuous belief.[15]

Similarly, the Karaites Salamon ben-Yeruḥam and Yeffeth ben-Ali, in their commentaries on the Bible, sought to dispute the Talmud and its followers. The latter wrote (on *Hosea* 14:3):[16] "Turn away from the line of approach [to understanding the Torah's *mitzvos*] that the men of the Diaspora invented,[17] creating *machlokess* and separate opinions among themselves."[18]

And so the Rambam addressed this issue and said: yes, there are disagreements about the proper ways to fulfill given *mitzvos*, and the opinions are the result of human analysis; but this does not conflict with the fact that there is an extant Sinaitically-revealed Oral Law that tells us, among other things, to understand some verses unliterally. For the disagreements merely revolve around how to interpret these unliteral renderings, but the renderings themselves, challenged by the Karaites, were never contested. They were, on the contrary, unanimously accepted principles—precisely because, as our Sages report, they did come from G-d.

In Context

By examining the question with which the Rambam prefaced the first passage we quoted at the beginning of the chapter,[19] we will see the context of the recurrent phrase "אין מחלוקת בהם," and it will become clear that it should be translated "there was no *machlokess* with oral laws," i.e., no contesting them, and not "there was no disagreement *about* oral laws." We will also see that the Rambam was apparently reacting to an intriguing development of his time: The Karaites, we know, totally denied the validity of the Talmud. Yet even the followers of the Talmud, no doubt due to the confusion

[15] *Encyclopedia Judaica*, 1971, Vol. 10, p. 766

[16] "קחו עמכם דברים ושובו אל ה'", Take with you words [of confession] and return to Hashem."

[17] Probably referring to the methods of Torah interpretation, whose Sinaitic origin the Karaites denied.

[18] The Karaites advocated a "simple" understanding of G-d's will solely through textual analysis of Scriptures. The fact is, however, that without an authoritative Oral Law, they themselves became terribly enmeshed in *machlokess* over the Scripture's meanings.

[19] *Introduction to the Talmud*, Hebrew pp. 11-12, English pp. 81-84.

introduced by the Karaites, evidently saw, in two of the Talmud's own passages, support for the Karaites' denial of an extant Oral Law.

The Rambam presents the question he is addressing as follows:

אם פירושי התורה, כפי אשר יסדנו, מקובלים מפי משה—כמו שאמרנו מדבריהם
(קפח: כפי הכללים שאמרנו, כשהזכרנו אמרם): „כל התורה נאמרו כללותיה ופרטיה
ודקדוקיה מסיני"—אם כן מה אלו ההלכות היחידים שנא' בהם „הלכה למשה
מסיני"?

If, as we have laid down as a principle, we are in receipt, from Moses, of the explanatory details for [performing] all the *mitzvos*—as we cited the Sages as saying ("All the Torah, [including] its general laws, its details, and its fine points, is from Sinai")—if so, what are those special laws which are described as *Halacha L'Moshe MiSinai*, Laws Given to Moses at Sinai?

In other words, How could the Rabbis have said that the explanations of all the *mitzvos* were given to us by Moses, when we know that only an exclusive group of explanations is called "Laws Given to Moses on Sinai"?

The First Challenge

The apparent contradiction may be rephrased and developed as follows: True, some passages of the Talmud state that all the Torah's details were given at Sinai. But the fact that the Talmud itself also labels only a select group of laws *Halachos L'Moshe MiSinai* indicates that its Sages did not really consider any other oral *halachos* literally to have come from Hashem.[20] It would seem that no other more-encompassing, divinely-revealed Oral Law ever existed, and the literal belief that one does exist is false.

Now, let us re-examine the words (quoted at the beginning of this chapter)[21] with which the Rambam begins his answer:

---

[20] The *Encyclopedia Judaica* (1971, Vol. 10, p. 766) describes the Karaites as claiming that "Tradition is accepted, provided that it is indispensable for the application of precepts contained in the text, for the clarification of ambiguities, or to make up for deficiencies in the concrete details of precepts; even so, however, its role remains restricted and subordinate." Perhaps the existence of a small body of laws known as "*Halachos L'Moshe MiSinai*" gave this view talmudic credence in the eyes of some, impelling the Rambam to clarify the true meaning of the term.

[21] From *Introduction to the Talmud*, Hebrew pp. 11-12, English pp. 81-84.

וזה עיקר יש לך לעמוד על סודו, והוא: שהפירושים המקובלים מפי משה כמו
שאמרנו אין מחלוקת בהם בשום פנים.

[The answer] is a fundamental principle which you must
master. As we said: [Regarding] the explanations received from
Moses' lips—there is no מחלוקת בהם.

The Rambam proceeds to give several illustrations of oral elucidations[22] and then explains that the *Halacha L'Moshe MiSinai* laws
differ from all the other oral *halachos* only in being unhinted to,
even through the principles of interpretation, in the Torah's verses.
That is his entire answer. Now, if "אין מחלוקת בהם" meant that there
are no disputes about oral laws, the answer would be irrelevant to
the question. The question challenged the claim of a Sinaitic origin
for the non-*Halacha L'Moshe MiSinai* explanations; why should
the answer concern *machlokos* about them? Once we translate "אין
מחלוקת בהם" as "there is no *machlokess with* them," i.e., no contesting them, the flow of ideas becomes evident: In the question, the fact
that only a select group of laws are called *Halacha L'Moshe MiSinai*
was taken to imply that no other *halachos* originated at Sinai: to
demonstrate the falseness of this inference, the Rambam points out
that the other oral laws, just as *Halachos L'Moshe MiSinai*, are
nowhere found to be ever contested, which indicates that they too
came from an indisputable Source. As the Rambam emphasizes after
his examples of uncontested non-*Halacha L'Moshe MiSinai* orally-
transmitted renderings of Scriptural laws:

. . . אין מחלוקת בהן שכולן פירושים מקובלים מפי משה, ועליהם ועל דומיהם אמרו
כל התורה נאמרו כללותיה ופרטיה ודקדוקיה מסיני.

There is no *machlokess* with them [i.e., they are never contest-
ed]. For they are all explanations we received from the lips of
Moses. And of them and those like them[23] the Sages said, the

---

[22] Which, not surprisingly, had been challenged by the Karaites: the non-literal
understandings of 'eye for an eye' (*D'varim* 19:21) and 'cut her palm' (*ibid.* 25:12),
the limited applications for the stated punishments in some cases of sexual immorality (*Vayikra* 21:9 and *D'varim* 22:20) and the identities of the apparently
ambiguous 'fruit of the glorious tree' and 'bough of a thick tree' (*Vayikra* 23:40).
[23] By "those like them" the Rambam is probably referring to all renderings criticized
by the Karaites for not following the simple meanings of the words, as they understood them.

overall rules and the details and minutiae of all the Torah were
said from Sinai.

When the Rambam gives these examples to illustrate his point,
he repeatedly remarks that no one contested the law as we know it.
He does not assert that in contradistinction to their details, no 'fundamental parts' of oral laws were ever forgotten or that there were
no disagreements about them.

As we continue reading the Rambam's words, we see how well
their line of logic flows as long as we consistently translate אין מחלוקת
בהם as "they are not contested." Following the paragraph just quoted, the Rambam categorizes the oral laws as follows:

החלק הראשון: הפירושים המקובלים ממשה שיש להם רמז בכתב . . . וזה אין בו
מחלוקת כלל, אלא כל זמן שיאמר אדם קבלתי כך וכך—אין לדבר עליו [קפח:
מסתלק כל ויכוח].

1. Explanations received from the lips of Moses and which are
hinted to in the Scriptures: Any such explanation has absolutely
no מחלוקת בו. Once one says, "So have I received," all debate
dissipates.

החלק השני: הדינים שבהם אמרו שהם הלמ"ס: ואין עליהם ראיה כמו שאמרנו, וזה
כמו כן אין חולק עליו [קפ"ח: זה ממה שאין בו מחלוקת].

2. Laws called *Halachos L'Moshe MiSinai*: These have no Scriptural indications . . . and concerning these, too, no one differs.

ולכך אומרים אם הלכה נקבל, ואם לדין יש תשובה.

Hence, the [Sages] say, "If it is a *halacha*, we must accept it. But
if it is a logical inference, we have a retort."

We also see from here that the Rambam accepts the possibility
that someone may be uninformed of the Sinaitic origin of a teaching
and that as long as he remains uninformed he may choose to contest
it, as with any law derived through analysis.

The Second Challenge

We have seen that underlying the question of defining the term
Halacha L'Moshe MiSinai was a larger challenge against Judaism's
insistence on possessing a widely-encompassing, Sinaitically-

revealed oral explanation of *all* the *mitzvos*. In the second passage quoted at the beginning of this chapter, the Rambam is addressing a second challenge to the validity of Judaism's claim, a challenge that touches upon the issue that we had temporarily put aside, the forgetability of Laws revealed at Sinai. The challenge claims as follows: Even if originally there *were* oral instructions—besides the *Halachos L'Moshe MiSinai*—revealed by G-d, they obviously had been long lost, because we see that the Sages often argued over the correct way to observe Scriptural laws. Surely, the argument goes, if they literally believed that the extant explanations came from Hashem, the Sages would never have contested them. The Karaites would claim that the reason the Sages had *machlokos* over the correct ways to fulfill the *mitzvos* is that any such traditions were of dubious authenticity and authority, and the Sages therefore felt free to disagree with them. The original, genuine oral laws obviously fell victim to the previous Sages' incompetence: they must have been poor listeners or unable to retain what they heard. Or, erroneous reception may have been at fault.[24] These explanations, the Rambam strongly objects, are fundamentally wrong.[25] *Machlokos* were due not to errors or loss of facts but to differing analyses of unlost information.[26]

In view of the fact demonstrated in this and the preceding chapter that numerous *machlokos* really are the result of loss (a fact to which, as we see concerning the shofar-blowing, the Rambam clearly agrees), some observations are in order concerning the Rambam's objection. Notice that the Rambam does not address the issue

---

[24] "Some may think that the laws that were disputed were also received from Moses' lips. They may conjecture that disagreements arose due to error about the *halachos* or lack of retention: that one of the disputants received the teaching (*kabballa*) correctly, whereas the other one erred in his receiving it, or forgot or did not hear all that he needed to hear from his teacher" (*Introduction to the Talmud*, Hebrew pp. 14-15, English pp. 88-90).

[25] "These are very repugnant thoughts. Such are notions of senseless people who do not understand matters of basic principle, and such words besmirch the people from whom we received the commandments. The entire conjecture is less than worthless" (*Introduction to the Talmud*, ibid.).

[26] "For the entire Received Explanation came from Moses. [Those who mistakenly attribute *machlokess* to forgetfulness or error] fail to distinguish between the corollaries [תולדות], matters determined through analysis [which can be, and are, contested], and the Basic Transmitted Mandates [which cannot be contested]" (*Introduction to the Talmud*, Hebrew pp. 14-15, English pp. 88-90).

of whether an oral law may be forgotten by all. He only objects to the suggestion that it was forgotten by *one* of a pair of opposing Sages, and that *machlokos* survived in the Talmud because that Sage continued to contest extant, admittedly accurate versions of surviving oral laws, instead of declaring "אם הלכה נקבל, If it is a *halacha*, we must accept it:" because ".... שכח. ... מפני שאחד מהם קבל קבלת אמת והשני one of them received a true teaching whereas the other . . . forgot." Whereas one Sage may have heard the lecturer correctly, another thought he heard the lecturer say something that wasn't actually said, or did not hear something that was said. For instance, perhaps the lecturer said that "an eye for an eye" *was* meant literally, but one disciple thought he heard him say it was *not* meant literally and he argued with the others, *refusing to accept correction*.

We can understand the vehemence with which the Rambam denounces these views. For in attempting to explain why disputes exist in the Talmud, these erroneous conclusions either (a) attribute incompetence to our Sages, demolishing, for all practical purposes, any claim to possession of an intact Sinaitic explanation of any *mitzva*, or (b) assert that there never *were* any revealed explanations of the Torah at all. The truth, the Rambam teaches us, is that *machlokess* was not the result of forgetfulness or error, but of differing analyses of identical, extant information. We add the explanation that in pursuit of the truth, the Sages were open to enlightenment by anyone who had more data, and willingly conceded error when warranted. Though it was entirely possible for a Sage to have forgotten information,[27] to have never been taught it, or to have erred in his reception or interpretation of it, he would not cling to his opinion if presented with facts showing him that it was only arrived at because of these deficiencies. Thus, the final versions of *machlokos* present-

[27] Nevertheless, mention must be made of the Sages' truly incredible ability to accurately memorize and retain information. Today, someone who can memorize the vowelization of the Torah, and the *trupp*, the cantillations with which to chant the words—though looking at the consonants—is considered accomplished. But one of the *minimum* requirements to enter the ancient yeshivas was to commit to memory the entire Scriptures—including the Prophets and Writings. It is considered an achievement to memorize a few pages of *Shas*. We struggle to follow its intricate argumentation, though the words are printed on the pages before us. Yet the *minimum* requirements to enter the ancient Yeshiva included memorizing the entire *Mishna* and commentaries and the ability to understand and memorize the yeshiva's proceedings. The scholars also memorized the *Mechilta*, the *Sifra*, *Sifray*, *Seder Olam*, *Sefer Yetsira*, *Pirkay D'Rebbi Eliezer*, and *braissos*. (Based upon Rabbi A. Miller's *Rejoice O Youth*, pp. 242-3.)

ed in the Talmud represent the fruits of honest investigation uncon-
tradictable by and based upon extant facts. They cannot be attributed to one side's lack of information or error therein.

The Rambam saw the crucial link that exists between understanding the Oral Law's rightful claim to authenticity and accuracy
and the need to grasp the real nature of *machlokess*. He therefore felt
compelled to make it clear that while there are disputes over details
of the Oral Law, there does exist a Sinaitically-revealed Oral Law
against which no Sage dared argue. The entire Talmud, the basis of
Judaism, stands on this principle of an unaltered tradition. Original
Judaism must be defended, through this principle, against the heretical movements that rise throughout history to challenge its integrity.

Additional Notes to Chapter 4

5. For example, a passage in *Yerushalmi Payah* 2:4 clearly states that a
   Halacha L'Moshe MiSinai, listed by the Rambam as no. 23, had been
   forgotten:

ר"ז בשם שמואל: אין למידין . . . מן ההלכות.

והתני ר' חלפתא בן שאול: היא שני מיני חטים, היא שני מיני שעורין.

אר"ז כך היתה הלכה בידן ושכחוהו (ומ"מ הגר"א מחק תיבת „ושכחוהו" והגה והזכרו ושנו
בברייתא לשתיהן—פ"מ). [ואח"כ הקשו על תירוץ זו דע"כ היה ע"י לימוד.]

Rebbi Zeyra said in the name of Shmuel: "One may not derive laws by
applying the interpretation rules to *Halachos L'Moshe MiSinai*. [One
may only apply the interpretation rules to things that are *written* in the
Torah; *Halachos L'Moshe MiSinai* are, by definition, unwritten.]"

But a *Braissa* reports that Rebbi Ḥalafta ben Sha'ul said: "The law that
'two species of wheat [have a special law regarding *Payah*,' which is a
Halacha L'Moshe MiSinai] applies to two species of barley, as well.*

---

* I.e., Tractate *Payah* 2:4 teaches that the amount of produce one must leave for the
poor at the edge, *payah*, of his field depends upon the number of species he planted.
From each species, he must leave one unit. Even if he had harvested several times
over the year, if he dealt with just one species, one unit from all the harvests is sufficient. Conversely, even if several species had all been harvested at one time, he must
leave a unit for every one of them. However, the *Halacha L'Moshe MiSinai* cited
here states that if one had planted several varieties of wheat, the rule changes: The
amount he must leave for the poor is calculated by the number of harvests, regardless of the number of varieties he planted. The *braissa* is reporting that the change
of rules applies not only to wheat but to barley—indeed all produce—as well.

[So we see that a law *was* derived from a *Halacha L'Moshe MiSinai* through an *Interpretation Rule* (viz., *hekesh*, *equation*)!]"

Answered Rebbi Zeyra: "That was the original *Halacha L'Moshe MiSinai* all along. It was just forgotten [and therefore not recorded in the Mishna. But it was recalled and stated in the *braissa*]."

6. The Rambam's explanation of this *Gemora* is all the more telling when we realize that not everyone accepts it. *Rav Hai Gaon*, who lived 200 years before the Rambam, maintained (in a *Responsa* written 949 C.E.) that the right way to sound the *shofar* had *never* been forgotten. All three ways were really optional, and each was fine as far as the Torah was concerned. They were all perfectly valid, acceptable and correct ways to fulfill the obligation of blowing the *teruah*. But, he explained, the Sages saw that the uninformed would *think* that the different Sages who suggested different ways were in dispute over the correct way. Therefore it was decreed that all three variations be combined. That way the practice for all Jewry would be uniform, and no misconception would take root. (This *Responsa* is quoted verbatim in the chapter entitled "The Control and Proliferation of Machlokos.")

   Rabbeynu Nissim, too, cites this explanation, alone (*Commentary on the Ryf, Rosh HaShonna* 34a). The *Ritva* also offers an explanation which does not resort, as the Rambam does, to saying that the original authentic way of shofar-blowing was lost.

   Thus, authorities earlier than the Rambam dismissed the explanation that the oral explanation of *shofar*-blowing had been lost. It is the Rambam who insists that an oral law given at Sinai could have been— and was—forgotten in later times.

7. As by Rav Yechiel Michael Halevy Epstein, in his *Aruch HaShulchan HaAssid*, Mossad Harav Kook, Jerusalem, 1969, *Hilchos Mahmrim, Siman 64*; Chaim H. Schimmel, *The Oral Law*, Feldheim, 1971, 1978, p. 34; and Michael Hecht, *Have You Ever Asked Yourself These Questions?* Shengold, 1971, p. 116:

   After listing two categories of Oral Law, namely *halachos* handed down by Moses which have Scriptural support, and *Halachos L'Moshe MiSinai*, Hecht writes, "The Rambam forcefully makes clear that in each of these categories no *machlokos* are found concerning any matter of fundamental importance."

   Schimmel: "[A]ccording to Maimonides, laws of Sinaitic origin are not subject to controversy, yet there are a number of controversies in the Talmud concerning *Halacha Le Moshe Misinai*. It seems, however, that disputes in *Halacha Le Moshe Misinai* concern only details which do not go to the root of the law. There is no case of *Halacha Le Moshe Misinai* [that consists of] one *Tanna* declaring an object *Kosher* or an act permitted and another declaring the identical object or act prohibited."

These two books are excellent, clearly-written works which I highly recommend.

8. "The Talmud's Sages, great and righteous scholars, received all their
explanations from great and righteous scholars. . . .

"And should someone suffering from a deviant temperament
attempt to cast doubt upon the authenticity of the Sages' report [that
their explanations were truly received from their previous mentors, in a
chain of tradition originating at Sinai] and to obscure things by citing
the many *machlokos* that exist—then you make him grate his teeth, as
well! Tell him that he is rebelling against the Great Sanhedrin! And tell
him how the Sages never in history disputed the [oral traditions
describing the] basic *mitzvos*. They only argued over their details. . . .
They did not argue over *whether* [from the verse 'And you shall speak
these words that I command at your laying down and at your getting
up'] there is an obligation to recite the *k'riass sh'ma* morning and
night. Over what did they argue?—Over '*As of when* does one recite
the Sh'ma in the morning.' And so it is with all their words."

12. The word *machlokess* originally had two meanings, one of which has
fallen somewhat into disuse since the Rambam's days: *Machlokess* can
mean (1) A debate (i.e., a pair of conflicting opinions) or (2) an objection against someone's opinion. Shmuel HaNaggid, in his מבוא התלמוד,
Introduction to the Talmud, defines the word "קושיא," which we know
is a piece of evidence that casts doubt on an assertion, as follows:

היא המחלוקת הבא על השמועות. ולא יחלוק החולק בהלכה מקויימת ואם היה
החולקים לרבים, הסימן מיתיבי. ואם ליחיד, איתיביה.

"It is the מחלוקת that comes against statements. The one who will
חולק will not do so with an הלכה מקויימת, established law [a term
he previously defined as referring to a law transmitted from
Moses]. The terms used for this are מיתיבי, they raised an objection, or איתיביה, he raised an objection."

Shmuel HaNaggid is obviously using the word *machlokess* in the sense of a
contesting of a statement and not a disagreement between Sages. A קושיא is
an objection brought against something; not a pair of conflicting opinions
about it.

Cf. *Bava Bassra* 122b and *Tosefos* there which calls an anonymous
statement followed by an individual disagreeing with it "סתם ואח"כ מחלוקת,
an anonymous teaching followed by a *machlokess.*"

In English as well, when we say there is an argument about an assertion, we can mean either that the argument concerns whether the assertion
is true, or that the argument is over its interpretation, both sides granting
the truth of the assertion, *per se.*

Chapter 5

Moses Was Not Expressly Given All Talmudic Literature or Law Details

We have pointed out that the need to analyze the Torah and tradition to clarify the *halacha* obviously presumes the prior absence of answers. Loss of answers originally given at Sinai explains this absence. Can it be suggested that there never *were* some answers, that some information was never specifically revealed at Sinai? Two fundamental teachings seem to oppose such a suggestion: (a) the teaching that Hashem told Moses everything ever to be known about the Torah, a teaching emphasized in many places, and (b) the teaching that Moses proceeded to teach all the details of *halacha* to the people.

A typical example of the first principle, as expressed in the Talmud *Yerushalmi* (*Megilla* 28a), is the following:

אמר ר' יהושע בן לוי: . . . מקרא, משנה, תלמוד ואגדה, אפילו מה שתלמוד ותיק
עתיד לחדש (הגר"א מוחק הגרסא „להורות") כבר נאמר למשה בסיני. מה טעם?
„יש דבר שיאמר אדם, ראה זה חדש הוא' (קהלת א'), משיבו חבירו ואמר לו, „כבר
היה לעולמים" (שם).

Rebbi Yehoshua ben Levi[1] said: "The Torah, the Mishna, the
Talmud and Aggada, even whatever a conscientious scholar will
in the future originate, was told to Moses at Sinai. 'There may
be something regarding which a person says, "Look! Here is
something new!" (*Kohelless* 1:10).' His friend can respond: 'It
has already existed long ago' (*Kohelless* 1:10)."

The second principle is expressed in the *Mechilta* on *Sh'mos*
(21:1), paraphrased and made famous by *Rashi's* commentary on
the verse:

אשר תשים לפניהם — אמר לו הקב"ה למשה לא תעלה על דעתך לומר אשַׁנֶה להם
הפרק וההלכה ב' או ג' פעמים עד שתהא סדורה בפיהם כמשנתה ואיני מטריח עצמי
להבינם טעמי הדבר ופירושו. לכך נאמר „אשר תשים לפניהם"—כשולחָן הֶעָרוך
ומוכן לאכול לפני האדם.

G-d told Moses, "Let it not enter your mind to say, 'I will teach
them the *perek* (chapter of *mishnayos*) and *halacha* (i.e., *mishna*) two or three times until they can recite it verbatim and
fluently, and I will not trouble myself to make them understand
the reasoning (טעמי) of the matter and its explanation.' . . . Present the *halacha* like a table fully set, with prepared portions
ready to be eaten."

So it would seem that all the contents of the Talmud were
handed down directly by Moses to the people. Yet, as we have seen,
Talmudic literature and its commentators plainly assume that the
Sages did extract from Scripture clarifications of *mitzva* observance
that they did not possess beforehand.[2]

Indeed, we have seen that the Rambam clearly states that *drashos* were used even in Moses' time to produce *halachic* clarification

---

[1] In the *Midrash Kohelless Rabba* (end of first chapter), this same statement is made
by Rebbi Yoḥonon bar Lakish.

[2] Furthermore, if the חידושים, new insights, were already known, then why did the
conscientious scholar consider them חידושים? Wasn't he just repeating what he had
been taught, things that everyone had already known?

and that he himself was not directly told all the details of law, not to
mention the entire contents of talmudic literature:

הנא לא כל מה שנמצא לחכמים שהוציא בהיקש משלש עשרה מדות נאמר שהוא
נֶאֱמַר לְמֹשֶׁה בְּסִינַי.

Behold, we cannot say that everything the Sages brought forth
through the Thirteen Principles of Torah Interpretation were
said to Moses at Sinai.[3]

Rashi, too, indicates that there were facts that the Sages were
able to uncover in addition to those which Hashem had told Moses.[4]
King Solomon teaches us (*Kohelless* 1:9) that "there is nothing new
under the sun." Rashi explains this to mean that there are no new
discoveries in the corporeal world. But, he continues, *there can be
totally new discoveries when it comes to understanding the Torah.*

בכל מה שהוא למד בדבר שהוא חליפי השמש אין בו חידוש. לא יראה אלא מה שהיה
כבר, שנברא בששת ימי בראשית. אבל ההוגה בתורה מוצא בה תמיד חדושי טעמים
כענין שנ' (עירובין נ"ד:) „דדיה ירווך בכל עת"—מה הדד הזה כ"ז שהתינוק
ממשמש בו מוצא בה טעם, אף דברי תורה כן. וכן מצינו במס' חגיגה שאמר ר"א בן
הורקנוס דברים שלא שמעתן אוזן במעשה מרכבה.

In everything one studies instead of "the sun," (i.e., instead of
the Torah)[5] there will be nothing new. He will see nothing but
that which already existed at the world's Creation. But one who
studies Torah will always find new טעמים [meanings, perceptions, senses], as it says (*Eruvin* 54b), "'Its breasts will satisfy
you at every time' (*Mishlay* 5:19)—Every time a suckling works
at his mother's breast he finds a [new] taste; so too is it with the
words of the Torah." And so we find in *Ḥaggiga*[6] that Rebbi
Eliezer ben Horkinus told of things regarding *Maaseh Merkava*
which no ear ever heard before.[7]

---

[3] *Sefer HaMitzvos*, beginning of *Shoresh Shayni*, p. 29 in our editions.

[4] Though not contradicting any facts Moses *had* been told, of course.

[5] "תחת," translated "under," is also used as "in place of" (as in "עין תחת עין, *Eye in
place of eye*"). Thus, "תחת השמש, under the sun," refers to everything other than the
Torah, either because the Torah is *above* the "world under the sun," or because the
Torah itself is called "שמש," sun, for the Light it provides.

[6] See Additional Notes at the end of this chapter.

[7] Rashi's contrast to non-Torah studies requires investigation. True, new discoveries about the physical world merely uncover facts that always existed. But "new

"Which no ear ever heard before" indicates that even Moses was not told these secrets. Indeed, the *Midrash Rabba*[8] declares that "דברים דלא נגלו למשה נגלו לר"ע וחביריו, Things were revealed to Rabbi Akiva that were not revealed to Moses," just as the rationale for the *Porra Aduma*, the red cow procedure, was revealed only to Moses. Can we apply this principle to more "mundane" matters as well, to give *pre-Rishonic* support to the thesis that information contained in the Talmud—*halachic* or otherwise—was also withheld from Moses?

Moses and Rabbi Akiva

Let us examine an *Aggada* (מנחות כ"ט:) which some interpret to mean that some information which constitutes a significant part of the Talmud indeed was not taught to Moses: the locations of the Scriptural allusions to specific oral laws. This *Aggada* reports that when Moses ascended on High to receive the Torah, he was shown the future Rabbi Akiva *darshonning*, expounding, the "crowns" on the letters of the Torah. Moses, unable to follow the discourse, was distressed. He regained his composure only when he saw Rabbi Akiva identify the source for a law as a *Halacha L'Moshe MiSinai*.[9] Yet if Moses was taught the contents of all talmudic literature, including all *halachic* details that future Sages would discover, how could the *Aggada* depict Moses as being unaware—to say the least—of Rabbi Akiva's discoveries?

The *Ohr HaHayyim* in his commentary on *Vayikra* 13:34[10] suggests that Moses knew all there is to know, both of the Written Torah and of the Oral Law, but he was not told what particular subtleties of the written text *hinted* at the oral laws.[11] This science of

truths" revealed through Torah analysis, too, had always existed latently within the Torah's words. Indeed, this is implicit in Rashi's comparison of new Torah perceptions to the "new" milk suckled by a babe.

[8] פרשת חקת י"ט:ו׳. See Additional Note 24 for the first part of this quote.

[9] See Additional Notes at the end of this chapter.

[10] Also the עץ יוסף on the עין יעקב on *Menachos* 29b.

[11] According to this, a possible explanation for Moses' relief upon hearing Rabbi Akiva reporting a *Halacha L'Moshe MiSinai* would be as follows: Being a *Halacha L'Moshe MiSinai*, evidently not one derived from the crowns of the Torah's letters but the technical kind which by definition is not connected to any *p'sukim* (see *Maimonides' Introduction to the Talmud*, p. 84), it was independent of any *drashos* Rabbi Akiva could develop, and could be known solely through Moses' teaching.

linking an oral law to written law was the forté of Rabbi Akiva and was the branch of knowledge that Moses lacked.[12]

Obviously, the *Ohr HaHayyim* was intent on attributing *no* lack of *halachic* information to Moses. He understood that Moses literally had been told all future *halachic* discoveries. Yet, according to his own solution, knowledge of the specific links between the oral laws and Scriptural verses—a large and integral part of talmudic literature—*was* withheld from Moses. Moreover, as discussed previously, the methods one chooses to link an oral law to Scripture produces differences in *halacha*, too.

Rashi

The *Rashi* on the passage under discussion (*Menachos* 29b) solves the problem immediately, without forcing recourse to the *Ohr HaHayyim's* assertion. Unlike the *Ohr HaHayyim*, *Rashi* understands the *Aggada* to be saying that Moses was unaware of the specific *halacha* that Rabbi Akiva reported. Rashi anticipated the obvious question: Rabbi Akiva himself reported the *halacha* in the name of Moses. How, then, could Moses have been unaware of it? Rashi's answer is:

נתיישב דעתו. של משה הואיל ומשמו אומר אע"פ שעדיין לא קיבלה.

"Moses was relieved"—since the law was stated in his name, though he had not as yet received it.

That is, the "preview" of the future was shown to Moses *before* he received the Torah—precisely as the words of the Talmud read: "כשעלה משה למרום." This event took place "when Moses ascended on high" *to receive* the Torah. Moses failed to understand Rabbi Akiva's lecture simply because he had not yet received the information upon which it was to be based. He was not yet told the verses, or the codes planted in them, or the laws at which they were to hint. This *Aggada* therefore has no bearing on the question of whether Moses was ever told all the details that anyone would ever discern from the Torah.[13]

Moses was relieved to find out that he himself would indeed make an exclusive contribution to the Oral Law.

12 See Additional Notes at the end of this chapter.

13 See Additional Notes at the end of this chapter.

Moses Was Not Taught Everything Explicitly

There is, however, a source clearly stating that Moses was not taught all law details, one by one. In *Sh'mos Rabbah* (41:6), Rabbi Avahu declares that Moses could not possibly retain all the Torah he was being taught until Hashem granted him that ability as a gift. He then continues:

> אר׳ אבהו . . . וכי כל התורה למד משה?! כתיב בתורה (איוב י״א:ט) „אֲרֻכָּה מֵאֶרֶץ, מִדָּהּ, וּרְחָבָה מִנִּי יָם. ״ ולארבעים יום למדה משה?! אלא כללים למדוהו הקב״ה למשה.

And did Moses actually learn the entire Torah [even through a special gift from Hashem]?! It (*Job* 11:9) says that '[the Torah] is vaster than the Earth . . . and wider than the Sea.' And in forty days Moses learned it all?! No. It was the *overall principles [alone]* that G-d taught Moses.

The details were not revealed even to Moses, for the infinite number of fine details were indeed beyond even Moses' ability to absorb. Even Hashem's special gift granted Moses the ability to retain only the "overall principles."[14]

Now, the body of 'overall principles' which Moses *was* granted obviously included the information we received from him: the laws of the Written Torah and the פירוש המקובל, the transmitted explanations. What then remains to be called the infinite number of "particulars" whose knowledge Moses was *not* granted? Evidently, the myriad details later to be discovered by future sages!

Included in the 'overall principles,' of course, are the י״ג מדות שהתורה נדרשת בהן, the classical Thirteen Principles of Torah Interpretation. These produce many of the "particulars" not specified by G-d to Moses.[15] Indeed, the מהרז״ו[16] on the *Midrash Rabba* identifies the 'overall principles' of our passage with these Thirteen Principles, and he identifies the unrevealed details with the many laws resulting from their application. He writes:

> „כללים למדוהו הקב״ה למשה״—אלו דרכי הדרשות. שכל מדה מלמדת לאין חקר.

---

[14] See Additional Notes at the end of this chapter.

[15] See Additional Notes at the end of this chapter.

[16] Rabbi Zev Wolf Einhorn, Vilna, 18th century, author of works involving the methods of Torah-interpretation.

These 'overall principles' [which *were* given to Moses] are identical with the *darcay ha'drash*, methods of Scriptural interpretation. For each of the rules of Torah interpretation produces an infinite number of teachings [which were *not* revealed to Moses].

It is over these 'particulars' that we see *machlokos* since they were not explicitly given over even to Moses.

Moses' "Knowledge": Potential

In what sense, then, can we understand those statements indicating that Moses was told of all future discoveries?

It would seem that such statements are meant only in a *potential* sense. The fine details affecting future circumstances were given to Moses potentially or implicitly, because these details were *extractable* from the explicit information and formulae he was given (e.g., the פירוש מקובל, revealed explanations, and the Thirteen Principles). In this sense they had already been "told" to Moses.[17] For, encountering any future situation, Moses could apply the rules of analysis and arrive at the correct *halachic* response.

Was Moses Told to Withhold Any Halachic Information He Did Master?

The *Tosefos Yom Tov*, in his *Introduction to the Mishna*, reconciles the fact of future discoveries with the principle that Moses was told everything on Mount Sinai in a similar, if not identical way:

אבל תועלת חבור המשנה וסיבתה היתה לפי שתורה שבע"פ שמסרה משה ליהושע ויהושע לזקנים וכו', אע"פ שהיתה ביאור התורה ומצותיה ביאור שלם, אין לך זמן ודור שלא יתחדש בהכרח ויפלא למשפט.

ואל תשיבני דבר ממה שאמרו בפ"ה דמגילה (י"ט:) מאי ועליהם וכו' מלמד שהראהו הקב"ה למשה דקדוקי תורה ודקדוקי סופרים ע"כ. שאני אומר שזה לא היה מוסר משה לאחרים כלל. ודקדוק לשונם כך הוא. שאמרו „מלמד שהראהו" ולא אמר „שמסר לו" או „שלמדו." שאילו אמר אחד מאלו הלשונות היה מתחייב מזה שהוא מסרם ויתנם ג"כ ליהושע. שהרי עינו לא צרה (שמצינו שסמך בשתי ידיו אע"פ שלא נצטוה אלא באחת). אבל אמרו „שהראהו." וזה דרך ראיה בלבד, לא בדרך מסורה. כאדם המראה דבר לחבירו לראותו, ואינו נותנו לו. וזה דקדוק נאה וענין אמיתי.

[17] See Additional Notes at the end of this chapter.

True, the Oral Law—which Moses handed over to Joshua, and
Joshua handed over to the Elders, and so on—was a *completely
full* explanation. Nevertheless, by necessity, there was no time
or era in which there was an absence of new discoveries and
halachic hearings and findings.

And do not attempt to contradict me on the grounds that the
Sages (in *Megilla* 19b) stated that G-d told Moses *dikdukay
Torah v'dikdukay soferim*, the details [to be] extracted by the
Sages. For I say that *Moses did not relay this to the others at all.*
It is not said that these details were "handed over" to him, or
"taught" to him. . . . but that he was "shown" them. . . . It was
like someone letting another view an object without, however,
actually letting him take it [to do with it as he pleases, such as
sharing it with others].[18]

Tosefos Yom Tov's reconciliation may be a new one: that Moses
was given specific answers to all *halachic* questions, but was made to
withhold them. Yet by the nature of his description of how G-d
made Moses withhold the information (". . . it was like someone letting another view an object without, however, actually letting him
take it [to do with it as he pleases, such as sharing it with others]"),
his explanation virtually merges into a reiteration of the principle
that Moses was not taught all *halachos* one-by-one, but was given
them implicitly, as developed above.

The Rambam states quite clearly that Moses withheld none of
the *halachos* revealed to him:

אף־על־פי שלא נכתבה תורה שבעל־פה, למדה משה רבינו כולה בבית דינו לשבעים
זקנים; ואלעזר ופנחס ויהושע—שלשתם קבלו ממשה.

Although the Oral Law was not written, Moses taught all of it,

---

18 What about the passages which *do* use the term, "ניתנו," "they were *given* to
him"? The *Tosefos Rishon L'Tzion* (in a note on this passage in the *Tosefos Yom
Tov*) observes that the term appears only in passages about facts *other* than דקדוקי
סופרים, facts which *were* meant for Moses to give over:
תוס׳ ראשון לציון: מדברים אלו מובן היטב סוגיא זו עם סוגיא דברכות (ה.) מאי דכתיב „ואתנה לך את לוחות
האבן כו׳"—„תורה" זו מקרא, „והמצוה" זו משנה, „אשר כתבתי" אלו נביאים וכתובים, „להורותם" זה גמ׳
מלמד שכולם ניתנו למשה מסיני. הנה כל השינויים בין ב׳ הסוגיות מבואר לפי מאי דאמר במגילה: דקדוקי
סופרים—הוכרח לומר שהראהו, משא״כ בברכות [דלא הזכיר כך] שפיר אמר שכולם נתנו כו׳ ויבא על הכוונה
שכתב . . . בסמוך, כיון שהכללות שבימיהם אמתים ומסורות להם ממשה רבינו ע״ה ומפני כן אלו ואלו כו׳.

in his *Bes Din*, to the seventy Elders; and Elazar, Pinchas and Joshua—the three of them—received it from Moses.[19]

Indeed, in view of the well-known rabbinic teaching (*Eruvin* 54b) cited by Rashi at the beginning of *parshas Mishpattim*, the suggestion that Hashem gave Moses *halachic* information and then told him to withhold it from the people is difficult to accept. In *Sh'mos* 21:1, Hashem tells Moses: "ואלה המשפטים אשר תשים לפניהם", These are the rulings which you shall place before them," and He proceeds to deliver a series of commandments. The rabbis teach that the phrase "which you shall place before them" would be uncharacteristically wordy for simply instructing Moses to tell the Jews these laws. Hashem was telling Moses something more:

אמר לו הקב"ה למשה לא תעלה על דעתך לומר אשנה להם הפרק וההלכה ב' או ג' פעמים עד שתהא סדורה בפיהם כמשנתה, ואיני מטריח עצמי להבינם טעמי הדבר ופירושו. לכך נאמר אשר תשים לפניהם כשלחן הערוך ומוכן לאכול לפני האדם.

Do not imagine that you are to simply teach them the chapter and the *halacha* [of each *mishna*] two or three times until they know it by rote. You must exert yourself so that they comprehend the טעמי הדבר, the concepts behind the matter, and its פירוש, its explanation. That is why I tell you that you must "set it before them." Present the *halacha* like a table fully set, with prepared portions ready to be eaten.

Evidently, whatever *halachic* information G-d gave Moses clearly, He commanded Moses to hand over to the people clearly, too.[20] The only reasons the Talmud gives for Moses not initially telling the people a *halachic* fact are that he was not told it (as above) or that he forgot it. Other passages[21] that give *no* reason can be explained the same way, without introducing the assertion that Moses was told to withhold the information.

Between G-d and Moses

There *are* Talmudic passages stating that G-d commanded Moses to

[19] Introduction to Mishneh Torah. See also at the beginning of the *Introduction to the Commentary on the Mishna*: "ילמדום פירושי המצוה ההיא הנתונה מאת השם", He taught them the explanations of that *mitzva* which was given by *Hashem*."

[20] See Additional Notes at the end of this chapter.

[21] See Additional Notes at the end of this chapter.

withhold information, but they are clearly not referring to *halacha*.
A passage in the *Talmud Yerushalmi* (*Avoda Zorra* 2:7, p. 11a)
reports:

> אר' יצחק: כתיב „ואותי צוה ה'." אותי! ו אותי?—נאמר לי דברים שנאומר לכם
> ונאמר לי דברים שנאמר בינו לבין עצמי.

> Said Rav Yitzchak: "It says (*D'varim* 4:14), 'G-d commanded
> also me . . .' Shouldn't Moses have phrased it 'G-d commanded
> me' without the word 'also'? Why did he say 'also me'?—
> Because Moses was alluding to the fact that 'some things told to
> me I will tell to you as well; but other things were meant to be
> just between G-d and myself.'"

The lines that follow this passage indicate that this private information consisted of deep secrets, רזי תורה, mysteries concerning the
Upper Worlds:[22]

> בשעה שתלמידים קטנים—כבוש לפניהן דברי תורה. הגדילו . . . —גלה להם רזי
> תורה. תני רבי שמעון בן יוחאי: „ואלה המשפטים אשר תשים לפניהם." מה הסימה
> הזאת, אינה נגלית לכל בריה, כך אין לך רשות לשקע את עצמך בדברי תורה אלא
> לפני בני אדם כשרין.

> When the disciples are young, withhold from them words of
> Torah. When they grow great . . . reveal to them the "Secrets of
> the Torah."

What Are the "Secrets of the Torah?

Apparently, our passage is speaking of the secrets of *kabballa*.
These mysteries were not taught to all the people. Even after a Sage,
through his own efforts, would distill these secrets from the Torah,
he was to disclose his findings only to qualified students. On the
other hand, for this very reason these lines may not be meant to
define the subject of the passage they followed—the information that
Moses was bidden to suppress. They may be only loosely related to
it, in that they also deal with something that should not be indis-
criminately divulged. For if these secrets are the *kabballa*, then certainly, by definition of the word (*kabballa* means "received [infor-
mation]"), Moses did not withhold them completely. Moses *did*

---

[22] Such as *Maaseh Merkava*, discussed in Ḥaggiga 13a and *ff.*

reveal to some the רזי תורה, the Torah's secrets, albeit to a select group of people. Our passage, however, is speaking of matters that were kept strictly between Hashem and Moses and given over to absolutely no one else.

Perhaps, then, the 'secrets' of our passage are the טעמי המצוות, the deep reasons behind the mitzvos, reasons that only a King Solomon could decipher.[23] We know that these matters Moses was told to disclose to no one.[24] Context can support this interpretation of our passage. The passage immediately preceding ours had applauded the Sages' policy of withholding the reasons (טעמים) for *their* decrees. Indeed, the *P'nay Moshe* paraphrases our passage accordingly:

שנאמר לי דברים שיש לי רשות לומר הטעם לכם, ודברים שאין לי לגלות הטעם.

Things were told to me whose underlying reasons (טעמים) I have permission to tell you, and things were told to me whose underlying reasons (טעמים) I cannot reveal.[25]

Moses' Knowledge Not on Final P'sak

Even if, as per the *Tosefos Yom Tov*, Moses was granted a brief exposure to all future discoveries, this exposure did not necessarily reveal to him the *p'sak* destined to win the majority vote in future Sanhedrins. The *Ritva* on *Eruvin* 13b and the *Tosefos Shantz* on *Aid'yos* (1:5) tell us that Moses was exposed only to all the *arguments* that future scholars were to present when debating those issues:[26]

„אלו ואלו דברי אלוקים חיים" (עירובין י"ג:)—שאלו רבנן צרפת ז"ל האיך אפשר

---

[23] *Bamidbar Rabba* 19:3.

[24] See Additional Notes at the end of this chapter.

[25] Only by stretching things a bit could this passage be used to support the thesis that G-d commanded Moses to refrain from revealing some *halachic* details to the people, although Moses himself knew them clearly, by suggesting that "טעמי המצוות" includes answers to *halachic* questions. True, "טעם," "reason," is usually understood to mean the rationale for a *mitzva*. But the specific factor that determines a case is also called a טעם, as in "שהיה [סומכוס] אומר על כל דבר ודבר של טומאה מ"ח טעמי טומאה ועל כל דבר ודבר של טהרה מ"ח טעמי טהרה, [Soomchos] would give 48 *reasons* to explain why something was *tomay* or *tahor*" (*Eruvin* 13b). See Additional Notes at the end of this chapter.

[26] Cf. *Yerushalmi* on *Sanhedrin* 4:2, *Midrash T'hillim* on 12:7, *Vayikra Rabba* on הביאני אל בית היין, and *Shir HaShirim Rabba* on ועוד ראיתי.

שיהא אלו ואלו דברי אלקים חיים זה אוסר וזה מתיר? ותרצו כי כשעלה משה למרום
לקבל התורה, הראו לו על כל דבר ודבר מ"ט פנים לאיסור ומ"ט פנים להיתר. ושאל
להקב"ה על זה ואמר שיהא זה מסור לחכמי ישראל שבכל דור ודור ויהיה הכרעה
כמותם. וכנכון הוא לפי הדרש. ובדרך האמת יש טעם סוד בדבר.

"The words of both sides of a halachic dispute are the words of
the Living G-d."—The Rabbis of France asked how they can
possibly both be the words of G-d when one side permits something that the other forbids. And they answered that when
Moses ascended On High to receive the Torah, they displayed
before him 49 points of argument to forbid each thing and 49
points of argument to permit it. When he questioned the Holy
One about this, he was told that the responsibility of determining the *halacha* will be given to each generation of Sages, and
the decisions will be in their hands. And there is a deep *kabballistic* concept behind this.

This source indicates that G-d did not divulge to Moses *answers*
to all issues, but only the arguments supporting all sides of the
issues. And he was told that, as each decision was a matter of analysis and judgment, the Sages of each generation's Great Sanhedrin
were expected to make each decision by *darshonning* the *p'sukim*
and comparing each case to previously set precedents. .... אלו ואלו,
These and those, does not mean that *both* statements were made by
Hashem in the sense of final decisions of law. Hashem did not say
that the final law is that something is at the same time both permitted and prohibited![27] Not at all. He simply said that the Sanhedrin of
each generation was to determine for itself those details of law not
presented to Moses in a decided way.

In fact, Moses' brief exposure, if any, to all future issues did not
necessarily supply him with a final *p'sak* even on those issues to be
faced in his own time. Some may have been left for him and his
Sanhedrin to decide through Torah analysis. Talmudic passages
relate that Moses arrived at an immediately relevant *halacha* through
reasoning with a *kal v'homer*.[28] Hashem approved of his conclusion.
We have already mentioned the Rambam's citation of *Eruvin* 13a to
prove that thousands of *halachos* were determined in Moses' days
through the Thirteen Principles of Torah Interpretation. Clearly

[27] Chapter Eleven will deal more fully with the concept of "ואלו אלו."
[28] *Shabbos* 87a and *Sh'mos Rabba* 19:3 ("נשא קו"ח בעצמו [משה]").

Moses had not been told these *halachos* beforehand.[29] The Talmud[30] tells us that Hashem withheld three immediately relevant *halachic* details from Moses until an event making them pertinent occurred. Not that there may have been other details that remained unaccounted for since no event occurred in Moses' days to make them pertinent. The Talmud controverts this very point, as *Rashi* makes clear (*Bava Bassra* 119a ד"ה וראויה היתא וכו'):

ולא תאמר אם לא דברו בנות צלפחד ולא נתחייב מקושש היו שתי פרשיות הללו חסרין מן התורה והכי נמי איכא למימר שהרבה מצות חסרים מן התורה לפי שלא אירעו המעשים.

And do not say that if the daughters of Zelophhad had not spoken up, and the wood-gatherer would not have been liable, [the rules revealed in] these two Torah-sections would have [ended up as being] absent from the Torah—and that one can say that many [*other*] *mitzvos* are likewise missing because no episodes occurred [to make them pertinent].

But although Moses' Joshua's or the Elders' Sanhedrin did eventually address those issues pertinent to them, if they were not specifically addressed by G-d, we have the theoretical possibility that later Sanhedrins could take issue with a former *p'sak*, as we will see in the following chapter.

Summary

Any disagreement among the Sages over a detail of a biblical law occurred when they lacked a statement by Moses which pinpointed the solution to their question. One reason for this lack, as developed in this chapter, is that in isolated cases Moses himself did not have the answers to hand down. When the Sages state that Moses was told everything that was to be known in the future, it means only that Moses was told this in an implicit way, as we have other sources

[29] *Why* should G-d have withheld information from those who urgently needed it? We can only conjecture. Perhaps this was to train the people and scholars of the Sanhedrin in deriving details from the Torah, so that they would master the science when a Moses would *not* be there to supply the answers. Or perhaps Hashem provided such challenges to the people because of His desire for them to be immersed in Torah study.

[30] See Additional Notes at the end of this chapter.

which declare that Moses was told only *general rules* (Rebbi Avahu
quoted in *Sh'mos Rabbah*), that he was given methods by which to
darshon law details from the Torah (*Nedarim* 38a according to the
Netziv) and used them (*Vayikra* 10:16-20), and that he was not
given the solutions to several halachic problems (*Ritva* and *Tosefos
Shantz*). Even details which had to be known immediately may have
been withheld from him (*Shabbos* 87a, *Sh'mos Rabba* 19:3, *Vayikra*
10:16-20) with Hashem desiring that he and/or his Sanhedrin con-
strue them through analysis of given data. This situation left room,
naturally, for different opinions to be voiced.

That's All?!

One question remains. If, as has been stated, the dictums saying that
Moses was told all the details of the Torah mean only that Moses
knew the Torah in general and had the tools to generate all future
teachings, then how does this show the superiority of Moses over
any of the other *talmiday chachmim* throughout the generations
who also knew the Torah in general and its principles of interpretation.[31] When *anyone* knows something in general, he in a sense
knows whatever others will derive from it.

The answer is that the purpose of these declarations is *not* to
describe Moses' genius or the power of his prophetic abilities. They
are not speaking in terms of what Moses knew, they are speaking in
terms of what the Torah is.

מקרא, משנה, תלמוד ואגדה, אפילו מה שתלמוד ותיק עתיד לחדש (כן צ"ל וגרסת
להורות נמחק—גר"א) כבר נאמר למשה בסיני. מה טעם? "יש דבר שיאומר אדם
ראה זה חדש הוא' וגו'" (קהלת א') משיבו חביריו ואומר לו, "כבר היה לעולמים"
.(שם)

The Torah, the Mishna, the Talmud and Aggada, even whatever
a conscientious scholar will in the future originate—all were told
to Moses at Sinai. "There may be something about which a
person says, 'Look! This thing is new!'" His friend can answer
him that "it has already existed long before."[32]

These dictums mean to tell us a very basic fact: Those ideas
which the prophets and the teachers and students of the *Mishna*,

---

[31] Certainly Moses must have been more adept than any future scholars at using
these tools, but the dictums do not address this point. They solely speak of the fact
that Moses was told everything they would discover.

[32] *Yerushalmi, Meggillah* 28a.

Gemora, and *Midrash* declare as Scripturally based truly *are* contained in the words of the Torah and are *not* their own new contrivances. Indeed, when the Rambam teaches the fundamental principle that the Oral Law was revealed at Mount Sinai, these are the statements he cites as his source.[33] They tell us not to imagine that the rabbis of the Mishna *invented* the laws and just called them Biblical, perhaps poetically attributing them to *p'sukim.* No. The Sages' concepts were literally drawn from the Torah, adding insights, subtracting none.

The spokesmen who enunciated this crucial point—Rebbi Yoḥonon,[34] Resh Lakish, Rebbi Neḥemia, and others—made it clear that Judaism has always maintained that the Oral Law was not an excuse for some Jewish law reforms, for changing and distorting the Torah given at Sinai. Whatever the Sages declared to be oral laws were not the fanciful inventions of rabbis who would use the Torah's verses as playthings for putting dubious stamps of approval on their own ideas. This fantasy, propounded by the Saducees and later by the Karaite[35] and Reform and Conservative movements,[36] conveniently allowed them to discard the oral laws and invent their own practices. Our Sages vigorously discredited this idea so that no mistake could be made. The biblical laws and ideas to be taught by the prophets and writers of *Nach,* the *Men of the Great Assembly,* the *Soferim,* the *Tannaim* and *Amoraim,* and even the *Rishonim* and *Acharonim,* Rebbi Yoḥonon and the others remind us, constitute the original intent of the Torah and not implantations upon it. Their laws and ideas were, indeed, inherent in what Moses had been told. The ideas were there in the Torah that Moses was given.

Nevertheless, as we mentioned, we will see in the following chapter that there is a fundamental difference between biblical law details that were explicitly received from G-d and those which were inferred from Scripture through the system of Torah-analysis: those inferred through analysis may later be challenged.

---

[33] Beginning of Rambam's *Introduction to Mishna Commentary* and his *Introduction to Mishneh Torah.*

[34] Rebbi Yoḥonon (bar Naphcha) is the author of many declarations basic to Judaism. One of the first of the *Amoraim,* he stood at the ship's helm during the crucial voyage over the transitional period between the era of the *Tannaim* and that of the *Amoraim.* He had the responsibility of ensuring that the fundamentals of Judaism would remain intact and saw to it that they were elucidated for posterity.

[35] See end of chapter "Rambam's Attack on Attributing Machlokess to Loss."

[36] See Epilogue.

Additional Notes to Chapter 5

6. In our texts of Ḥaggiga 14b, praises are heaped upon Rebbi Elazar ben Aruch—not Rebbi Eliezer ben Horkinus—for his dissertation on *Maaseh Merkava*. The phrase "דברים שלא שמעתן אזן", things which no ear ever before heard" does not appear. However, this phrase does appear, and in reference to Rebbi Eliezer ben Horkinus, in *Ahvos D'Rebbi Nosson* 6:3, though it does not specify that the subject he spoke on was *Maaseh Merkava*. (In *B'rayshis Rabbah*, a different subject is indicated.) Nevertheless, Rashi's point remains. Discoveries were made which were never before known. (I am indebted to Rabbi Moshe Friedman, שליט"א, for finding this source for me.)

9. א"ר יהודה א'רב בשעה שעלה משה למרום מצאו להקב"ה שיושב וקושר כתרים לאותיות. אמר לפניו רבונו של עולם מי מעכב על ידך. א"ל אדם אחד יש שעתיד להיות בסוף כמה דורות ועקיבא בן יוסף שמו שעתיד לדרוש על כל קוץ וקוץ תילין תילין של הלכות. אמר לפניו רבש"ע הראהו לי. א"ל חזור לאחורך. הלך וישב בסוף שמונה שורות ולא היה יודע מה הן אומרים. תשש כחו. כיון שהגיע לדבר (אחד) אמרו תלמידיו רבי מנין לך אמר להן הלכה למשה מסיני. נתיישבה דעתו.

Rav Yehuda said in the name of Rav: "At the time that Moses ascended to the Above, he found the Holy One Blessed-be-He sitting and attaching crowns to the [Torah's] letters. He said before Him, 'Master of the World! Who is forcing you?' [G-d] replied, 'In the future there will be a certain man—and Akiva ben Yosef is his name— who in the future will expound (*darshon*) many mountains of *halachos* concerning every tittle.' [Moses] said before Him, 'Show him to me!' [G-d] replied, 'Turn back!' [Moses] went and sat in the last of the eight rows [of seats in Rabbi Akiva's lecture hall], and didn't know what the discussants were saying. He felt faint. [But] when they came to a certain [*halacha*] the students asked [Rabbi Akiva], 'Rebbi, what is your source for this?' He replied to them, 'It is a *Halacha L'Moshe MiSinai.*' [Upon this, Moses] regained his composure."

12. This is similar to the Ramban's explanation (in his commentary on *Shoresh Shayni* of the Rambam's *Sefer HaMitzvos*, page 43 in our editions) for the existence of *machlokos* over laws derived through a *gezeyra shavva* (a classic rule of Torah interpretation in which information is carried over between Torah passages containing similar terminology), despite the rule that one can *darshon* a *gezayra shavva* only if that *gezayra shavva* was a *kabbala*, tradition, going all the way back to Moses. The Ramban explains that Moses was given only *partial* information, such as what words were meant to be paired for a *gezayra shavva*. But more than one pair of *p'sukim* might contain these words, and Moses was not told which ones were meant. The *Ohr HaHayyim* would extend Moses' incomplete knowledge of specifics to

all the kinds of *drashos* that could connect *p'sukim* to the oral explanations.

13. Likewise, Rashi's explanation of this *Aggada* makes unnecessary Rabbi N. Scherman's beautifully expressed solution to our problem (*Artscroll B'rayshis, Mesorah*, NY, 1977). In his interpretation of the *Maharal's* commentary (*Overview*, p. li), Rabbi Scherman answers that Moses did know the methods of Torah interpretation. But he didn't need them. His "depth of understanding was such that he intuitively knew every individual law(-detail) associated with the commandment. [He perceived the details] as aspects of one whole." The gist of the Torah's law-system was so deeply engrained within him that he could "sense" the correct answer to any halachic problem. Only later generations would need to use the rules of interpretation to uncover details which Moses was able to determine intuitively. When Moses was told to witness Rabbi Akiva deducing new details from the Written Law, he "had to descend from his august pinnacle of Torah greatness . . . [and] was bewildered by this unfamiliar method of uncovering the laws [used by Rabbi Akiva]" (*ibid.*).

14. The *Netziv* (Rav Naftali Tzvi Yehuda Berlin, 19th century commentator) understands still another source, *Nedarim* 38a, to be saying that Moses, not explicitly told all future discoveries, was given the tools by which to generate *halachic* discoveries from Scripture:

אר' יוסי בר' חנינה: לא ניתנה תורה אלא למשה ולזרעו, שנ' „פסל לך," „כתב לך."
מה פסולתן שלך, אף כתבן (כתב של לוחות) שלך. ומשה (אעפ"כ) נהג בה טובת עין
ונתנה לישראל.

מתיב רב חסדא: . . . [והכתיב] „ . . . למען תהיה לי השירה הזאת לעד בבני
ישראל."

אלא פיפולא בעלמא.

Rebbi Yosay b'Rebbi Ḥannina said: "The Torah was given to Moses and his descendents, alone. For the Torah says, 'Carve out for yourself' the tablets for the Ten Commandments and also, 'Write for yourself' the words of the Torah. That is, just as the tablets are for you, so are the words. Nevertheless, Moses, a generous person, gave it to Israel.

Rav Ḥissda questioned this: "It says, . . . 'This Song shall be my testimony for the Jewish People (that they should learn the Torah).'"

"(Then I'll modify my statement.) What was originally meant solely for Moses was the *pilpul*, alone."

The other commentators, however, seem to understand the skill under discussion (i.e., *pilpul*) to be the ability to extract profound, perhaps *kabballistic*, concepts.

15. It might seem that the mere fact that Moses was taught the science of deriving laws from Scripture already proves that Hashem held back from telling him the derivable laws. However, this is not necessarily so. In addition to generating laws, there are other uses for this tool. One, there is the task of finding the Scriptural hints for the Oral Laws. If Moses was not taught what the hints were, he, too, would need the interpretation rules to discover them. Two, he, and especially his descendents, would need this system in the event that some details become forgotten (see chapter entitled "Loss of Halachos"). Indeed, we do know of one instance (*Vayikra* 10:16-20) in which Moses admitted that his brother Aharon's use of the interpretation rules was sounder than his own in reconstructing a law he (Moses) forgot (*Zevachim* 101a).

17. Cf. *Ramban* on *Sefer Hamitzvos, Shoresh Rishone, siman* 7, regarding the justification for counting rabbinical decrees among the 613 *mitzvos* that 'the Jewish people were given as commandments at Sinai':

שכיון שנאמר למשה בסיני שיקבלו עליהם ישראל מצות ב״ד הגדול ובאו הם ותקנו את אלו, כבר נאמרו כלם למשה בסיני אין הפרש ביניהם באמירת סיני אלא שזה בפרט וזה בכלל.

Since it was said to Moses at Sinai that Israel should accept upon itself the commandments of the Great Sanhedrin, and the latter came and decreed these [rabbinical ordinances], they were all quite already given to Moses at Sinai. There is no difference between them in the aspect of being said at Sinai except that this was said specifically and this in general.

20. Indeed, Moses was quite generous with the information he was given, as is demonstrated in *Nedarim* 38a:

אמר רבי יוסי בר׳ חנינא, לא ניתנה תורה אלא למשה ולזרעו—שנאמר „כתב לך . . . פסל לך," מה פסולתן שלך אף כתבתן שלך—ומשה נהג בה טובת עין ונתנה לישראל, ועליו הכתוב אומר, „טוב עין הוא יבורך כי נתן מלחמו לדל" (משלי כב:ט).

Said Rebbi Yosay b'Rebbi Ḥannina: "'Torah' [later in the passage defined as *pilpul*, i.e., the science of extracting the Torah's secrets] was given [by G-d] only to Moses and his descendents [i.e., the Levites to be descended from him], as it says, 'Write *for yourself* . . . hew out [the tablets from the mountain] *for yourself* . . .,' which means that just as you alone will have had the [original tablets] that are shattered, you alone will have 'Torah.' But Moses conducted himself generously with it and gave it to Israel. Regarding Moses Scripture says, 'The one who has a kind eye—he shall be blessed, for he gave of his bread [often a metaphor for Torah] to the poor' (*Mishlay* 22:9)."

21. An example of a passage wherein Moses did not reveal information

that was immediately relevant to his generation, but with no explanation why:

The *Talmud Yerushalmi Payah* 1:1, p. 2b) quotes four very frequently mentioned *Amoraim* Rebbi Tanhuma, Rav Huna, Rebbi Yohonon, and Rebbi Bennaia:

רבי תנחומא בשם רב הונא: "ובצלאל בן אורי בן חור למטה יהודה עשה את כל אשר
צוה אותו משה" אין כתיב כאן. אלא: "אשר צוה ה' את משה."—אפילו דברים שלא
שמע מפי רבו הסכימה דעתו, כמה שנא' למשה מסיני.

רבי יוחנן בשם רבי בנייה: "כאשר צוה ה' את משה עבדו, כן צוה משה את יהושע,
וכן עשה יהושע." "לא הסיר דבר מכל אשר צוה אותו משה" אין כתיב כאן, אלא
"(את) [צ"ל מכל] אשר צוה ה' את משה.—אפילו דברים שלא שמע מפי רבו,
הסכים דעתו כמה שנא' למשה בסיני.

Rebbi Tanḥuma said in the name of Rav Huna: "The verse (*Bamidbar* 38:22) does not say, 'And Beẓallel . . . did everything that *Moses* commanded *him* to do [in constructing the *Mishkan (Portable Temple)*].' It states that he 'did everything that *Hashem* commanded *Moses* to do.' Even regarding those things which he was *not* told by his master [Moses], his mind deduced exactly what [Hashem on Mount] Sinai had *told Moses*."

Rebbi Yoḥonon said in the name of Rabbi Bannaia: "The verse (*Joshua* 11:15) reads, 'Exactly as *Hashem* commanded Moses, Moses commanded Joshua; and Joshua did exactly as commanded.' It does not [go on to] read, 'He did not neglect a thing from all that *Moses* commanded *him*.' It reads, rather, '[He did not neglect a thing] from all that *Hashem* commanded *Moses*!' He deduced exactly that which [Hashem on Mount] Sinai had told Moses, even though Moses had not, in turn, told it to him."

24. As in the following *Midrash Rabbah* (*Ḥukas* 19:6):

"ויקחו אליך פרה אדומה." א"ר יוסי ברבי חנינא, אמר לו הקב"ה למשה לך אני
מגלה טעם פרה אבל לאחר—חקה. . . . דברים המכוסין מכם בעולם הזה עתידים
להיות צופים לעולם הבא . . . כבר עשיתי [בענינים אחרות] לר"ע וחביריו: דברים
דלא נגלו למשה נגלו לר"ע.

G-d told Moses: "To you I am revealing the reason for the *Red Cow*, but for anyone else—it is a חוק, a decree that must be followed although it seems to have no rationale. . . . [It is one of those] matters which are covered over in this world, destined to be revealed in the *Next World*. . . . I have done [this with other matters] for Rabbi Akiva and his colleagues: Matters not revealed to Moses were [to be] revealed to Rabbi Akiva."

(Remarkably, this implies that the טעמי המצוות, the rationales for the *mitzvos*, are even more closely guarded than the *kabballa*, which was at least revealed to Moses for transmission to select individuals. The rea-

son for such secrecy over the authentic reasons behind the mitzvos are
discussed in *Pesikta Rabba* 14 in relationship to King Solomon.)

25. The difference between the two uses of the word טעם can be illustrated
as follows: The טעם, rationale, for refraining from proscribed activities
on Shabbos may be to publicize that G-d created the world in six days
and ceased creating on the seventh. Let's say a certain individual feels
he can best accomplish this by driving through the streets on Shabbos
in a van that has a sign attached reading "Remember the Sabbath!" But
the טעם of "Shabbos observance" in the other sense of the word—a
definition and legal parameter-type of "Shabbos observance"—
prohibits this. Even if an individual feels uncomfortable with restrictions and they disturb his concentration on spiritual thoughts, the legal
parameters of that which constitutes Shabbos observance override his
personal method of fulfilling the rationale-type טעם. (One may suggest
a "טעם" for the precedence of the "legal parameter" טעם over the
"rationale-type" טעם: uniformity is necessary. Totally variant practices
would destroy the message meant to be communicated.)

30. *Bava Bassra* 119a regarding the laws of inheritance (Cf. *Sanhedrin* 8a)
and the punishment for the wood gatherer, and *Sifray* on *Bamidbar* 9:7
regarding *Pesach Shayni*. *Sanhedrin* 8a reads as follows:

כדתניא: ראויה פרשת נחלות שתיכתב על ידי משה רבינו אלא (הא שלא נאמר לו פרשת
נחלות עד שבא מעשה לפניו ולא ידע מה להשיב—ע' פרש"י ד"ה נענש משה) שזכו בנות
צלפחד ונכתב על ידן. וראויה היתה פרשת מקושש שתיכתב ע"י משה רבינו אלא שנתחייב
מקושש ונכתבה על ידו, ללמדך שמגלגלים חובה על ידי חייב וזכות על ידי זכאי.

A *braissa* states: "The [rules revealed] in the *parsha* dealing with laws
of inheritance (*Bamidbar* 27:6-11) really would have been [told to
Moses on Mount Sinai and] written by him [in normal imperative form
as are most commandments. The reason that they were not revealed
until an actual issue arose to make these rules—unknown to Moses—
pertinent is] only because the daughters of Ẓelophḥad [who raised the
issue (*ibid.*)] were deserving of [being mentioned in the Torah and having the law] written through them. And the [rule revealed] in the
parsha about the man who gathered wood on Shabbos really would
have been [revealed to Moses on Mount Sinai and] written by Moses
our Teacher [in normal imperative form] except for the fact that the
wood-gatherer became liable to punishment. It [the specific punishment to be meted out for this act] was therefore written through [a
narrative about] him. This was to teach you that one should associate
odious matters with the blameworthy and honorable matters with
those of repute."

Chapter 6

Disputes over Drashos Previously Accepted by Sanhedrin

As discussed previously, *drashos* of Biblical verses can be used to do two things. They can be used to demonstrate indications for laws already known, laws that were revealed at Sinai, and they can also be used to *generate* previously unknown, or forgotten, law details. The Rambam states a surprising principle regarding this second function: Law-details that had been newly generated through a *drash* could be overruled by a later Great Sanhedrin, if it determines that a different *drash* is more valid.[1]

ב"ד גדול שדרשו באחת מן המדות, כפי מה שנראה בעיניהם, שהדין כך, ודנו דין, ועמד ב"ד אחר ונראה לו טעם אחר לסתור אותו הרי זה סותר דן כפי מה שנראה בעיניו, שנאמר, „אל השופט אשר יהיה בימים ההם," (כלומר) בית דין שבדורך (ממרים ב:א).

---

[1] See Additional Notes at the end of this chapter.

If, using its judgment, a *Bes Din Gadol (Great Sanhedrin) dar-shonned* through any of the 13 Rules of Torah Interpretation[2] that the *halacha* is like so, and it ruled accordingly, and another *Bes Din [Gadol]* arose which saw reason to overturn the previous decision, it [the second *Bes Din Gadol*] overturns and rules according to what is seen by its [own] eyes. "You shall bring the matter to the judge who will be in those days" (*D'varim* 17:9)—The Court that rules in your generation [is the one to follow][3] (*Mahmrim* 2:1).

Apparently, during the time of the Great Sanhedrin, each Sanhedrin related to its succeeding one data specifying which of the *drasha*-backed halachos originated through their *drashos* and which had originated at Sinai, thereby making known which *halachos* could be changed and which could not be tampered with.

Thus, we do not find a law generated by one Great Sanhedrin's *drash* tested for compliance to a *drash*-generated decision by a previous *Great Sanhedrin*.[4] But to avoid misunderstandings, it must be emphasized that the reversals we speak of can be made only by a *Great* Sanhedrin. No individual Sage, or even any *Bes Din*, may contradict a decision pronounced by any Great Sanhedrin. And the reversals we speak of affect only details known to have *originated* through the rules of Torah interpretation and not directly from Sinai.[5] Only after exhaustive investigation revealed that no known *kabballa* completely answered a certain *halachic* question was an analysis of Scriptural verses brought forward to determine the law:

כשהיה בית דין הגדול קיים . . . כל דין שנולד בו ספק לאחד מישראל, שואל לבית
דין שבעירו. אם ידעו—אמרו לו. אם לאו—הרי השואל עם אותו בית דין או אם
שלוחיו עולין לירושלים ושואלין לבית דין שבהר הבית. אם ידעו—אמרו לו. אם
לאו—הכל באין לבית דין שעל פתח העזרה. אם ידעו—אמרו להן. ואם לאו—הכל
באין ללשכת הגזית, לבית דין הגדול, ושואלין. אם היה הדבר—שנולד בו הספק
לכל—ידוע אצל בית דין הגדול—בין מפי הקבלה, בין מפי המדה שדנו בה—
אומרים מיד. אם לא היה הדבר ברור אצל בית דין הגדול—דנין בו בשעתן, ונושאין
ונותנין בדבר עד שיסכימו כולן, או יעמדו למנין וילכו אחר הרוב, ויאמרו לכל

[2] The Rambam uses this term to refer to any of the interpretation rules. See the first *Shoresh* of *Sefer HaMitzvos*.
[3] See Additional Notes at the end of this chapter.
[4] See Additional Notes at the end of this chapter.
[5] See Additional Notes at the end of this chapter.

השואלים: כך הלכה. והולכין להן. משבטל בית דין הגדול, רבתה מחלוקת בישראל.
זה מטמא ונותן טעם לדבריו, וזה מטהר ונותן טעם לדבריו; זה אוסר, וזה מתיר
(ממרים א:ד).

Whenever a Jew faced a *halachic* quandary, he would present
the dilemma to his local *Bes Din*. If its judges already knew the
law, they would advise him of it. If not, they would go together
with the questioner to Jerusalem and present the problem to the
Court at the Temple Mount. If the judges of that Court already
knew the law, they would say so. Otherwise, all would go to the
Court at the doorway to the Temple courtyard. If that Court's
judges already the law, they would tell them. Otherwise, all
[three courts and the petitioner] would go to the Great Sanhedrin at the Marble Chamber and present the question there. If the
Great Sanhedrin had the solution, whether it was a known law
preserved from the time of Moses or whether the law had been
determined through a *drash* (by a previous Great Sanhedrin), it
would be told to them promptly.

However, if the solution was not already clear to the Great Sanhedrin, they would deliberate over the issue there and then.
They would discuss it either until they reached a unanimous
conclusion, or until they would take it to a vote and follow the
majority. They would then declare to all: "This is the *halacha!*"
and go on to their other proceedings (*Mahmrim* 1:4, based on
the *braissa* in *Sanhedrin* 88b).

Machlokos Over Matters Already Practiced by Jewry

Since one Great Sanhedrin could knowingly disagree with a previous one over Biblical laws, we have a possible explanation for the
occurrence of disputes about *mitzva*-details[6] that surely were practiced a specific way by Jewry before the days of the participants in
the *machlokess:* The previous practice was known, but since it was
known to had been established by a *drash*[7] and members of the
present *Great Sanhedrin* saw grounds to question that *drash*, they

---

[6] Such as the correct design of *tsitsiss*, a *machlokess* between *Bes Shammai and Bes
Hillel* (*Menahos* 41b and *B'choros* 39b), or the proper position within which one
should recite the nighttime *K'riass Sh'ma*—reclining or not—another *machlokess*
between *Bes Shammai* and *Bes Hillel* (*Brachos* 1:3).

[7] Either because the original minimum requirements were forgotten, though given
at Sinai, or because Hashem had originally left the details to be determined by the
Great Sanhedrin of Moses' and all future generations' times.

debated the merits of their suggested *drash* with others who defended the original one. Additionally, if the challengers' opinion held
sway, we would have a *machlokess* between one Great Sanhedrin
and a preceding one.

Ruth

The *Brisker Rov*[8] uses the Rambam's principle to solve a difficulty in
the *Book of Ruth*. When Ruth's closest relative refused to marry her
(*Ruth* 4:6), he explained, "I cannot redeem [Ruth's property if that
means I must marry her], lest I ruin my future children" (נחלתי, "my
inheritance," means "my children"—*Rashi*). His fear was based on
the Biblical prohibition against marrying a Moabite, a descendent of
Moab. The children of such a union would suffer the stigma of
illegitimacy. He continued to refuse to participate in such an act
despite the fact that Boaz assured him that the prohibition was only
against marrying a Moabite, and not against marrying a Moabitess.
The Great Sanhedrin, of which he was head, *darshonned* "מואבי ולא,
מואבית," "'Moabite' but not Moabitess," teaching that a Jewish male
may marry a Moabite female.

The *Brisker Rov* poses a difficulty with this Scriptural account.
If Boaz declared in the name of the Great Sanhedrin that there is a
drash of "'Moabite' but not Moabitess," how could the relative dismiss it? And why was his only concern the stigma upon his *children*
were he to marry Ruth? If he held that the marriage was *halachically*
prohibited, why did he not simply refuse on *that* count?

The answer that the *Brisker Rov* gives illustrates our point: The
relative was not concerned about personally transgressing any prohibition by marrying Ruth. He knew that if the Great Sanhedrin
darshons "'Moabite' but not Moabitess," then that is the law and
the Will of G-d. His fear was that since this understanding of the
verse apparently was based on a *drash*, a *later* Great Sanhedrin
might disagree and decide that there is no distinction between a
Moabite and Moabitess. His only concern was for tragic consequences that could possibly affect his offspring.

Indeed, this *drash* **was** later challenged by Doe'aig Ha-Edomi
when he contested David's appointment to the throne (*Yevomos*

---

[8] In *Hiddushay Marran RYZ Halevy*, by Rav Yitzchak Zev Halevy Solovetchik,
Jerusalem, 5741.
[9] *Mamzerim* are children born of incestuous or adulterous unions.

76b-77a). "Before you ask whether David has the qualities to be king," he argued, "ask if he is qualified [meets the legal criterion— *Tosefta Sanhedrin perek* 4—of first being allowed] to marry into the Jewish People: He comes from a Moabitess!" When confronted with the Sanhedrin's *drash* of " 'Moabite' but not Moabitess," he countered with an array of arguments against its validity. We don't say " 'Mitzri' and not *Mitzris*" or " 'mamzer' but not *mamzeress*," that the restrictions in marriage to Egyptians or *mamzerim* are limited to marrying their men, though the wording of the verse refers to them only in the masculine! So why say, " 'Moabite' but not Moabitess"?

But this was a mistake on the part of Doe'aig, as Yesser HaYissra'aylee retorted. "It is a *kabballa*, a law preserved [from the lips of Moses] by the Sanhedrin of Shmuel, that only *male* Moabites are forbidden to marry into Jewry." Ruth's relative shared the same error.

In other words, had the limitation of the prohibition to males been the *result* of a *drash*, then it would, indeed, be challengeable by a later Great Sanhedrin. But it was not. The law was a *kabballa* from Moses of an explanation that was given by Hashem Himself. It therefore could never be changed. The *drash* was the kind that *supported* the known law, not the kind that *generated* a law.[10]

Only Theory?

Armed with the Rambam's principle, one may anticipate answering how many disputes in the Talmud arose: namely by explaining them as situations wherein which one Sanhedrin decided to challenge the *drash* of a previous one or wherein which the members of a Sanhedrin were disputing whether to do so. However, we are confronted with a disappointment. There is no passage in the Talmud which clearly indicates such a background for any *machlokess*. All the classical scholars, in their attempts to find a Talmudic source for the Rambam's principle, are hard put to produce any historic record of a Great Sanhedrin actually exercising their alleged power to con-

---

[10] An anonymous, contemporary scholar, in בריכת המעיין, published by עם התורה (אגודת ישראל באה"ב, שנת 1982) explains further why Ruth's relative still shunned marrying her, even after Boaz informed him of the unchangeable nature of this law. He was afraid that though *he* now knew that this was not a *drash-generated* law, the Great Sanhedrin of a future generation might forget this fact, leaving his offspring in the predicament he had originally envisioned. As we see from the incident with David and Doe'aig HaEdomi, this danger was real.

test an earlier one's *drash*-generated law. Most sources cited by the scholars show only the *permissibility* for a Great Sanhedrin to do so.

One passage which does at first seem to indicate the occurrence of the kind of reversal under discussion is in *Bava Bassra* 21a. It reads as follows:

בתחילה מי שיש לו אב מלמדו תורה, מי שאין לו אב לא היה למד תורה. מאי
דרוש—"ולמדתם אתם": ולמדתם אַתֶּם. התקינו שיהו מושיבין מלמדי תינוקות
בירושלים. מאי דרוש—"כי מציון תצא תורה."

> Originally [the law was], "He who has a father [the father] teaches him Torah." Whoever did not have a father did not learn Torah. What did they *darshon?*—"And you shall teach them, your sons" (*D'varim* 11:19) [wherein the word for "them" is written in such a way—חסר—that it can be read "אתם," you, emphasizing that the teaching of your sons must be done by *you*, the parent]. [Later, however] they decreed that school-teachers must be placed in Jerusalem. What did they *darshon?* "For out of Zion shall go forth Torah, and the Word of Hashem from Jerusalem."

Apparently, there was an original *halacha* based upon one *drash* and then a later *halacha* based upon a different *drash*, providing a historical instance of the uprooting of a law generated by *drash*. The passage continues with two more historical changes in the education system, giving explanations, not *drashos*, as their source. This indicates that the first two stages, in contrast to the second two, were indeed products of *drashos* and not human pedagogic wisdom. However, the evidence is not conclusive. Though "they dar-shonned" normally indicates a bona fide *drasha*, "they decreed," referring to the second stage, normally indicates a rabbinical origin for the law, which points to the *drasha* in question being a mere *asmachta* for the rabbinical *takkonna*.[11] And so we remain with no certain documented occurrence of one Sanhedrin uprooting the *drash*-generated biblical law of an earlier one. One finds that the norm was a desire to conform to previous practices, not to contest

---

[11] Rabbi Avigdor Miller (*Torah Nation*, p. 161) describes the decision to place teachers throughout Jerusalem alone to have taken place in the days of Ezra, when the Jews returned to Jerusalem after the seventy-year exile in Babylon. (It would follow that the problem of which the passage then speaks—that orphans outside of Jerusalem lacked a formal education—developed later when the population spread.)

them. Perhaps this was simply because no Sanhedrin ever did find cause to contest a previous Sanhedrin's *drashos*.[12] Each Sanhedrin was happy to discover how earlier and greater Sanhedrins *darshonned* and did not desire to exercise its power of repeal. Or perhaps this is because the *Gemora* only presents us with the final interpretations and judgements as they stood at the close of the Talmud and sees no purpose in recording interpretations previously held but ultimately rejected. Indeed, the Talmud deals hardly at all with events surrounding *halachic* decisions before the time of the Second Temple, not to mention information on their *drashic* backgrounds. In the Mishna, the earliest picture we possess of any kind of *halachic* debate takes place near the end of the Second Temple period. At that time, circumstances prevented the Sanhedrin from fully functioning[13] and it could not vote on changing any laws. The few times afterwards that all the Sages could gather together, they concentrated on clearing up and preserving the original version of the laws—not on questioning them.[14] On the other hand, history is not over yet. Perhaps when the prophet Eliyahu comes in Moshiach's time and reestablishes the Great Sanhedrin, we shall see the Rambam's principle in action.

Where in the Talmud?

If there is no mention of the Rambam's principle in the Talmud, on what did he base it? True, there may be no record of one *Bes Din Gadol* having been constrained from differing with another's *drash*. No talmudic passage *contradicts* the Rambam's assertion. Yet, familiarity with the Rambam's method and style makes it clear that he would not advocate a position simply because it cannot be contradicted by Torah-sources.[15] We shall describe several attempts that

[12] See Additional Notes at the end of this chapter.

[13] See Chapter, "The Control and Proliferation of Machlokess."

[14] As we will see later, this "permission to overturn" does not presently exist. It remains, like the subject of בן סורר ומורה, the rebellious son (*D'varim* 21:18-21), or זקן ממרא, the rebellious elder (*D'varim* 17:12), a subject to study only for שכר לימוד, the rewards of Torah study, not for practical application.

[15] Also, the Rambam does not invent *drashos*. There must have been some *Midrash* which explicitly attached the Rambam's concept to the *posuk* "ובאת אל השופט אשר יהיה בימים ההם, You shall come to the judge who will be in those days," as the Rambam did. Yet we know of none. Perhaps it existed but is no longer extant.

have been made to find a source for the Rambam's dictum in the extant literature.

- ## *The Kessef Mishna*

  The *Kessef Mishna*, the classical commentary on the Rambam, points out that we constantly see later *Tannaim* deciding issues concerning *drashos* differently than earlier ones did, and later *Amoraim* differing with earlier *Amoraim*. (Why *Amoraim* do not differ with *Tannaim* will soon be discussed.) Apparently, then, it was presumed that the later authorities were allowed to disagree with the earlier ones—and this presumed understanding would serve as a basis for the Rambam's position.

  The *Doros HaRishonim*,[16] as well as HoRav Tzvi Hirsch Ḥayos,[17] rejects the *Kessef Mishna's* explanation, calling the viewpoints expressed and challenged across the generations irrelevant. There was never any question that opinions of individuals can be contested. The Rambam is speaking of a much more serious matter: overturning a *drash* promulgated by a *Great Sanhedrin*.

- ## *"The First Mishna and the Later Mishna"*

  We might anticipate support for the Rambam from those *mishnayos* which conclude, "This was the משנה ראשונה, the first *mishna*, but the משנה אחרונה, the later *mishna*, states such-and-such." Apparently there was a decision originally made part of the Mishna, yet overturned before the Mishna was canonized. If these decisions were based upon variant *drashos*, then we would have located a proof text for the Rambam.

  Rav Tzvi Hirsch Ḥayos[18] notes that we can attempt to provide support for the Rambam only from "First" and "Later" *mishnas* that concern Torah laws.[19] But, he points out, even in all such cases, it is not clear that the "First

---

[16] Part Four, p. 516.

[17] *Kol Kissvay Maharatz Ḥayyos*, Yerushalayim, 5708, p. 385 (bottom).

[18] *Mishpaht HaHora'ah*, chapter six, pages 384, 385, 392.

[19] These include *Pesachim* 88a, *Nedarim* 66b, *Sanhedrin* 27b, *Nazir* 6:1, 35b, 37a. See *Addendum III*.

Mishna" is describing a decision of a *Great Sanhedrin*. It may only be describing what had been the opinions of individual scholars or heads of local courts, before the matter was thoroughly discussed and voted upon by the supreme law body, the *Great Sanhedrin*. These *mishnas* say only that "בראשונה היו אומרים," at first they used to say such-and-such, until they came and taught otherwise." Evidently, these "unofficial" decisions were around long enough to gain entry into the remarks of the *mishna* recited by the people. Nevertheless, such "uncanonized" opinions could surely be debated upon by later authorities.

In *Doros Harishonim*, Rav Yitzchak Isaac Halevy, too, explains the designations "First" and "Later Mishna" in a way that eliminates them as proof texts for the Rambam. According to Rav Halevy, neither the "First Mishna" nor the "Later Mishna" ever directly analyzes the Torah's verses. Each merely interprets the words of an even earlier Sanhedrin, and this makes their dispute irrelevant to the Rambam's formula.

• *Changing Measurements*

There is another possible proof text for the Rambam's thesis which Rav Ḥayyos and Rav Halevy, as well as the *Aruch HaShulchan HaAssid*[20] (*Hilchos Mahmrim* 64), all cite with approval. It is a passage in *Yoma* 80a (also in *Yerushalmi, Payah* 1:1) that states:

אר' אלעזר: „האוכל חֵלֶב בזמן הזה, צריך שירשום את השיעורין שמא יבא ב"ד אחר וירבה בשיעורין . . . דלא מחייבי קרבן עד דאיכא כזית גדול. (ופרש"י, האוכל כזית בינוני אל יכתוב מחוייבני חטאת, אלא יכתוב בינוני כזית בינוני אכלתי, שמא יבא ב"ד ויפטרנו מקרבן, ונמצא מביא חולין לעזרה).

Rebbi Elazar said: "Now we must wait for the Temple to be rebuilt in order to bring sacrifices to atone for having unwittingly eaten forbidden fat. Therefore, if a person does eat some, he should record the *amount* that he ate rather than merely recording that he is obligated to bring an offering in the future. For the Temple may be rebuilt in his days, and the new *Bes Din Gadol*

[20] HaGaon HoRav Yechiel Michal Halevy Epstein, *Mosaad HoRav Kook*, Jerusalem, 1969.

may decide that only a *larger* amount obligates and entitles one to bring a sacrifice. [For it is forbidden to bring into the Temple vicinity animals that are not totally necessary for sacrificial purposes.]"

By writing down the *amount*, one can compare it to the amount agreed upon by the new *Bes Din Gadol* and see whether he is still obligated (and allowed) to bring a sacrifice. This advice presumes that a later *Great Sanhedrin* has the right to contest an earlier *Great Sanhedrin's* interpretation of Torah terminology, which would be a proof text for the Rambam.

Furthermore, the Talmud proceeds to report that Rebbi Yoḥonon disagrees,[21] maintaining that one needn't record the amount of forbidden food eaten. He claimed that the original interpretation of the *k'zayyis* size originated as a *Halacha L'Moshe MiSinai*, making it incontestable by anyone. So here we have precisely the distinction described by the Rambam: Explanations originating at Sinai cannot be changed, but explanations generated by Scriptural analysis *can* be changed. The issue in dispute here is: What was the origin of this statement?

• *Idolaters' Cooking Oil*

Rav Ḥayyos cites more sources: The Sanhedrin of the *Amora*,[22] Rebbi Yehuda Nessia, permitted the use of oil produced by idolaters, reversing a former prohibiton. The discussion in the *Gemora* (*Avoda Zorra* 36a) clearly indicates that it was unacceptable for a Sanhedrin to reverse a *decree* issued by an earlier, superior one,[23] but that it *was* acceptable to reconsider a former, superior Sanhedrin's prohibition-generating interpretation of the *Torah*.

א"ל שמואל לרב, „בשלמא לדידי דאמינא זליפתין של כלים (פי' דס"ל דמדאורייתא
כלים נותנים טעם אפי' לפגם)—אסורים. . . . אלא לדידך דאמרת דדניאל גזר עליו,
דניאל גזר ואתא ר"י הנשיא ומבטל ליה?! והתנן אין ב"ד יכול לבטל דברי ב"ד חבירו
אא"כ גדול ממנו בחכמה ובמנין!"

[21] ע' יפה' עינים שם

[22] עי' ר"ן

[23] When the prohibition was originally adhered to by Jewry.

Shmuel said to Rav: "According to my opinion—that gentile oil was prohibited on the assumption that [by Scriptural authority] non-kosher ingredients absorbed by the gentile's cooking utensils escape into his oil and make it unkosher as well, even though the absorptions had already spoiled—all is understandable. But according to you—that [the oil does not thereby become unkosher, and the prohibition against it was] Daniel's decree [intended to limit socializing with gentiles][24]—how could Rebbi Yehuda *Nessia* later[25] permit it? 'One *Bes Din* is not allowed to nullify the words of a fellow *Bes Din* unless it is superior to it in wisdom and number!'"

We have interpreted Shmuel to be holding—as does another *Tanna*, Rebbi Shimmon (*Avoda Zorra* 68b)—that the original prohibition of idolaters' cooking oil was based upon a *drash*. Rav Ḥayyos apparently assumes this to be so, and this results in Shmuel plainly making the Rambam's distinction, without challenge. Here would be a case where historically it *did* happen that a *Bes Din Gadol* reversed the *drash* of an earlier and superior one.

This theory is hurt, however, by the fact that *Tosefos* maintains that Shmuel disagrees with Rebbi Shimmon's opinion. The authoritative *Rishon* therefore constructs a complex explanation of this passage which does not involve Scriptural interpretation at all. True, the Rambam very possibly may have understood the passage as Rav Ḥayyos did. But as long as this passage can be understood without it being a proof for the Rambam's formula, we cannot be sure that it was his proof text.

The two remaining passages cited by Rav Ḥayyos as proof texts[26] also apparently lack the strength of the third source we mentioned, which remains the only compelling one so far.

● *Contesting a Kal V'ḥomer*

Another attempted proof comes from the first *mishna* in

---

[24] Daniel was a leader when the Jews were exiled from Israel to Babylon (3338) to remain among gentiles for 70 years.

[25] Rebbi Yehuda Nessia flourished circa 4010 (260 CE), after the close of the *Mishna*, seven centuries after Daniel.

[26] *Yerushalmi Moed Kotton* 2:3 (בקש רבי), *Megilla* 5b (א"ר אבא בן ממל אילו היה לי כו'), (לעקור את תשעה באב וכו').

chapter five of *Sota* and its *Gemora* commentary (29a).
Both Rav Ḥayyos (*Sota*) and the *Ohr Somayach* (a commentary on the Rambam, *loc. cit.*) cite it. The *mishna*
reads:

בו ביום דרש ר"ע, ,,ו[כל]כלי חרש—אשר יפול מהם (מהשרצים) אל תוכו—כל
אשר בתוכו יטמא.' אינו אומר ,טמא,' אלא, ,יטמא.'—לטמא אחרים. למד על ככר
שני שמטמא את השלישי."

א"ר יהושע: ,,מי יגלה עפר מעיניך, רבן יוחנן בן זכאי, שהיית אומר, ,עתיד דור אחר
לטהר ככר שלישי, שאין לו מקרא מן התורה שהוא טמא.' והלא ר"ע, [תלמיד]
תלמידך, מביא לו מקרא מן התורה שהוא טמא, שנ', ,כל אשר בתוכו יטמא'!"

גמ': ומאחר דאין לו (מקרא מן התורה) למה טמא (לפי ריב"ז)?—אר' יהודה א'רב:
,,מן התורה אין לו; מדין קל וחומר יש לו . . . ודור אחר פריך . . . יש בהן צד חמור.
וריב"ז צד חמור לא פריך."

On that day Rabbi Akiva expounded: "'Whatever is contained
in earthenware vessels, into which will fall [sh'ratzim, crawling
creatures], will make impure' (*Vayikra* 11:33). It does not say *is*
impure, but, *will make* impure: It makes other things impure.
This teaches that food that became טמא because it was in a vessel
that had become impure, itself causes other things to have 'third-
degree' impurity."

Rebbi Yehoshua said: "Who will roll the dirt [of your grave]
from your eyes, O Rebbi Yoḥonon ben Zakkai! You used to say,
'[I am afraid that] some generation will declare third-degree as
ritually pure, since there is no verse in Scripture that spells out
that it is impure.' Hasn't Rabbi Akiva, your [disciple's] disciple,[27]
cited a verse that states it is impure?!"

GEMORA: If Rebbi Yoḥonon ben Zakkai thought there is no
verse for it, then why *did* he consider it impure?

Rebbi Yehuda said in the name of Rav: "There is no explicit
verse, but the law can be inferred through a *kal v'ḥomer* which
others may consider technically invalid [through צד חמור]."

Rabban Yoḥonon ben Zakkai expressed fear about
future generations: They may fail to recognize that if a
container is touched by a *sheretz*, any food the container
holds—though the food had no direct contact with the

---

[27] The speaker, Rebbi Yehoshua, had himself been one of Rebbi Yoḥonon ben
Zakkai's disciples. And he had Rabbi Akiva as *his* disciple.

sheretz—conducts *tum'ah* to another piece of food. His fear emerged because the law at hand was based on a *kal v'homer drash* and he perceived an apparent fault in the *drash* that a future *Great Sanhedrin* might accept and thereby nullify the law.

Rabbi Akiva, the disciple of his disciples, removed the fear by pointing out a *drash* against which Rebbi Yehoshua felt sure no substantial objection could be raised and which supported Rabban Yohonon ben Zakkai's opinion.

Clearly, the Talmud assumes that later Sanhedrins could challenge decisions based upon *drash* by earlier ones: Rabban Yohonon ben Zakkai's fear was not that his *drash* and law would be forgotten; his fear was that the future *Bes Din Gadol*, aware of his Sanhedrin's[28] *drash*, would nevertheless disagree with it based upon a פירכא, a logical objection to, his *kal v'homer*. Perhaps this passage is one which led the Rambam to his formula.

• *The Ohr Somayach*

The *Ohr Somayach* presents an original and brilliant proof to support the Rambam:

In *Sanhedrin* 88b we are given four illustrations of *zaken mahmray*, a rebellious Sage, a Sage who continues to teach or practice a Scriptural law according to his own interpretation, despite the opposing consensus of the *Bes Din Gadol*. The punishment in such cases is execution (*D'varim* 17:12).

In one illustration, the dissenting Sage declares that his analysis of an issue brought him to a certain conclusion, whereupon the *Bes Din Gadol* informs him that they had been taught—they have a *kabballa*—otherwise. In another, the Sanhedrin and the Sage are each in possession of contradictory *kabballos*. In the third illustration, the *Bes Din* and dissenting Sage disagree on how to analyze an issue.

In the fourth case, the dissenting Sage reports that he possesses a *kabballa* that the law is one way, yet the Great Sanhedrin declares that its own *analysis* shows that the law

---

[28] Rabban Yohonon ben Zakkai was the leader of Jewry at the time of Yavneh. See Additional Notes at the end of this chapter.

should be a different way. Even here, the Sage is considered a *zaken mahmray* if he does not submit to the Sanhedrin's decision.

Now, the *Ohr Somayach* asks forcefully, who is not qualified to testify that he possesses the *kabballa* of the former Great Sanhedrins' decisions? Isn't the entire tractate *Aid'yos* replete with testimonies, given by individuals, which determined for everyone previous decisions and practices? Once someone reports a decision of a previous Great Sanhedrin and he is investigated and found to be a reliable witness, isn't the present Sanhedrin obligated to follow his *kabballa*, since the Sanhedrin lacks the benefit of one for its own opinion? Why should the dissenting Sage face capital punishment for insisting on following and promulgating a teaching which he knows to have been the accepted *halacha*?!

If someone did possess a tradition going back to Sinai, the *Bes Din Gadol* certainly would have accepted and followed it. Obviously, the Talmud cannot be speaking here of a teaching originating at Sinai. Neither can it be referring to a rabbinical *gezayra* or *takkonna*, for one is considered a rebellious Sage only if he disputes a Sanhedrin's interpretation of *Scriptural* law. Only one possibility remains: the Scriptural explanation given over to the dissenting Sage was not an explanation going back to Sinai, but one generated by an earlier *Bes Din's drash*, which the *mishna* presumes is changeable.

This *mishna* makes no comparisons regarding the Great Sanhedrins' abilities. And so we have an ingenious source for the Rambam's declaration that a *Great Sanhedrin* can overturn a law, even if it had been decreed by a superior *Great Sanhedrin*, if that law had originally been generated through *drash*.

The *Ohr Somayach* proceeds to apply the Rambam's principle to a passage (*Pesachim* 66a) which is otherwise puzzling. When Hillel came to Israel, where the *B'nay Besayra* were temporarily in charge of Sanhedrin-related affairs, the Sages debated whether the *korban Pesach*, Passover eve sacrifice, could be offered on *Shabbos*, despite the *Shabbos* interdictions involved. Hillel offered numerous *drashos* permitting the ritual, but the *B'nay Besayra* found fault with every one (*Yerushalmi, Pesachim* 6:1). Finally,

Hillel declared that the source for his decision was a
kabballa he had received from his mentors, Shmaya and
Avtalyon, the former heads of the Great Sanhedrin. Upon
hearing this, the *B'nay Besayra* deferred and permitted the
offering to take place on *Shabbos.*

The *Ohr Somayach* comments that it is not at all rare
for Passover eve to occur on *Shabbos.* How could a question about the practice have arisen? The *Ohr Somayach*
suggests that the sacrifice had indeed been offered on *Shabbos* in the past, and everyone remembered that it had previously been permitted. People did forget, however, that
the permission originated as a clarification specified at
Sinai. They thought that the permission was generated
through a *drash.* Therefore, the *B'nay Besayra* understood
that they could—and must—differ with the previous ruling
if they found fault with the *drashos* that generated it. Lacking any Scriptural basis to override *Shabbos* restrictions
for the sake of the Passover eve sacrifice—finding Hillel's
drashos to be uncompelling—they questioned the propriety
of continuing the procedure. Finally Hillel informed them
that the *drashos* he had presented to them were not the
source for his stand. The true source was a *kabballa* (originating at Sinai, according to this explanation) from the
previous Sanhedrin. Even if the *drashos* he found were
faulty, the law was genuine. Perhaps further research
would produce the Scriptural indication for the law.

This presentation presumes that the Sages must have
remembered the *halacha* and nevertheless considered it dis-
putable. But this presumption conflicts with the *Gemora*
text itself (*Yerushalmi Pesachim* 6:1) which implies that the
halacha was forgotten.[29] It declares that though the event
described was unnatural, Hashem miraculously caused it to
occur in order to bring about awareness of Hillel's greatness:

א״ר אבון, והלא א״א לשני שביעית (שמיטות) שיחול י״ד להיות בשבת?! ולמה
נתעלמה הלכה מהן?—כדי ליתן גדולה להלל (שיודע מה שלא ידעו כולם ויהיה נשיא
בישראל).

---

[29] Rabbi Moshe Friedman, a *yungerman* at the Yeshiva of Staten Island, has pointed
out to me the commentary באו חשבון printed in back of our tractates ערכין. This commentary offers a new interpretation of the passage.

Said Rebbi Avoon: "Isn't it impossible for two cycles of seven years to pass by without the 14th [of *Nissan—Passover eve*] falling out on a *Shabbos*?! [That is, certainly this situation occurred before within memory!] *Why was the halacha hidden from them?*—To attribute greatness to Hillel!"

● *Horios*

Another source for the Rambam's dictum is suggested by Rav Moshe Feinstein, z''l:[30]

Mesechta Horios teaches that if a Great Sanhedrin reverses its decision and the majority of Jews followed the original ruling, the nation must bring a sin offering.[31] The required "majority of Jews" is formed by adding together all those individuals who unwittingly sinned,[32] even if only some of them had sinned one period, and others sinned in another.

Horios 3a-b raises a hypothetical problem:

הורו ב"ד שחלב מותר, ועשו מיעוט הקהל, ומת אותו ב"ד, ועמד ב"ד אחר, וחזרו
....?והורו ועשו מיעוט אחר ... אליבא דמ"ד צבור מייתי—מאי?

A *Bes Din [Gadol]*[33] had promulgated that a certain kind of fat is *kosher*,[34] but only a minority of Jewry had acted upon that decision; then the members of that *Bes Din* all passed away to be replaced by others who also instructed the people the same way, and [this time] a different minority of them actually ate the fat . . .

---

[30] *Dibros Moshe, Shabbos,* p. 131. This proof was also independently suggested to me by Rabbi Moshe Freidman. See also *ibid. Yevomos, perek 4, Ha'ara 59.* Rav Feinstein mentions other sources cited in our text and considers the possibility that the power of uprooting was not restricted to the Great Sanhedrin of Jerusalem and also the possibility that the Sanhedrin of Messiah's time may not have the power to uproot *drash*-generated *halachos* of the past.

[31] *Vayikra,* 4:13.

[32] According to the opinion that the obligation to bring a sacrifice rests and depends upon the people who followed the original ruling and not upon the *Bes Din* which promulgated the ruling.

[33] This passage is not following the opinion of Rebbi Yehuda, the only one who holds that even the decision of a minor *bes din* (של שבט אחד) if changed would necessitate this sacrificial offering.

[34] The *Gemora* is speaking of the kind of fat which the Torah prohibits through *drash,* not explicitly. The פר העלם דבר של צבור offering, which *mesechta Horios* is about, is not brought for an explicitly stated prohibition.

[but then the second *Bes Din* reversed their decision, rendering the fat unkosher].

צבור הא קאי, או דלמא ידיעה דההוא ב"ד דהורו בעינן?

[Do we say that since] the [same] Jews are still present [to make up a proper majority, the offering is brought]; or perhaps [we should say that to require an offering] the Sanhedrin which had made the original ruling must be [alive and] aware of the reversal. The problem remains unsolved.

In other words, what if the Sanhedrin's judges died out without ever retracting their decision and only the new judges eventually decided on a reversal? In order to form a majority, do we count the individuals who sinned during the tenure of the first judges, or do we count only the individuals who sinned during the tenure of the judges who eventually made the reversal?

Though the *Gemora* leaves the question unsolved, we do see that the *Gemora* readily accepted the idea that a later Sanhedrin can disagree with and overturn a *drash* made by a previous one. (And the second *drash* is valid enough to obligate the nation to bring an offering for following the original ruling.)

Not Good Enough

Were these the Rambam's sources for his principle? Perhaps. But as a rule, his own wording usually reveals his sources by closely resembling them. This feature is lacking in any of the passages we have cited. However, sometimes the Rambam's paraphrasing is of a post-talmudic, i.e., *Gaonic* authority, and such is the case with the passage in question: *Rav Hai Gaon*[35] says what the Rambam says, using as his basis a talmudic passage that no one else has suggested.

- *Rav Hai Gaon*

  In his work, *Mussar HaDayyanim, Ethics for Judges,*[36] the

---

[35] 4699-4798 (939-1038 CE). Last of Gaonim, son of Rav Sherira Gaon, head of Pumbedisa talmudic academy, leader of World Jewry.

[36] This work is not extant, but the passage under discussion appears in the commentary יד רמ"ה on *Sanhedrin*. My attention was drawn to it by a reference in the

Gaon Rav Hai, too, states that regarding *drashos* even a *Bes Din* which is not superior has the right to overturn a previous *Bes Din's* decision. His proof is a passage in *Bava Bassra* 130b:

אמר להו רבא לרב פפא ולרב הונא בריה דרב יהושע: „כי אתי פסקא דדינא דידי
לקמייכו, וחזיתי ביה פירכא—לא תקרעוהו עד דאתיתו לקמאי. אי אית לי טעמא—
אמינא לכו; ואי לא—הדרנא בי. לאחר מיתה—לא מיקרע תקרעוהו, ומגמר נמי לא
תגמרו מיניה. לא מיקרע תקרעיניה: דאי הואי התם, דלמא הוה אמינא לכו טעמא.
מגמר נמי לא תגמרו מיניה: דאין לדיין אלא מה שעיניו רואות.‟

Said Rava to Rav Pappa and Rav Huna b'ray d'Rav Yehoshua: "If you should find an objection against any decision of mine, consult me before nullifying it. If I can defend it, I will; otherwise, I will retract. And after I die, do not nullify any decision, but neither must you adapt it [to similar cases]. Do not nullify it, because were I still alive I might be able to defend it. But neither must you apply it [to similar cases], because *a judge can only depend upon his own perceptions.*

Assuming that Rava's decisions represented those of the Sanhedrin he headed, his instructions are most puzzling. The *mishna* (*Aidyos* 1:5), cited previously, declares:

אין בית דין יכול לבטל דברי בית דין חבירו עד שיהיה גדול ממנו בחכמה ובמנין

No Sanhedrin may overturn the decision of another [former one] unless it is greater in both wisdom and number.[37]

On the basis of this mandate, the Talmud[38] rejects the possibility that any Sanhedrin rescinded the decrees of an earlier one—even had the original reason for the decree seemed to render it obsolete. Apparently, this mandate renders unnecessary Rava's request to his students to refrain

---

קונטרס „גנזי הספרי‟ by Horav Yaakov Bezallel Zolty, printed in the *Sifra With the Commentary of Rabbeynu Hillel*, published by Shachne Kolidetsky in conjunction with *Mosaad HoRav Kook*, 5738.

[37] Since a Great Sanhedrin must always number 71, there are various explanations of the requirement for a "greater number." The Rambam explains it to mean a greater number of Sages, not part of the 71, who had concurred with the majority opinion (even before it became nationally binding through vote.)

[38] *Megilla* 2a, *Moed Kotton* 3b, *Gittin* 36b, *Avoda Zorra* 36a.

from nullifying his decisions, and it controverts his maxim
that "a judge can only depend upon his own perceptions"
and need not be bound to apply to future cases the principles promulgated by earlier Sanhedrins.[39]

Rav Hai answers that the prohibition against Sanhedrins rescinding past decrees refers only to past *takkonnos*
and *gezeyros*—post-Mosaic decrees.[40] **But in all other
areas—such as Scriptural laws determined through
drashos[41]—a Great Sanhedrin has full power to overturn
its earlier and greater counterpart.[42]** It appears quite certain
that the *p'sak* of Rav Hai Gaon was the Rambam's source.
We see that Rav Hai Gaon states exactly what the Rambam
was later to write. Furthermore, the Rambam's wording,
"כפי מה שנראה בעיניו", [the Sanhedrin rules on the matter]
according to what is seen by its [own] eyes," is unmistake-
ably paraphrasing the words "מה שעיניו רואות", "[the judge
rules on the matter according to] what his eyes see," of the
Gemora passage (*Bava Bassra* 131a) upon which Rav Hai
Gaon based his position.

Amoraim's Deference to Tannaim

And this should close the subject. However, one difficulty remains.

---

[39] The Sanhedrin of Rava was the only one of his time, and had the status of the *Bes
Din Gadol B'Yisroel, The Great Sanhedrin.*

[40] Indeed, although in *Aid'yos* 1:5, the phrase, "אין בית דין יכול לבטל דברי בית דין חבירו
אא"כ גדול ממנו בחכמה ובמנין, No Sanhedrin may overturn the decision of another
[former one] unless it is greater in both wisdom and number.," appears without any
specific application, the other five times it appears (*Gittin* 36b, *Avoda Zorra* 36a,
Mo'ade Kotton 3b, *Megilla* 2a), it is specifically in reference to rabbinical decrees.

[41] The Rambam explicitly contrasts *drashos* to גזירות ותקנות. Rav Zolty, in the work
that cites Rav Hai, also paraphrased the Gaon as referring to matters "שדרשו באחת מן
המדות, that they *darshonned* by using the [13] Rules of Interpretation." Evidently, as
long as the science of *drash* was known to the Sages, judging the meaning of
p'sukim and the proper way to *darshon* them was conceptually identical to judging
the nature of present situations and deciding how to apply precedents to new cases
(מדמה מילתא למילתא). This explains why the Rambam uses the term סברה, *logic*, when
referring to matters of *drash.*

[42] לשון הי"ד רמה (סנהדרין ל"ג.): . . . וההיא דתנן בעדיות דאין ב"ד יכול לבטל דברי ב"ד חבירו אא"כ גדול
ממנו בחכמה ובמנין—כתב הרב האי גאון ז"ל בספר מוסר הדיינים דלעולם יכול ב"ד לבטל דברי ב"ד חבירו
ואע"פ שאין גדול ממנו בחכמה ובמנין. ומייתי לה ראיה מהא דאמר להו רבא. . . . והא דתנן אין ב"ד יכול . . .
מוקים לה בגזירות ותקנות ב"ד והרי מסתבר.

Any student of *Gemora* knows that there is a basic understanding that the *Amoraim*, later authorities, do not and cannot contradict any *halacha* stated by the *Tannaim*, the Sages of the *Mishna*. Yet, according to the Rambam and Rav Hai Gaon, why can't the *Amoraim* question *drasha*-generated decisions recorded in the *Mishna* by Rebbi Yehuda HaNassi's Sanhedrin, and, as a Sanhedrin, overturn them?

True, the Rambam reports[43] that the *Mishna* became the recognized version of the Oral Law; all future generations devoted their efforts to its analysis. But there is no hint of *why* this was so. He does not even write of any formal agreement to accept all the *Mishna's* rulings as final, as he writes concerning the *Gemora* in his introduction to the *Mishneh Torah:* "‏. . . וכל אותם הדברים שבגמ' הסכימו‎ ‏עליהם כל ישראל‎, All Jewry agreed to all the words of the Gemora." What he does say is, "‏ואולם לא היו אלה הברייתות כלם כצחות דברי המשנה ולא‎ ‏כתקון ענינים וקוצר מליה ועל כן היתה עיקר ר"ל המשנה . . . והיא המכובדת אצל הכל‎, None of the texts written by the *Tannaim* matched the *Mishna* [of Rebbi Yehuda HaNassi] in eloquence, organization, and conciseness. It therefore became the principle text . . . esteemed by all." But this is a description of the literary quality of the work. It has no bearing on the incontrovertablity of all *halachos* it contains.

We are familiar with the statements, cited elsewhere,[44] which say that the later generations were greatly inferior to the earlier ones. However, the talmudic generations to which this principle applied are specified, and no contrast is made between that of Rebbi Yehuda HaNassi and the following one.[45] And anyway, the Rambam's point is precisely that a Sanhedrin can disagree with an earlier one, despite its own inferiority.

The *Kessef Mishna* suggests that at the closing of the *Mishna*, the Sages and all Jewry accepted the *Mishna* upon themselves as the final authority. The *Chazon Ish* is emphatic that it was obvious to each era—*Tannaitic, Amoraic, and Rishonic*—that it could not com-

---

[43] *Maimonides' Introduction to the Talmud*, pp. 22-23 in Hebrew Section, English Section p. 144.

[44] Viz., in the chapter "Disciples Disagreeing with Their Mentors," subsection "The Descent of the Generations."

[45] One contrast is between two generations of *Tannaim* (that of Rebbi Elazar ben Shamua—Rebbi Yehuda HaNassi's rebbi—to that of Rabbi Akiva); the second contrast is between the generation *after* Rebbi's (that of Rebbi Oshia) to that of the generation *before* Rebbi Yehuda HaNassi's—that of Rebbi Yehuda HaNassi's rebbi, Rebbi Elazar ben Shamua.

pare with the preceding one. But neither of these Sages presents a source stating this recognition of inferiority as the reason for the *Amoraim's* refusal to differ with the *Mishna*.

Instances in Which Amoraim Did Disagree with Tannaim

Furthermore, there are some areas within which *Amoraim* did not refrain from vying with *Tannaim*.[46] *Amoraim* differed with *Tannaim* concerning the Scriptural indications for laws.[47] We find an instance of an *Amora* who felt he better understood a *Tanna's* words than that *Tanna's* own contemporaries.[48] Granting that it is relatively innocuous to disagree when no *halachic* matter is at stake, the question still remains: If the *Amoraim* really felt so intellectually inferior to the *Tannaim*, how could they feel capable of understanding a *Tanna's* intentions better than *Tannaim* had, or of grasping the reason for a *halacha* better than a *Tanna?* Moreover, *Amoraim* sometimes declare even *halacha* to follow no individual *Tanna*, but to be a "hybrid" construction of the opinions of different *Tannaim*. No individual *Tanna* would subscribe to such a *halacha*. Why did the *Amoraim* feel free to do this?

An Original Suggestion

I propose that the reason the *Amoraim* abstained from disagreeing with the *Tannaim* is not based on their degree of inferiority but upon a principle elucidated by Rebbi Yoḥonon in a *Gemora Yerushalmi* commenting on *Payah* 2:5.

The *mishna* teaches that the number of *payah* donations[49] one must give depends upon the number of species he planted. From each species, he must donate one unit. Even if he had harvested several times over the year, if he dealt with just one species, one donation unit from each of the harvests is sufficient. Conversely,

---

[46] See *Pesicha L'Meseches Ahvos L'Meiri, Hotsaas Mechon HaTalmud HaYisraeli HaShalem, Yerushalayim 5728*, p. 47, s.v. נתמעטו הלבבות ועם כל זה.

[47] See Additional Notes at the end of this chapter.

[48] See, in the chapter "Disciples Disagreeing With Their Mentors," the citation from *Gittin* 37b, and the comment of the רש״י citing *Rosh HaShonna* 30b. See too, in Additional Notes to Chapter 3, note 48.

[49] *Payah* means "edge [of a field]." *Vayikra* 19:9 requires one to leave unreaped some produce from the end of his field for the poor.

even if several species had all been harvested at one time, he must donate a unit for every one of them. However, if one had planted several varieties of the same species, the rule changes: He donates according to the number of harvests:

הזורע את שדהו מין אחת, אע"פ שהוא עושהו שתי גרנות—נותן פאה אחת. זרעה שני מינים, אע"פ שעשאן גורן אחת—נותן שתי פאות.

הזורע שדהו שני מיני חטים, עשאן גורן אחת—נותן פאה אחת; שתי גרנות—נותן שתי פאות.

Appended to this ancient *mishna* is a passage of later origin (*Payah* 2:6) reporting an occurrence in the time of Rabban Gamliel:

מעשה שזרע ר' שמעון איש המצפה לפני (ס"א: ובא) רבן גמליאל ועלו ללשכת הגזית ושאלו. אמר נחום הלבלר, מקובל אני מרבי מיאשה, שקבל מאבא (ס"א: מאבין), שקבל מן הזוגות, שקבל מן הנביאים, הלכה למשה מסיני בזורע שדהו שני מיני חטים, אם עשאן גורן אחת—נותן פאה אחת; שתי גרנות—נותן שתי פאות.

Rebbi Shimmon *Ish HaMitspi* was planting two varieties of wheat. A question arose over how to treat these,[50] so he and Rabban Gamliel brought the issue before the Great Sanhedrin. There, Nahchum HaLavlar reported that he was in receipt of a report from Rav Meesha, who in turn had received that report from Abba, who in turn received that report from the *Zuggos*,[51] who received the information from the Prophets as a *Halacha L'Moshe MiSinai*, that the number of *payah* donations one must give for two varieties of one grain [etc., etc., quoting the original *mishna*.]

This is the *mishna* as it stood at its closing by Rebbi Yehuda HaNassi. Now, the *Yerushalmi Gemora* quotes a statement by Rebbi Yohonon, one of the earliest *Amoraim*, and the head of the entire Jewish people in his time. I suggest this statement answers why the *Amoraim* unanimously refrained from disagreeing with any *mishna*.

אמר רבי זעירא בשם רבי יוחנן: „אם באת הלכה תחת ידיך ואין את יודע מה טיבה,

---

[50] Perhaps he questioned the logic of the *mishna* (which treated two varieties of one grain in a peculiar way) and, assuming it was based on faulty Scriptural analysis, decided to challenge it.

[51] The last of whom were Shammai and Hillel and the first of whom were Yosay ben Yo'ezer and Yosay ben Yohonon.

אל תפליגינה לדבר אחר. שהרי כמה הלכות נאמרו למשה בסיני וכולהן משוקעות
במשנה."

אמר רבי אבין: "ויאות הוא! ,שני מיני חיטים' אילולי שבא נחום ופירש לנו—יודעין
היינו?!"

Said Rebbi Zeyra in the name of Rebbi Yoḥonon: ''If you come
across a *mishna* whose reason you cannot understand, do not
brush it aside and replace its law with another one. For many
laws were told to Moses at Sinai, and all of them are lodged
throughout the *Mishna*.''

Said Rebbi Abbin: ''How true! For behold the *halacha* regarding
''two varieties of one grain'' [as a prime example]! If Nachum
HaLavlar had not come and explained to us [that it was a *halacha L'Moshe MiSinai*], would we ever have known?!''

This passage shows two things. For one, Rebbi Yoḥonon had to
instruct his fellow, and following, *Amoraim* to refrain from rejecting
a *mishna*. That implies that until then, the *Amoraim* had not accepted such a policy of restraint.[52] He had to give them a *reason* not to
reject an incomprehensible *mishna*. Without this special reason,
they could indeed dispute a *mishna*. And the special reason was not
their inferior intellectual abilties.

Secondly, the explanation Rebbi Yoḥonon *did* give for his
instructions provides us with the reason for the deference of the
Amoraim to every *halacha* of the *Mishna*: namely, the *halacha* may
have originated with Hashem at Sinai.[53] Thus, even if the *halacha*
was associated with a *drash*, it was the kind searched for as a *remez*,
an indication for a law already stated by Hashem, and not one that
generated the law.

Persecutions, expulsions, and Rome's increasingly harsh iron
rule made it necessary for Rebbi Yehuda HaNassi's *Bes Din* to take

---

[52] His warning did not refer to גזירות ותקנות שגזרו, post-Mosaic decrees by the Sages,
because they are obviously not *Halachos L'Moshe MiSinai*, and overturning such
decisions had already been forbidden by the *Mishna* itself (אין ב"ד יכול לבטל דברי ב"ד
חבירו אא"כ כו').

[53] Though "שני מיני חיטים, two varieties of grain" is a technical *Halacha L'Moshe
MiSinai*—i.e., there is no indication in the Torah for it—in the context of Rebbi
Yoḥonon's warning, *any* law that came from Sinai is obviously meant, so that we
should take "*Halacha L'Moshe MiSinai*" here in its broader sense: a law given at
Sinai, whether it was to be associated to a Scriptural verse or not.

advantage of its historically unique period of respite and fix the *Mishna* text to save the Oral Law from possible oblivion. Evidently, the same tumultuous state of affairs had also caused an actual, not merely potential, obscurity about the laws to develop: The Sanhedrin lost track of which laws had originated with *drashos*, permitting challenge, and which laws had really originated from Sinai, precluding question. Even if the law in question was not a *minhag* or *takkonna*, which could be reversed only by a superior *Great Sanhedrin*, it may very well have been an absolutely uncontestable law, one given by Hashem to Moses.[54] It now became impossible to exercise the power to differ with **any** *halachos*, for the Sages no longer knew *which* of the *halachos* they could overturn. This new situation, immediately following the formulation of the *Mishna*—the time of Rebbi Yoḥonon, at the beginning of the era of the *Amoraim* (c. 4000, 250 CE)—explains why *Amoriam* necessarily refrained from differing with any *halachos* stated in the *Mishna*. It also accounts for why matters that did not fundamentally affect such *halachos*, such as the specific Scriptural indication for the agreed upon law, were still open to challenge.

Similarly, the above situation had no bearing on the ability of *Amoraim* to dispute *drashos* in the *Mishna* which produced *halachos* definitely not specified at Sinai. This would explain passages such as the following in *K'reesos* (15a):

אר"ע, „שאלתי את ר"ג ואת ר' יהושע . . . הבא על אחותו ועל אחות אביו ועל אחות
אמו—מהו? חייב על כולן או חייב על כל אחת ואחת?"

. . . אמרו לו, „לא שמענו. אבל שמענו ,הבא על ה' נשיו נדות בהעלם אחת, שהוא
חייב על כל אחת ואחת.' ורואין אנו שהדברים ק"ו."

גמרא: [היינו] ומה הבא על ה' נשיו נדות בבת אחת—שהן שם אחת—חייב על כל
אחת ואחת, אחותו שהיא אחות אביו שהיא אחות אמו—שהן ג' שמות—אינו דין
שיהא חייב על כל אחת ואחת?!

איכא למיפרך: מה לה' נדות שכן גופן מחולקין!

אלא אמר קרא, „ערות אחותו גלה," לחייב על אחותו שהיא אחות אביו שהיא אחות
אמו.

---

[54] Rava, cited above, was an *Amora*, who lived long after the *Mishna* was closed. Since his *drashos* generated law-details not given in the *Mishna*, they were therefore technically subject to challenge. Thus his instructions to his disciples not to overturn any of *his drasha*-generated laws formed a special request.

MISHNA: Rabbi Akiva asked Rabban Gamliel and Rebbi Yehoshua, "How many prohibitions would one be culpable [to bring a sin-offering] for if he would commit incest with his sister, who is simultaneously his father's sister and his mother's sister[55]—one or three?"

They replied, "We have not received a tradition concerning such a case. However, we *have* learned that even if due to only one misconception of *halacha*, one had relations with each of his five wives while they were *niddos*, he must bring five sin-offerings. And it seems that this principle would apply to your case *kal v'homer*, even more so."

GEMORA: The *kal v'homer* reasoning is as follows: The case of five wives involves five instances of the identical prohibiton, yet the sinner is required to bring five offerings. Rabbi Akiva's case involves prohibitons separately labeled in Scripture. All the more so should the sinner have to bring more than one sin-offering! But this reasoning is faulty! Perhaps the crucial reason the man with five wives brings five offerings is the fact that he acted with five separate women. But in Rabbi Akiva's case, only one woman was involved!

Rather [the solution to Rabbi Akiva's problem is not through a *kal v'homer* but another method of *drash*]: Scripture says "The nakedness of his sister he revealed," a redundant verse. This [is the source] that the sinner in Rabbi Akiva's case must bring three offerings.

Here we see the *mishna* propounding a *drash* to generate a clarification of law, and the *Gemora* finding fault with it, approving instead of an original *drash* to generate the clarification. Although the law was stated in the *Mishna*, since the *Mishna* itself disclosed that neither the law nor the *kal v'homer* producing it were received from Sinai ("We have not received a tradition concerning such a case"), both were open to challenge by *Amoraim*.

Our theory also explains how an *Amora* can declare a law to be a hybrid of the opinions of two *Tannaim*, although no *Tanna* subscribed to it. Since each side's opinion was disputed by the other, it is clear that each was known by the *Tannaim* not to have been received from Sinai.[56] Relying upon this fact, the *Amora* could offer

[55] The case is hypothetically possible if the subject's parents had also committed incest.

[56] "נפלה המחלוקת והעיין בדבר שלא נשמע בו הלכה, *Machlokess* and analysis arose [only] on that which its *halacha* was not heard" (*Introduction to the Talmud*, p. 14 in Hebrew section). See chapter entitled "Loss of Halachos."

from them and base new decisions upon them," but not that they were free from being contested.

4. However, we do find the validity of *Tannaitic drash*-generated laws tested for compliance to the actions of people in *Nach*. (*Nach*: The *Prophets and Writings*, the part of the Bible covering the events of the 1,000 years following those in the *Five Books of Moses*. The authorities of those days, too, could derive *d'oraissa* law details by *darshonning* only the *Five Books of Moses*. As the Rambam explains in the introduction to his *Mishna* commentary, no new Torah was revealed after Moses, and prophecy was no longer a means of deriving Torah laws.) Thus, Rebbi Yehuda in *Succa* 37a (לגבי מחלקותו ברבי מאיר באם יש לדרוש קל וחומר דצריך הסכך להיות נעשה מד' מינים) is expected to conform his *drash*-generated opinion with practices mentioned in the Books of the Prophets (in this case, the Book of *Neḥemia*). Similarly, (as Rabbi Moshe Freidman found for me) in *Makkos* 22a-b (לגבי אם יש לדרוש "מספר ארבעים", דקרא כארבעים חסר אחת) Rebbi Yehuda supports himself against his protagonists with a practice referred to in *Zecharia* 13:6. And in *Moed Kotton* 7b, Rebbi Yehuda (or Rebbi) is found conforming his opinion to a פסוק in *Yeḥezkiel* 44. (In Bava Metsia 47a, Rebbi Yehuda wishes to reconcile קנין חליפין practices with those of Boaz, but it is not clear that the *Gemora* is dealing with a matter of *drash*, nor even if the entire matter is indeed a simple דאורייתא issue—see ערך חליפין, אינצייקלופידיה תלמודית). See next note.

5. Perhaps the practices narrated in *Nach* (see above note) could not be contradicted by any *Tannaitic Sanhedrin* because these practices were known to have originated not as *drashos* but as *kabballos* from Hashem at Sinai. Even a *Great Sanhedrin* would not contradict such facts. Or perhaps, regardless of its origin, the recording of a practice in *Nach* thereon rendered it irreversible. (I.e., perhaps once Hashem gave the prophet permission to record a law, it gained official and permanent status even if it was originally *drash*-generated.)

12. In fact, the commentaries explain the *Jerusalem Talmud* (*Payah* 1:1, page 1b) to mean that any *Bes Din* that puts "proper effort" into its decisions is guaranteed accuracy in its findings. This would certainly discourage any *Bes Din* from contesting an earlier one, since that earlier one couldn't be wrong! This may be the thought behind the Rambam's intriguing statement at the very beginning of *Hilchos Mahmrim*, that "עליהן הבטיח תורה," if it is to be translated, "The Torah gave an assurance" about the Sages' accuracy. However, tractate *Horios* deals specifically with the sacrifices that a *Bes Din* must bring after finding it was mistaken in a decision. Is it a description of something that was never to happen? Evidently not, as this matter is not listed among those which have been declared to be merely academic. Besides, the Rambam clearly states in his *Hakdama L'Payrush*

his own opinion, as long as it did not oppose the ideas upon which both *Tannaim* agreed (since that upon which all *Tannaim* agree may again be something received from Sinai).

All details in the *Mishna* known not to be *kabballos,* and all rabbinical decrees not yet voted upon by a *Tannaitic* Sanhedrin, were challengeable. On such issues, an *Amora* could conceivably differ with a *Tanna.* As we mentioned above, there were rare instances in which *Amoraim* exercised this power.

Additional Notes to Chapter 6

1. In this aspect, *halacha* treats rabbinical law more stringently than Biblical law! The Rambam tells us (*Introduction to Payrush HaMishnayos; Hilchos Mahmrim* 2:1) that *gezayros*—precautionary measures introduced to ensure that Biblical prohibitions would not be transgressed—could never be rescinded by any Sanhedrin, no matter how great it is and no matter whether the original reasons for the *gezayros* still seem to exist. *Takkonnos, enactments,* and *minhagim, practices,* once instituted, can only be voided by a Great Sanhedrin superior בחכמה ובמנין, in wisdom and number" which according to the Rambam (*Hilchos Mahmrim* 2:2,3) means, superior in expertise and in the number of contemporary Sages who had decided the law the same way the Sanhedrin finally did. Only then can the new ב"ד overturn the ruling of the previous one.

3. This makes puzzling another statement of the Rambam (beginning of *Hakdama L'Payrush HaMishnayos* [English translation, *Introduction to the Talmud,* p. 73; Hebrew section p. 10]). Regarding the Torah-transmission from the days of Joshua and on he states: "והיו חכמי כל דור משימים דברי הקודמין עיקר, והיו לומדים מהם ומחדשים ענינים. והעיקרים המקובלים לא נחלקו בהם, Every generation's Sages treated the earlier ones' words as axiomatic. They would learn from them and base new decisions upon them. And they never contested the received principles." Yet here he states that previous decisions *were* challengeable. But we can solve this problem if we understand the uncontestable "עיקרים המקובלים," received principles, to be referring to the פירושים המקובלים which Moses received at Sinai. This interpretation is supported (דיקא נמי) by the fact that the Rambam wrote *two* sentences. One, about the "עיקרים המקובלים," received principles, about which he says, "לא נחלקו בהם, they were never contested," and another about "דברי הקודמין, the earlier Sages' words," about which he states, "היו לומדים מהם ומחדשים ענינים," they would learn

HaMishnayos (*Introduction to the Talmud*, p. 124), regarding the contents of tractate Horios that "it is impossible for flesh and blood not to err" ("וכאשר השלים מוסר הדיינים [במס׳ אבות] החל לבאר שגיאותיהם. כי כל מי שיש בו" טבע בשר ודם אי אפשר שלא יטעה ויחטא"), and so he evidently considered it inevitable for even the Sages of the Sanhedrin to sometimes err.

28. Whether Rabban Yoḥonon ben Zakkai was also the *Nassi* is a controversial subject. The *Doros HaRishonim* maintains that he was not. Perhaps this is why he does not cite this passage as a proof text for the Rambam. He may hold that Rabban Yoḥonon ben Zakkai was only voicing his personal opinion, not that of the Great Sanhedrin. However, from the fact that Rabban Yoḥonon ben Zakkai was concerned only with the disagreement of *future* generations, it would seem that the Great Sanhedrin of his own generation nevertheless concurred with his *drash*.

47. Rava, a fourth-generation *Amora*, declared that the *drashos* found for laws by Shmuel, a first-generation *Amora*, were better than those found by early *Tannaim*: "Said Rav Yehuda in the name of Shmuel, 'Had I been there, I would have told them, "My [*drash* in support of the law] is better than yours!"' . . . Said Rava, 'Fault can be found with all of them except for Shmuel's. . . . As the saying goes, "One grain of pepper is sharper than a basketful of melons!"'' (*Yoma* 85b, *Megilla* 7a and *Ḥaggiga* 10a, concerning three independent laws and their *drashos*.) In *Megilla*, Rav Yosef, a third- generation *Amora*, offers still another *drash*.

48. Likewise, we find an *Amora* differing with a *mishna* over the reason for a *halacha*: See *Gittin* 11b, where *Tosefos* (ד״ה בגיטי נשים אבל לא בשחרורי עבדים) quotes Rebbi Yoḥonon in the *Yerushalmi*, and the commentary *Korbon HaEyda loc. cit.* (Admittedly, the passage may be interpreted differently, as it is by *Shiray Korban*, but the plain understanding is as the *Korban HaEyda* has it, that Rebbi Yoḥonon is criticizing the *mishna*'s reason for a law and is providing a different one.) [Incidentally, *Tosefos*' wording of his principle in *Succa* 24a, (ד״ה רבי יהודה ור״ש אוסרין) easily lends itself to the wrong translation: "We find many instances in which the *Gemora* does not consider the real reason to be the one explicated in the *mishna*." By examining his proof texts one can see that he merely means that the *Gemora* often gives a non-literal interpretation of a *Tanna*'s opinion.]

It would also be difficult to counter our proof from *Gittin* 11b by arguing that Rebbi Yoḥonon had the authority of a *Tanna* and cannot be an example of an *Amora* differing with a *Tanna*. This assertion can be supported by only one passage (*Nazir* 65a) which refers to Rebbi Yoḥonon as a *Tanna*, but *Tosefos* (ד״ה הוא דאמר) states that this is referring to Rebbi Yoḥonon ben Nuri, not our Rebbi Yoḥonon ben Naph-

cha. The *Meiri* (on *Kesubos* 8a) entertains the possibility that we consider Rebbi Yoḥonon like a *Tanna* (i.e., not only Rav, to whom, as
mentioned elsewhere, this status is often granted in the expression "תנא
הוא ופליג, he is a *Tanna* and disagrees [by right with another]), but in his
Introduction to Ahvos he, like *Tosefos* (*Kesubos* 8a) ד"ה רב תנא הוא
ופליג), attaches that stature only to Rav.

Chapter 7

Errors On The Receiving End

We have seen that in the same sentence in which the Rambam criticizes those who attribute *machlokess* to forgetfulness, he criticizes those who blame it on error or on failure to be present when crucial information was presented.[1] Differences of opinion, he insists, are due solely to different ways of analyzing facts that were heard in the same way by all. Thus, even where it may seem that an opinion stemmed from its proponent lacking complete information, such as through his being absent from the lecture hall during the presentation of crucial data, that is not the case.[2] However, some observations are called for.

Receptional Vs. Analytical Error

First, we have already established that over time some details of *mitzva*-performance were forgotten, necessitating analysis to reconstruct them, and that if *machlokess* resulted, *someone* was coming to a conclusion at variance with the original fact. The Rambam could not be objecting to the possibility of error in this sense.

---

[1] See Additional Notes at the end of this chapter.
[2] See Addendum IV.

Rather, he is speaking about the accuracy of communication between the Sages when communication existed. The kind of error the Rambam rules out is error in reception. That is, error in correctly hearing words spoken. He does not consider conclusions based upon logically valid analysis of the facts to be within the realm of "error."[3]

Permanent and Final Opinions Vs. Opinions in Formation and Under Consideration.

Furthermore, we proposed that the Rambam, in declaring the phenomenon of "error" foreign to *halachic* analysis, is speaking only of the analysis behind the conclusions in their final form, those presented to us as the final opinions accepted by the Talmud. While the analysis was proceeding, however, it may have drawn conclusions that by the time of the Talmud's closing were ultimately to be revealed to have been factually incorrect.[4] We said this because we see that before the closing of the Talmud, opinions were investigated for error and sometimes discredited as erroneous. There are *Gemoras* which, after considering all the data, openly and definitively declare that an *Amora* was mistaken about some fact, with comments such as "הא דר׳ פלוני בדותא, that report of so-and-so's opinion is a fiction"[5] or "קא טעי רבא בד׳ זוגי, Rava erred concerning [his interpretation of the *mishna*" (*Yevomos* 2:2)].[6] A *Gemora* even declares that a *Tanna*,

---

[3] See Additional Notes to this chapter for the Rambam's words, wherein he also explains that when the Talmud attributes *machlokos* to scholars' failure to apply themselves sufficiently, this should be understood not as denigrating their ability to listen properly and register and retain the words spoken, but as a description of their relative deficiency in analytical skills.

[4] It is true that the Sages' extraordinary desire for Torah-knowledge and for success in all branches of G-d's service was rewarded with extraordinary supernatural assistance (רוח הקדש) that provided them with a miraculous abundance of mental energy and a largesse of genius. But supernatural inspiration is not Torah. After Moses, no Torah could be given by prophecy. Each Sage utilized his genius according to his free will, and always had the opportunity to err (condensed from *Rejoice O Youth*, pp. 244-246).

[5] *Bava Kamma* 67b and other citations listed there. See Additional Notes at the end of this chapter for explanation of the word "בדותא."

[6] *Yevomos* 19a. On the other hand, we must keep in mind that even the *Talmud's* declaration that someone was wrong in his analysis may sometimes be but the verdict of the *Bes Din* of Ravina and Rav Ashi, the final narrators of the Talmud's presentations. The proponent of the rejected opinion nevertheless may well have continued to maintain his position, if not for his obligation to bow to the decision of the Supreme *Bes Din*.

Rebbi Yehuda, disagreed with a very early *mishna's Tanna* only
because he misunderstood him![7] In a passage in Ḥullin (133a) a Sage
explicitly states that one of his students misinterpreted him:

אמר רב יוסף, „האי כהנא דאית ליה צורבא מרבנן בשבבותיה ודחיקא ליה מילתא,
ליזכי ליה מתנתא, ואף על גב דלא אתי לידיה, במכרי כהונה ולויה."

רבא ורב ספרא איקלעו לבי מר יוחנא בריה דרב חנא בר אדא . . . עביד להו עגלא
תילתא. א"ל, רבא לשמעיה, „זכי לן מתנתא, דבעינא למיכל לישנא בחרדלא." זכי
ליה. רבא אכל; ורב ספרא לא אכל (משום דלא מטא לידיה דשמעא—פרש"י).

אקריוה לרב ספרא בחלמא:

„מ.עֲדֶה־בֶּגֶד בְּיוֹם קָרָה חֹמֶץ עַל.נ נָתֶר וְשָׁר בּ.בַשִּׁרִים עַל.ל לֵב רָע"
(פרש"י: כן האומר דברי תורה למי שאינו יודע להבין בהן).

אתא לקמיה דרב יוסף. א"ל, „דלמא משום דעברי אשמעתא דמר, אקריין הכי." אמר
ליה, „כי אמרי אנא—באחר; שמעא—בעל כרחיה מזכי. וכי אמרי אנא—למאן דלא
אפשר ליה; הא—אפשר ליה. ואלא מ"ט אקריין הכי? כלפי רבא! ולקריין לרבא,
רבא נזוף הוה." (פרש"י: כלומר על רבא שלא ידע להבין בטעמו של רב יוסף הקרוהו
לרב ספרא כך.)

Rav Yosef said, ''A 'popular *kohane*' [to whom many people
donate the *kohane*-gifts and who is therefore oversupplied] can
and may grant the food to be donated to him—even if it had not
yet reached his hands—to a poor scholar [although one cannot
usually grant others something he himself does not yet pos-
sess].''

Rava and Rav Safra visited the house of Mar Yuchna b'ray
d'Rav Ḥanna bar Adda. He prepared for them fine meat. Rava
said to the servant [who was a *kohane*, to whom the host always
gave his food donations], ''Please grant me your donation; I
would like some special meat.'' He did so. Rava ate it, but Rav
Safra did not [for he maintained that regardless of the case, a
kohane cannot give over that which he has not yet received].

Rav Safra [then] had a dream in which they recited to him the
verse (*Mishlay* 25:20), ''As inappropriate as delicate clothing on
a wintry day, . . . is it to teach the beautiful songs of Torah laws
to a mind below par.''[8]

He came to Rav Yosef and said, ''Perhaps I dreamed this because

---

[7] *Rosh HaShonna* 30a. See additional notes at the end of this chapter.

[8] In a more literal sense, this verse is explained as meaning, ''As inappropriate as
delicate clothing on a wintry day . . . is it to sing before someone in an evil mood.''

I transgressed your teaching [permitting the food designated for the *kohane* even before the *kohane* received it]."

He replied to him, "I was only speaking of a case where the *kohane* was acting voluntarily. In your case, he was virtually forced. And I was only speaking of a case where there was no other way for the poor scholar to be fed—unlike your situation. The criticism in your dream was being directed at Rava [for giving my teaching too broad an interpretation]!"

The student, we see, clearly misinterpreted his rebbi's teaching. The rebbi himself declared him to be mistaken in interpreting his teaching too broadly.

Another example of a student erroneously interpreting his mentor's words too broadly is recorded in Ḥullin 110a:

כי סליק רבי אלעזר, אשכחיה לזעירי. אמר ליה, "איכה תנא דאתנייה לרב, ,כחל'?"
אחוייה [בני המקום] לרב יצחק בר אבודימי. אמר ליה, ,...אנא כחל של מניקה
שניתי לו; ומפלפולא של רבי חייא שנא ליה ,כחל' סתם."

פרש"י ד"ה ומתוך פלפולו של ר' חייא. "שהוא מחודד מאד, ומבין מעצמו וכסבור
שתלמידיו מחודדין כמותו. . . . שנה לו סתם, וסבור שיבין רב שאין אסור אלא
מניקה. ולא הבין." ע"כ פרש"י. (וע' מהר"ם שי"ף ולפע"ד אולי כוונת הגמ' דרב
היה שומע כשרב יצחק בר אבדומי היה מלמד את מאמרו לרבי חייא.) פי' תוס':
"וטעה בדבריו והיה סבור דמכח ברייתא הוה בא לחלוק על משנתנו."

This passage tells us that when Rebbi Elazar heard that Rav prohibited eating a cow's udder because it is a mixture of meat and milk, he asked to speak to Rav's teacher. The teacher declared that his disciple [Rav] was mistaken: What had happened, he explained, was that Rebbi Ḥiyya had indeed stated that a cow's udder is forbidden, but thought it to be self-understood that he was referring only to a *nursing* cow's udder, which is, naturally, full of milk. Rav erred (as *Tosefos* says) and thought he meant that any udder is *always* forbidden and taught that as Rav Ḥiyya's p'sak.

Even authorities of the stature of Rav and Shmuel could be misinformed about another's opinion due to initial lack of communication (Ḥullin 111b):

איתמר: דגים שעלו בקערה (מן הצלי). כשהיו רותחין נתנן לתוך קערה שאכלו בה
בשר—פרש"י): רב אמר אסור לאכלן בכותח. ושמואל אמר מותר לאכלן בכותח
[דנותן טעם לפגם הוא].

. . . רבי אלעזר הוה קאים קמיה דמר שמואל. אייתו לקמיה דגים שעלו בקערה, וקא

אכיל בכותח. יהיב ליה ולא אכיל. אמר ליה [שמואל לר"א], „לרבך (רב) יהיב ליה
ואכיל, ואת לא אכלת?!"

אתא לקמיה דרב, א"ל, „הדר ביה מר משמעתיה?" א"ל, „חס ליה לזרעיה דאבא בר
אבא [היינו שמואל] דליספי לי מידי דלא סבירא לי (פרש"י: לא היו דברים מעולם)!"

An *Amora* taught: "[Concerning] fried fish served hot on a
plate from which meat was eaten—Rav said, 'It is prohibited to
eat them dipped in a dairy dip,' but Shmuel permitted them to
be eaten dipped in a dairy dip [because he maintains that the
day-old taste of meat in the plate does not exude its *halachic*
(i.e., *fleishig*) status (into the *milchig* dip) although the fish
dipped into it is hot].' "

Rebbi Elazar was standing in front of Mar Shmuel when they
brought Shmuel fried fish served hot on a plate from which
meat was eaten, and he ate it with a dairy dip. Shmuel offered it
to him and he did not eat it. Shmuel said to him, "Your *rebbi*
[Rav] was offered it and he ate, and you do not eat?!"

Rebbi Elazar came to Rav and said, "Have you retracted your
opinion [and now permit this]?" He replied, "May the child of
Abba bar Avva [*viz.*, Shmuel] be silenced for attributing to me
something that I do not maintain (Rashi: such a thing never
was)!"

Although Shmuel was obviously victim to a simply confused
and wrong report concerning Rav (perhaps as the result of
someone's misinterpretation), we maintain that this in no way contradicts the Rambam's position that error is foreign to the phenomenon of *machlokes*. For, as we have noted, faulty opinions formed
through erroneous reports were only tentative. This is because, as
we have stated in a previous chapter and illustrated in this one, the
Sages pursued the truth and through discussion and investigation
opinions based on factual error would not endure.[9] The faulty report

---

[9] It is this process of ferreting out errors that belies the comparison of the transmission of the Oral Law to the game of "telephone." In that game, a message is given to
one person, who then retells it to the next on line and so on. The amusing result is
the corruption of the message by the time it is retold by the last person. But crucial
to this game is its rule that each time the message must be given in secret without
benefit of review with the previous transmitter. The transmission of the Oral Law,
in stark contrast, was seriously and responsibly conducted by men who constantly
reviewed and challenged each other's understanding, often checking with the original sources.

would not be the basis of the final *machlokos* authoritatively presented to us in the Talmud. If the Sage himself found out his mistake he would retract; if the mistake was found by later generations, they would discredit the opinion. The process of discussion and challenge by self, peers, superiors and successors, sometimes leading to the retracting or discrediting of opinions, was apparent in some of the passages already cited.

Bava Metsia 66b contains an example of one authority tactfully correcting two others' misunderstanding of an academy's teaching:

אמרי ליה מר ינוקא ומר קשישא, בני דרב חסדא, לרב אשי: „הכי אמרי נהרדאי
משמיה דרב נחמן, כו'." א"ל, …„דילמא הכי קאמריתו . . ."

Mar Yenuka and Mar Kashisha, sons of Rav Ḥissda, said to Rav Ashi: "The scholars of Nehardea say the following in the name of Rav Nachman..." He [raised an objection against their report and] said, "Perhaps you mean to say *this*...?"

Bava Metsia 72b demonstrates the clarification of a Sage's opinion through one of his disciples possessing more information than another:

אמר רב ששת, אמר רב הונא: „אין לווין על שער שבשוק."

אמר ליה רב יוסף בר חמא לרב ששת „ . . . ומי א"ר הונא הכי? והא בעי מיניה מרב
הונא כו' [ואמר דלווין על שער שבשוק]!"

מעיקרא סבר רב הונא אין לווין; כיון דשמעה להא דא"ר שמואל בר חייא א"ר
אלעזר, לווין, אמר איהו נמי לווין.

Rav Sheyshess said: "Rav Huna said, 'It is prohibited [on the grounds of usury] for someone to borrow money promising that if unable to pay cash by the due date he will repay with the amount of merchandise that it can buy at the time of the loan [even if at the due date more money would be needed to buy that amount].'"

Rav Yosef replied to Rav Sheyshess: "... Did Rav Huna say this? But when Rav Huna was asked [such] a question ... [his answer implied that one *may* borrow on such terms]!" The answer is that originally Rav Huna objected [as reported by Rav Sheyshess], but once he heard that Shmuel bar Ḥiyya said in the name of R' Elazar that such terms are permitted, he [conceded error and] also said so [as reported by Rav Yosef].

Accusations of Error in Analysis

Since analysis could produce erroneous conclusions, it follows as only natural that those engaged in *machlokess* would consider their opponents to be mistaken in their analysis, and we should not be surprised to find that, at least before consensus is reached, they openly criticized each other's assertions. A case in point is a critical comment by Rav concerning Levy.[10] Accusations by one authority that another's analysis is faulty are legion,[11] ranging from the respectful, "לפום חורפא שבשתא, His penetrating analysis misguided him,"[12] to the apparently biting "אמינא כי ניים ושכיב רב אמר להא שמעתתא, I say that Rav made that statement when he was falling asleep,"[13] and "כמדומה לי שאין לו מוח בקדקדו, It seems to me that he has no brains in his skull."[14]

An interesting passage in *O'hollos* 16:1[15] presents Rabbi Tarfon

---

[10] Refer again to Addendum IV.

[11] *Teshuvos Ḥavvos Ya'ir, teshuva* 152, explains that none of the following criticisms were motivated by malice and that in fact their formulation even implied high expectations of the one criticized.

[12] לפום חורפא שבשתא, *His penetrating analysis misguided him*

This expression appears twice in the *Bavli* (*Bava Metsia* 96b and *Needa* 33b) and the similar "אגב חורפיה לא עיין בה, Because of his sharpness [being involved in another area of study at the time—*Rashi* and *Rashbam*] he neglected to analyze [the material carefully enough]," appears another two times (*Eruvin* 90a and *Bava Bassra* 116b)—each time, incidentally, at the top of the page. Every time it is an accusation that Rommi bar Ḥamma posited a pointless question, an accusation made by his colleague Rava (except once when our text reads, "רבה," Rabba, instead of רבא, Rava). There are different interpretations whether the emendation of the question, to make it acceptable, is being offered by the critic or is the *Gemora's* comment. (Interestingly, Rava and Rommi bar Ḥamma were both disciples of Rav Ḥissda, and they both married his daughter, Rava doing so after Rommi bar Ḥamma. The *Gemora* and commentators do not specify whether Rommi bar Ḥamma passed away or divorced his wife. [See account in *Bava Bassra* 12b and *Yevomos* 34b, *Rashi* ד"ה אבתריה.])

[13] אמינא כי ניים ושכיב רב אמר להא שמעתתא, *I say that Rav made that statement when he was falling asleep*

This expression appears in eight places, each describing a separate incident, and all feature Rav Sheyshes criticizing a statement made by his *rebbi*, Rav: *Yevomos* 24b, 91a, 109b; *Bava Kamma* 47b, 65a, 67b; *Bechoros* 23b; *Needa* 60a.

[14] כמדומה לי שאין לו מוח בקדקדו, *It seems to me that he has no brains in his skull.*

This expression appears in *Yevomos* 9a and *Menachos* 80b, both times as Rebbi's response to a question posed to him by his disciple, Levy.

[15] Explained here according to the Rambam's commentary on the *mishna*.

declaring the analysis by another *Tanna* to be mistaken (טועה) and Rabbi Akiva defending it.

כל המטלטלין מביאין את הטומאה בעובי המרדע.

אמר רבי טרפון, "אקפח את בני שזו הלכה מקופחת! ששמע השומע וטעה. שהאיכר עובר והמרדע על כתפו, והאהיל צדו אחד על הקבר, וטמאוהו משום כלים המאהילים על המת."

אמר רבי עקיבא, "אני אתקן שיהו דברי חכמים קיימין: שיהו כל המטלטלין מביאין את הטומאה על אדם הנושאן בעובי המרדע ועל עצמן בכל שהן, ועל שאר אדם וכלים בפותח טפח."

The *tum'ah*, ritual impurity, that emanates from a corpse that is located beneath one end of any movable kind of object [such as a pot, for example] מביאין [normally taken to mean: spreads onto any item or person located anywhere else beneath that object] if that object is thick as an ox-goad [i.e., even if it is only one-third the width of a *tefach*, a handbreadth, rather than a full *tefach*, the standard specification for an *ohel*, covering].

Rabbi Tarfon said, "May I be bereft of my sons if this *halacha* is not bereft! [It is bereft of truth—*Rambam*; this *mishna* is in error—*Rosh*.] [To effect contamination, the object must have the *full* width of a *tefach*.][16] The listener made a mistake! [He heard that the Sages declared a certain farmer *tomay* in the following case:] The farmer was passing by, carrying one end of his ox-goad on his shoulder, and [at a certain moment] its other end was situated directly over a grave. [The author of the erroneous statement thought that the cause of *tum'ah* was the fact that the farmer was under the same object—the ox-goad—that was over the grave and concluded that an ox-goad's thickness is a sufficient amount for the specification of an *ohel*, a covering]. But the real cause was the fact that he was *touching* [the ox-goad, which was] an object that itself contracted *tum'ah* by hovering over a grave. [A hovering object of such small proportions can, indeed, contract *tum'ah* itself and transfer it to that which it touches, but it cannot transfer *tum'ah* to that which is under it. It must have at least the full width of a *tefach* to do that.]

---

[16] *Tum'ah* spreads more easily onto a person who *touches* an object that contracted *tum'ah* by hovering over a corpse than onto one who is merely *located under* the same object that the corpse was under. Specifically, even if the hovering object is merely one-third a *tefach* wide, it will spread the *tum'ah* to someone touching it, whereas it must be at least a *full tefach* wide to spread the *tum'ah* to someone merely located beneath the same hovering object.

Said Rabbi Akiva, "I will adjust and correct things so that the words of the Sages will stand as they are: [The *mishna* means:] The *tum'ah* that emanates from a corpse that is located beneath one end of any movable kind of object [such as a pot, for example] is caused to spread *onto a person who carries* that object if it is as thick as an ox-goad [i.e., one-third of a *tefach* wide, and it spreads over the entire object itself *regardless* of its width, and it spreads onto other people and utensils *under* the ox-goad if its width is a full *tefach*]."

In his commentary on this *mishna*, the Rambam explains that though Rabbi Tarfon called the *Tanna* mistaken, he did not question the *Tanna's* accuracy in registering the information he heard, but he did question his *analysis* of it. R'Tarfon concluded that his predecessor must have described his analysis of what he had been taught, rather than having plainly reported the teaching in its original words. Rabbi Tarfon therefore "reconstructed" the statement which, in his opinion, must really have had been heard but then misinterpreted. Rabbi Akiva, on the other hand, maintained that the *Tanna* did merely report what he had heard, and that the teaching simply had to be properly understood:[17]

> When Rabbi Tarfon heard this statement . . . he was astounded and declared that there is an erroneous law [in this *mishna*], and that this *halacha* is less than true . . . Furthermore, he explained how the mistake came about, and he explained that the mistake arose because the listener heard the Sages declare *tum'ah* in this case, but attributed the judgment to the wrong cause, the real cause of the *tum'ah* being etc. and etc.

Thus, we come to the following conclusions concerning the Rambam's stand on errors by the Sages:

1. Our Sages did not think they heard things that were not said.

2. Before the closing of the Talmud and its investigation of opinions and/or discussion of peers with each other, opinions based upon incorrect facts, erroneous reports

---

[17] It is noteworthy that in any event, both Rabbi Akiva and Rabbi Tarfon could not accept the *Tanna's* statement at face value, without some "adjustments" ["תקון"], because as such it contradicted all other information they possessed.

and mistaken analysis were possible. The Rambam's denial of errors occurring does not apply here.

3. After discussion and/or investigation, such errors were weeded out and retracted or discredited. It is from this point and on that the Rambam condemns the idea that an authority's opinion is the result of deficient analysis or failure to obtain available data. The remaining opinions were based upon precise analysis of the facts, alone.

4. Disputants even at this point, however, could still accuse each other of wrongly analyzing the facts, and even the Talmud might discredit someone's analysis based upon what it feels is a more logical approach or a better interpretation of the facts.

The Rambam's only objection is that if it could have been proved[18] that someone's opinion was based upon his being absent from part of a lecture or a mistake over the very words of a statement, if it could have been shown that an interpretation of a statement was eventually denied by that statement's very author, then it would be an insult to the integrity of our Sages to suggest that any of them refused to yield his position—particularly concerning *halachos* that were (orally) documented to have originated with Moses. In those instances where a Sage might have tentatively misinterpreted, misapplied, misheard, forgot or failed to be present for a lecturer's remark, he would certainly stand corrected by the other listeners. The final positions of the Sages and all enduring *machlokos* were based solely upon different interpretations of the same facts.

Variant Versions and Reports

However, there are some *machlokos* that do not seem to be matters of analysis but simply matters of bad reception by the reporters of the statement, and there is every indication that neither side admit-

---

[18] The word "proved" is essential. We must keep in mind that an accusation of error in analysis may be the opinion of the accuser alone, whereas the accused himself may well continue to maintain his stand. As we mentioned before, even the *Talmud's* declaration that someone was wrong in his analysis may be but the verdict of the *Bes Din* of Ravina and Rav Ashi, the final narrators of the Talmud's presentations.

ted a mistake and neither side is discredited by the *Gemora*. The *Gemora* often gives us variant, even opposite, versions of narrative concerning what someone said (״איכא דאמרי האי ואיכא דאמרי האי״), as well as opposite reports by two disciples of their mentor's position on an issue. These situations apparently indicate a definitely concrete and permanent error on *someone's* part.

Placing the Quotation Marks

Some such problems can be solved simply by properly placing the "quotation marks." The two *talmidim* are *not* each claiming to have heard a different statement from their *rebbi*. What may seem to be *part* of a quote may actually be merely an *added explanation* to it. For example, a passage in *Bava Kamma* 56b reads:

איתמר: שומר אבידה . . . ר׳ יוסף אמר כשומר שכר דמי—בההיא הנאה דלא בעיא
למיתבי ליה ריפתא לעניא הוי כשומר שכר.

Rav Yosef *said*, someone who had found a lost object and is now safekeeping it [until the owner can be found] is legally considered a *paid* watchman.[19] For through the financial gain of being exempt from giving away bread to a pauper who comes to his door, it is as if he is being paid for his services.

At this point, the reader would assume that Rav Yosef was the author of the entire statement. But by reading on, it becomes obvious that it's not so:

איכא דמפרשי הכי: רב יוסף אמר כשומר שכר דמי, כיון דרחמנא שעבדיה בעל
כרחיה, הילכך כש״ש דמי.

There are others who explain as follows: Rav Yosef said that he is like a paid watchman. Since the Torah put a service upon him without his volunteering, he is therefore like a paid watchman.

It now becomes obvious that the second part of the statement originally attributed to Rav Yosef ("For through the financial gain, etc.") was not quoting Rav Yosef at all, but was an explanation tagged on for why he held as he did, probably contributed by some

[19] Being a *paid* watchman places responsibilities upon him, regarding loss of the object, from which an *unpaid* watchman is exempt.

disciples. *What* the explanation was, was a dispute among them. The "quotation marks" must end before the explanation begins. This alone can explain many apparently discordant reports of what an authority said. If two scholars differ on the reasoning behind an authority's remark, it could appear in the *Gemora* as a *machlokess* in the form of two authorities quoting their teacher differently. Analysis will reveal which part of the quotation is really a quotation and which is an explanation.

Conflicting Reports

Still, some Talmud passages do make it seem impossible to deny that gross, sensory errors were responsible for enduring *machlokos*. Such passages plainly state that two Sages are each claiming to have *heard* opposite remarks from their teacher, and neither one will give in to the other's testimony.

- *Bava Metsia* 46b-47a:

אמר רבה, אמר רב הונא: מכור לי באלו—קנה, ויש לו עליו אונאה.
רב אבא, אמר רב הונא: מכור לי באלו—קנה, ואין לו עליו אונאה.

Rabba said: Rav Huna said, [In a case where a buyer has some coins in his hands and simply says to the seller] "Sell me the item for these" [if the seller takes the money without bothering to ask how much it is]—it is a sale [and neither can coerce the other to retract]. And there is *no* obligation to compensate for underpay or overcharge.

Rav Avva said: Rav Huna said, [In the same situation of] "sell me the item with these"—it is a sale [exactly as above]. But there *is* an obligation to compensate for underpay or overcharge.

- *Bava Metsia* 66a:

א"ל ריש גלותא (לרב נחמן), „רב יהודא קרע לשטרך." א"ל, „דרדקא קרעיה?! גברא רבה קרעיה! חזא ביה טעמיה וקרעיה!"
איכא דאמרי: ... א"ל: „דרדקא קרעיה! דכ"ע לגבי דידי בדינא דרדקי נינהו!"

The *Resh Galusa*, Exilarch, told Rav Nachman [concerning a document of transaction whose language was composed to treat a complicated legality], "Rav Yehuda tore up the document you composed [implying that it was written faultily]!" He replied, "Do you think a mere child tore it up?! It was a great person who tore it up! He must have seen a reason to declare it invalid, and so he tore it!"

Others report the event as follows: ... He replied, "A mere child tore it! For in comparison to me, everyone else is a child [in the realm of judging the validity of documents]!"

The *Gemora* is replete with variant reports by Ulla and Rabbin on statements by their teacher, Resh Lakkish. Here is just one example:

A *mishna* (*Bava Metsia* 8:4) states that if a flood transplanted someone's tree into another's property, the new fruits grown should be shared by both people. Ulla and Rabbin report a qualification taught by their teacher:

- *Bava Metsia* 101a (top of page):

אמר עולא, אמר ריש לקיש: לא שנו אלא שנעקרו בגושיהן ולאחר ג'.

. . . א'רבין, אמר ריש לקיש: לא שנו אלא שנעקרו בגושיהן ובתוך ג'.

  Said Ulla, "Resh Lakkish said: The *mishna* is only speaking of a case in which the uprooted tree still had a clump of the original soil attached to its roots, and [the necessity to share first begins only three years after [the transplanting took place]."

  Said Rabbin, "Resh Lakkish said: The *mishna* is only speaking of a case in which the uprooted tree still had a clump of the original soil attached to its roots [as above], and [the necessity to share exists only] within the first three years after [the transplanting took place]."

- A similar example, involving Rabba and Rav Yosef, appears in *Gittin* 38b:

אמר רבה אמר רב: המקדיש עבדו—יצא לחרות.

ורב יוסף, אמר רב: המפקיר עבדו—יצא לחרות.

מ"ד מקדיש (רבה)—כ"ש מפקיר. מ"ד מפקיר (רב יוסף)—אבל מקדיש, לא;
דילמא לדמי קאמר.

  Rabba said: "Rav said: If one declares his slave 'holy'—the slave goes free."

  Rav Yosef said: "Rav said: If one declares his slave to be ownerless—then the slave goes free."

  Narrative: The one who maintains that the slave goes free when his owner declares him 'holy' all the more so will consider the slave free if the master declares him to be ownerless; the one who maintains that for the slave to go free one must declare him ownerless, maintains that if one declared the slave 'holy,' the slave will not go free. His opinion is that the master may well claim to have meant merely to donate the slave's cash value to the Holy Temple.

In each of these passages, two disciples are quoting their mentor in diametrically opposed ways. This is the final form of *machlokess* to be recorded in the *Gemora*, which means that this *machlokess* endured, no retraction was made, and no grounds were found by which to reject the validity of either opinion. Both statements could not have been simultaneously heard by the two disciples and cannot be explained as a matter of properly placing quotation marks. Was there a reception problem among these Sages? How does the Rambam deal with this?

"I Have a Kabballa—מקובל אני"

Once again, we shall refer to the Rambam's commentary on the last *mishna* in *Aid'yos* (8:7)[20] to see his approach to such situations. We will see that when it is stated that someone "heard" or "said" something, it is not necessarily meant literally. It can mean that this was the *understanding* someone had of the facts, based upon his analysis of them.[21]

א״ר יהושע: „מקובל אני מרבן יוחנן בן זכאי, ששמע מרבו, ורבו מרבו, הלמ״ס, שאין אליהו בא . . . אלא לרחק המקורבין בזרוע, ולקרב המרוחקין בזרוע . . .".

ר׳ יהודה אומר: „לקרב, אבל לא לרחק.".

ר״ש אומר: „להשוות המחלוקת.".

וחכמים אומרים: „לא לרחק, ולא לקרב, אלא לעשות שלום בעולם.".

Rebbi Yehoshua said: "I have a *kabballa* from [my teacher] Rabban Yoḥonon ben Zakkai, who heard from his mentor, who heard from *his* mentor, in a chain of tradition going all the way back to Moses, that Elijah [the prophet] is coming only to thrust away those who are [unlawfully] close and to bring in those who are far away. . . . "

Rebbi Yehuda [Rebbi Yehoshua's student's student] said: "To bring in, but not to thrust away."

Rebbi Shimmon [a colleague of Rebbi Yehuda] said: "To straighten out disputes."

And the [majority of] Sages say: "Not to thrust away, and not to bring near, but to produce harmony in the world."

Here, Rebbi Yehoshua had definitely reported that he was told a fact by a most reliable source. Yet the rest of the Sages gave different

---

[20] This passage was already quoted in a previous chapter to demonstrate the Rambam's stand on *machlokess* regarding Sinaitic *halachos*.

[21] The very fact that there is a disagreement is the Talmud's way of revealing that the "quotations" are not verbatim.

opinions. Why didn't they accept his testimony? If they had proof to the contrary, why didn't he retract?

Fortunately, the Rambam himself comments on this *mishna*. This commentary is a key to understanding the Rambam's approach towards *machlokess* and conflicting reports of *kabballos*.

The Rambam states:

לא נשמע ממשה רבנו ע"ה זה הלשון. אבל שמע ממנו זה העניין לפי שמשה ספר
בביאת המשיח. ולשון התורה, "אם יהיה נדחך בקצה השמים וגו' ושב ה' אלקיך את
שבותך וגו' ומל ה' אלקיך וגו'" וזולת זה. והגיד להם ג'"כ מפי הגבורה בהקדמותיו
וסבותיו ושיקדים אותו האיש לישר לו הארץ והוא אליהו והודע להם שהאיש ההוא
לא יוסיף ולא יגרע בתורה אבל יסלק ויסיר החמסים בלבד. ואין בזה מחלוקת ולא
הכחשה. אבל נפלה המחלוקת ברעות שיסיר—מה הם.

This wording [that Rebbi Yehoshua stated] was not heard from Moshe *Rabbeynu*, ע"ה. However, the matter [in general] was heard from him, because Moshe described the coming of the Messiah . . . and that Elijah will precede him to straighten out the world for him . . . and with this there is no *machlokess* or denial. But *machlokess* did arise over just what evils he is going to eliminate.

All involved knew that Rebbi Yehoshua himself did not *mean* that he had a *kabballa* originating with Moshe *Rabbeynu* spelling out the improvements Elijah is to bring. The Talmud did not bother to explain this, because once we see the Sages arguing on a point, it becomes manifest that it was known not to be a *kabballa*. By determining the facts agreed to by all, we come closer to knowing what information was actually handed down to the protagonists.

When the Talmud states that someone "said" something, it can really mean that it is known, somehow—either by an explicit remark, or, as will be shown, by an analysis of his remarks or actions and any other evidence—that he was of that opinion. When there is a conflict of reports of what someone said, therefore, it is merely a dispute over what he must have *meant*, or what he *held*.

"אמר"—A Paraphrase, Not a Literal Quotation

The citation we brought used the words "מקובל אני, I received," as meaning, "this is how I understand." Likewise, a quotation complete with the introduction "אמר, he said," may not be a quotation at all, but an abstraction of a known opinion. For example, let us look at its use in *Yevomos* 18a:

רבן גמליאל אמר: אין זיקא, ומותר לבטל מצות יבמין. דתנן:

ר"ג אומר, אם מאנה—מאנה; ואם לא מאנה—תמתין עד שתגדיל ותצא הלזו משום
אחות אשה."'.

Rabban Gamliel said: [Prior to performing *yibbum*,[22] the widowed sister-in-law's marital relationship [with the surviving brother] is not yet established [and he does not yet gain the restrictions he would have as her husband. Therefore, if he chooses to marry her mother he does not transgress the prohibition of cohabitation with one's mother-in-law]. And it is permitted to [thereby] nullify his obligation to perform *yibbum* [by thus making her his step-daughter, forbidding her to him even through *yibbum*.]

[We know that Rabban Gamliel said this] because of a *mishna* that states: "[If one was married to a minor—which marriage is only of rabbinical status—and this minor happens to be the sister of his brother's wife, if his childless brother's wife dies, a *yibbum* situation is created. It is true that one may not perform *yibbum* with his own wife's sister; but here she is Biblically a *yibbum* candidate whereas his marriage is only of rabbinical status. Must he divorce his present wife to perform the Scriptural requirement?] Rabban Gamliel says [no]: 'If the minor wife decides not to remain tied to him [the prerogative of a minor wife], she may decide so [and he may then perform *yibbum* with his brother's wife.] Or, he can wait until his minor wife becomes an adult and allow his thusly-attained Biblical status of being her husband nullify the *mitzva* to perform *yibbum* with her sister.'"

[Thus we can see that Rabban Gamliel said, "Prior to performing *yibbum*, the widowed sister-in-law's marital relationship [with the surviving brother is not yet established, and it is permitted to nullify the *mitzva* of *yibbum*."

Here, even though it is stated that Rabban Gamliel "said," ",אין זיקה, ",ומותר לבטל מצות יבמין," the proof brought is a statement of his which did not contain those words at all. Those words were only the *Gemora's abstraction* of the concept behind Rabban Gamliel's decision.

---

[22] As explained once before, if someone dies leaving a childless widow, his brother has the *mitzva* to beget children with that widow, even though she is his sister-in-law, a relation with whom marriage is otherwise forbidden. This *mitzva* is called *yibbum*.

The Talmud itself sometimes points out that when an *Amora* "quotes" a teacher, he may merely be voicing his opinion about what his teacher holds. Indeed, the Talmud uses this fact to reconcile contradictory "quotations." Here is a passage from *Bava Metsia* 38b:[23]

איתמר: רבי אבא ברבי יעקב: אר׳יוחנן—הלכה כרשב״ג.

(ורבא אמר רב נחמן—הלכה כדברי חכמים.)

והא אמרה ר׳יוחנן חדא זימנא![24] דאמר רבה בר בר חנא: אר׳יוחנן: כל מקום ששנה רשב״ג במשנתנו, הלכה כמותו, חוץ מערב, וציידן, וּרְאָיָה אחרונה.

אמוראי נינהו, ואליבא דר׳יוחנן. (פרש״י: רבה אמר בכללא אר׳יוחנן, ור׳אבא אמר לאו בכללא אמר רבי יוחנן, אלא יש מהן שהלכה כמותו.)

A statement by an *Amora*: Rebbi Abba bar Rebbi Yaakov: Said Rebbi Yoḥonon: This *halacha* is as Rabban Shimmon ben Gamliel decided [and not as the other Sages].

But Rebbi Yoḥonon already once said [even more than] that! For Rabba bar bar Ḥanna said: Said Rebbi Yoḥonon: *Everywhere* Rabban Shimmon ben Gamliel appears in our *Mishna* . . . the *halacha* is as he decided.

The answer is that the two statements were made by different *Amoraim*, [variantly] *interpreting* Rebbi Yoḥonon.

Rashi explains:

Rabbah [bar bar Ḥanna] said that Rebbi Yoḥonon's blanket statement was meant to be taken as such, whereas Rebbi Abba [bar Rebbi Yaakov] said Rebbi Yoḥonon did not mean it to be a blanket statement and only meant that there are *some* mishnas where the *halacha* follows Rabban Shimmon ben Gamliel.

Despite the use of the word "אמר, said," by the two *Amoraim*, they were not really *quoting* Rebbi Yoḥonon, but giving their understanding of his statement.

This shows that an *Amora* may seem to be *quoting* someone, but

---

[23] Similar examples appear in *Shabbos* 5b; *Gittin* 38a, 75a; *Bava Kamma* 69a; *Bava Metsia* 38b; *Bava Bassra* 11a (re: Rabban Shimmon ben Gamliel), 108a; *Sanhedrin* 31a; *Bechoros* 24a.

[24] בכתובות הלשון: ומי אר׳יוחנן הכי (בהא לחודא—פרש״י)?

in reality is *paraphrasing* the authority according to his own under-standing. And another *Amora* may understand him differently, and therefore quote him differently. The *Gemora* does not always spell it out, as it did here. For it presumes the talmudic student's realization that no Sage "heard" differently from another. Our Sages were not such poor listeners.

"It Was Only Inferred—לאו בפירוש איתמר, אלא מכללא"

Moreover, we can find a presentation of a dispute over an issue, complete with each opponent's opinion delved into and developed, and yet the Talmud later may reveal that one of those opinions was never really voiced, only inferred, and really not held. The expres-sion used for this is: "לאו בפירוש איתמר, אלא מכללא, It was not stated explicitly, but inferred"—despite the original use of the word "אמר."

For example, a passage in *Bava Metsia* 36a begins:

אתמר: שומר שמסר לשומר—רב אמר פטור, ור׳יוחנן אמר חייב.

> A remark by an *Amora*: If damage occurs to an item that one was designated to guard, after he took the liberty of designating someone else to guard it[—is he responsible for the loss or not?]

> Rav said he is not responsible. Rebbi Yoḥonon said he is respon-sible.

It appears to be a very ordinarily formulated *machlokess*, which the *Gemora* goes on to develop quite elaborately:

אמר אביי: „לטעמיה דרב, לא מיבעיא שומר חנם כו׳ וכו׳, אלא אפי׳ כו׳ וכו׳;
לטעמיה דר׳יוחנן כו׳ וכו׳"

> Said Abbaye: "According to the principles to which Rav is herein subscribing, it is needless to say that his decision holds true for someone who was originally guarding the item without pay . . . but even etc., etc. According to the principles to which Rebbi Yoḥonon is herein subscribing . . ."

Yet the *Gemora* continues—

א״ר חסדא: „הא דרב לאו בפירוש איתמר אלא מכללא. דהנהו גינאי כו׳ וכו׳ ואתא
לקמיה דרב ופטריה. ומאן דחזא סבר משום שומר שמסר לשומר פטור (פרש״י: אחד
מן התלמידים ששמע מפיו דפטריה סבר שומר שמסר לשומר פטור כו׳). ולא היא.
שאני התם וכו׳."

Rav Ḥissda said: "That 'remark' by Rav was not heard verbatim, but was inferred. For something once happened . . . and the case came before Rav, and he absolved the defendant from payment. Someone (viz., one of his disciples—Rashi) who saw this *thought* that Rav decided as he did because he held that if a person who was appointed to guard something designated someone else to do it, his legal responsibility does not become greater than it was originally [so as to become responsible for loss or damage through unforeseeable circumstances]. But it is not so. This was a special case."

Clearly, the *Gemora* finds it quite acceptable to say that although a statement plainly says, "Rabbi So-and-so *said* such-and-such," it is not necessarily meant to be taken literally.[25]

Indeed, from the *Gemora's* perspective, as long as there is proof from some authority's decision that he follows a certain formula, it can be plainly stated that he "said" that he holds that formula. This is so even if that authority never in his life uttered that formula.

Even more: If the inference from a Sage's words or actions is compelling, the *Gemora* will question the need to point out that the "quotation" was not verbatim: "וכי מכללא, מאי?!, And if it was not said explicitly—what of it?!" In the words of Rashi (in *Ḥullin* 94a):

מה לנו אי אמר מכלל או בפירוש? הא מהא כללא שפיר שמעינן!

What is it to us if it was implicitly or explicitly stated? It is a good inference, regardless![26]

The Talmud expects those who study it to approach it with the assumption that its Sages operated intelligently and responsibly. We are expected to "read between the lines" and realize that passages reporting the outbreak of an enduring *machlokess* signal differences not in how authorities heard, misheard, or did not hear identical information but in how they analyzed it. The Rambam's telling complaint against those who reach false conclusions about the cause of *machlokos* was not that these people are ignorant of the Talmud but that they begin with a simplistic understanding of the statements they read and an unappreciative attitude towards the diligence, care and punctiliousness with which our Sages devoted their lives to preserving and understanding the word of G-d.

[25] See Additional Notes at the end of this chapter.
[26] See Additional Notes at the end of this chapter.

Additional Notes to Chapter 7

1. אבל מי שיחשוב שהדינין שנחלקין בהם כמו כן מקובלים מפי משה, וחושבים שנפלה
המחלוקת מדרך טעות ההלכות או השכחה או שאחד מהם קבל קבלה אמת והשני טעה בקבלתו
או שכח או לא שמע מפי רבו כל מה שצריך לשמוע . . . זה דבר מגונה מאד. והוא דברי מי
שאין לו שכל ואין בידו עיקרים. ופוגם אשר נתקבלו מהם המצוות. וכל זה שוא ובטל.

Some may think that the laws that were disputed [Hebrew: שנחלקין בהם]
were also received from Moses' lips. They may conjecture that disagreements arose due to error about the *halachos* or lack of retention:
that one of the disputants received the teaching (*kabbala*) correctly,
whereas the other erred in his receiving it, forgot [what he was taught]
or did not hear all that was necessary from his teacher. . . . This is a
very repugnant thing to say. These are words of senseless people who
do not understand matters of basic principle, and such words besmirch
the people from whom we received the commandments. The entire
conjecture is less than worthless. (*Introduction to the Talmud*, Hebrew
p. 14, English pp. 88-89.)

3. אבל מה שאמרו „משרבו תלמידי שמאי והלל שלא שמשו כל צרכם רבתה מחלוקת בישראל"
ענין זה מבואר: . . . כאשר רפתה שקידת התלמידים על החכמה ונחלשה סברתם נגד סברת הלל
ושמאי ובהם נפלה מחלוקת ביניהם בעיון על דברים רבים שסברת כל אחד ואחד מהם היתה לפי
שכלו ומה שיש בידו מן העקרים. . . . ועל דרכים האלו נפלה המחלוקת; לא מפני שטעו
בהלכות ושהאחד אומר אמת והשני שקר.

As for their statement (*Sanhedrin* 88b), "From the time that the students
of Shammai and Hillel increased, who did not attend [their teachers] as
much as was necessary, *machlokess* increased in Israel," the meaning is
clear: When the disciples' scholastic diligence was enfeebled and their
reasoning abilities grew weak compared to those of Hillel and Shammai,
machlokess arose among them in the analysis of many things. For each
one's reasoning ability was in accordance with his mind and the axioms
he possessed. . . . This is how *machlokess* arose—not because they erred
about the *halachos*, and that one was telling the truth and the other a
falsehood (*Introduction to the Talmud*, Heb. pp. 15-16, Eng. p. 89).

We may add that this decrease in analytical skills was largely a factor
of historical circumstances: the increased persecution, expulsions and
executions under the Romans. (*Rashi* on *Bava Metsia* 33b, *Iggeress Rab
Sherira Gaon*, and the Rambam's *Introduction* to his *Mishneh Torah*.)
The Rambam is quick to add that the deficiency was not so great as to
make their conclusions less profound. We are only speaking, he reminds
us, of their skills as compared to those of Shammai and Hillel.

5. The *Ritva* explains the meaning of the word "בדותא" in *Bava Metsia* 71b
by quoting *Rashi*:

„פרש"י: ,לא אמרה רב אשי מעולם; אלא אחד מתלמידיו אמרה מעצמו, או דמשמע מכללא
וטעה, ובדאוה על שמו.''

''Rav Ashi never said it. One of his disciples said it in his own name, or
inferred it from something Rav Ashi said, and people concocted the idea
that Rav Ashi actually said it.'' He then adds, ''וכן הלשון הזה מתפרש בכמה
מקומות, and so can this expression be explained in many places.''

See also *Bava Metsia* 9a, where the word used is ''ברותא,'' with a 'ר in
place of the 'ד. A marginal note cites the ערוך as explaining, ''פי' במקום שטעו
חכמים ולא דברו כהלכה לא רצה לגנותם ולומר טעו אלא אמרו ברותא היא כלומר דעת חיצונות
היא—ערוך ערך בר ד'., Where the Sages erred, the Talmud did not want to deni-
grate them by declaring that they erred, and therefore it said, it is ברותא,
from the root 'בר, outside,' which means that they were reporting an un-
accepted opinion.''

7. *Rosh Hashonna* 30a:

משנה: התקין רבן יוחנן בן זכאי כו'.

גמ': רב נחמן בר יצחק אמר, ,,רבן יוחנן בן זכאי בשיטת רבי יהודה אמרה ... ''
והא מפליג פליג עליה! דתנן (סוכה מ"א., מנחות ס"ח.), ... התקין רבן יוחנן בן זכאי כו'.
א"ר יהודה, ,,והלא מן התורה הוא ... דכתיב כו'."
התם רבי יהודה הוא דקא טעי. איהו סבר ריב"ז מדרבנן קאמר. ולא היא. מדאורייתא קאמר ...
מאי ,,התקין"—דרש והתקין.

MISHNA: Rabban Yoḥonon ben Zakkai decreed a *takkonna* . . .
GEMORA: Rav Nachman bar Yitschak said: He was interpreting a
Scriptural verse in accordance with the *halachic* position Rebbi Yehuda
was later to maintain.
[The *Gemora* objects to Rav Nachman's statement:] How could that be?
Rebbi Yehuda disputed Rabban Yoḥonon ben Zakkai on this point, for
another *mishna* states, ''Rabban Yoḥonon ben Zakkai decreed, etc. But
Rebbi Yehuda objected: It is a Scriptural law [and not a rabbinical *takkonna*, decree]!''
[The Gemora answers:] Rebbi Yehuda was mistaken. He thought Rabban Yoḥonon ben Zakkai meant to enact a *rabbinical* decree [since the
mishna used the term ''התקין, he decreed,'' to describe it]. But that was
not so. The *mishna*, too, was speaking on the Scriptural level. Rabban
Yoḥonon *darshonned* the law, and [by the word ''התקין,'' the *mishna*
merely meant that he] ''decreed'' upon Jewry the fact that due to new
circumstances the Scriptural law again applied.

25. Using the cross-references printed in the *Gemora's* margins (מסורת
הש"ס), I compiled a list of no less than 22 times that the *Gemora Bavli*
itself points out that a reported statement was not made explicitly, but
inferred. Four of those 22 times refer to a passage that read, ''אתמר: רב
אמר כה וכה'' (all four, incidentally, actually concerning רב) and six con-

cern a passage that plainly read, "אמר ר' פלוני כה וכה." There is no difference whether the passage is introduced by the word "אתמר, It was
stated by a talmudic authority" or "אמר, So-and-so said." The remark
can still be an individual's wording based upon his opinion of an
authority's stand, and not a verbatim quote of that authority. Also,
there is no difference in this respect whether the "quotation" is introduced by the words, "א״ר פלוני משום פלוני, Rav So-and-so said in the
name of So-and-so" or simply "אר' פלוני א״ר פלוני כה וכה, Rav So-and-so
said that Rav So-and-so said." Only Rashi in Ḥullin 113a explains
that "משום, in the name of," is used when the quote came second-hand,
not directly from the source named, and the רש״ש there points out difficulties with this comment. *Tosefos*, in *Brachos* 34a (ד״ה אמצעית) and in
Ḥullin 14a (ד״ה אר'הונא), and the *Rashbam* in *Bava Bassra* 114b offer
other distinctions between "אמר פלוני" and "אמר פלוני משום פלוני."

Three times we find it recorded that ר' זירא asked ר' יעקב בר אידי if
what he stated in the name of ר' יהושע בן לוי was heard explicitly, and we
also find ר' יוסף questioning רבה בר בר כהנה the same way about his quote
of ר' יוחנן.

26. This can help solve a problem: Rebbi Eliezer is praised (*Succa* 27b,
28a) because "לא אמר דבר שלא שמע מפי רבו לעולם, He never said anything
he did not hear from his mentor." What is so praiseworthy about this?
The function of *Tannaim* and *Amoraim* was not merely to parrot what
they learned, but to analyze, to מדמה מילתא למילתא, to apply their learning to new situations and to teach their discoveries to the people (והא,
כל התורה כולה דמויי מדמינן ליה!"—ב״ב ק״ל:, וסוטה כ., רש״י ד״ה והדר אתא לקמיה
סברא למיסבר (דר״ע). Someone who merely knew how to repeat past teachings was considered dangerous (שמורין . . . התנאים מבלי עולם הן—סוטה כ״ב.
משנתן הלכה מתוך). Furthermore, we *do* find Rebbi Eliezer voicing his own
opinion (מהרש״א על יומא ס״ו:, ועי' ב״מ פ״ב:, רבי אליעזר אומר . . . ותמיה אני כו',
(ומ״מ לא היה זה בדבר פסק הלכה.

An answer comes from *Rabbeynu Yona* who, commenting on the
Ryf (*Brachos* 27b), explains that the meaning of "האומר דבר שלא שמע מפי
רבו, one who says something not in the name of his *rebbi*," is: one who
states something in his *rebbi's name* which he had not actually heard
from him. Perhaps this was what Rebbi Eliezer avoided in the extreme,
and from all that has been shown above, we can see that this was
indeed unique and praiseworthy in its own way, eliminating any confusion that might be caused by the principle of "ואי מכללא, מאי?," practiced by the other Sages.

Chapter 8

Making Room for Analysis—and Error

Since, in general, *machlokess* developed because a teacher's remarks could be taken in more than one way, we remain with a fundamental question: Why didn't the Sages always spell out exactly what they meant and leave no question about their intentions?

Teaching Through Brevity

To answer this question, another very basic principle must be introduced. The Sages—in accordance with the dictum (*Pesahim* 3b and *Hullin* 63b) "לעולם ישנה אדם לתלמידו דרך קצרה, One must always instruct his disciple in a succinct way"—spoke as concisely as possible. Brevity not only saves time, but it also facilitates quicker manipulation of the facts by the listener, which makes for more efficient thinking. The scholars listening in to the lectures were capable of filling in unspoken details through context and prerequisite information.

For example, once a speaker defined his terms, he would continue to refer to his concepts in concise "code words."[1] This is a

---

[1] See *Bava Metsia* 64a, quoted in Addendum IV, in which after the initial description of the case, Rav proceeded to refer to it by the word "קרי," and the listeners were expected to understand his reference.

normal and necessary procedure that is common to all fields of
endeavor. Each profession and pastime has its own jargon, which
takes involved ideas and converts them into short units of speech. In
everyday discussion we immediately recognize meanings in sentences which in a literal sense are cryptic, and fellow tradesmen com-
municate to each other with terms that to others sound foreign.
("Turn on the juice!" says one electrician to another.) The computer
revolution has certainly introduced single words that stand for concepts previously needing full sentences to convey. Similarly, the
Sages intentionally left it to their able students to fill in the details of
remarks that to others would seem entirely unfathomable.

אמר רב חסדא, „הא מילתא מגברא רבה שמיע לי—ומנו, רבי אמי: ,לא אסרו כלה
אלא מפני כלה.' . . . השתא סברתה מדעתי: לא אסרו כלת בתו אלא משום כלת בנו"
(יבמות כ"א).

Rav Ḥissda said, "I heard the following statement from a great
man—namely, Rebbi Ahmmi: 'They prohibited [a man from
marrying] a daughter-in-law [after the death of her husband]
only as a precaution against [him marrying] a daughter-in-law.'
. . . For now, I will explain it according to my own analysis:
They prohibited a man from marrying his *daughter's* daughter-
in-law as a precaution against his marrying his *son's* daughter-
in-law" (Yevomos 21b).

Similarly, the Sages intentionally consigned to their students the
task to determine whether a statement was meant to be taken un-
equivocally or in a modified way, literally or figuratively. As long as
a teacher thought his disciples might *possibly* be able to discover the
proper understanding of a matter, he might refrain from explaining
it to them, as in this passage:

קתני עולין לו מן המנין. משום דיצא—חל עליה נזירות?! אמר שמואל, „כגון כו'."
אמרו ליה רב כהנא ורב אסי לרב, „מאי טעמא לא מפרשת לן כהלין מילי?" אמר
להון, „אמינא דלמא לא צריכיתו" (נזיר י"ט.).

Shmuel explained a certain *mishna*. Rav Kahana and Rav Assi
asked Rav [Shmuel's contemporary], "What is the reason you
did not explain this to us in this way?" He answered them, "I
thought perhaps you would not need me to" (Nazir 19a).

Nevertheless, although the lecturer might hope that his disciples could decipher his intents, he also expected them to ask for clarification if necessary:

תני רב יוסף כו' א"ל אביי „עד האידנא מאי טעמא לא פריש לן מר?"

א"ל, „לא הוה ידענא דצריכי ליה, ומי בעיתו מינאי מילתא ולא אמר לכו?!"[2]
(סנהדרין י: ומגילה כ"ג.).

Rav Yosef stated a teaching. Abbaye (his disciple) asked him, "What is the reason the teacher did not explain this to us until now?"

He answered him, "I did not know you needed me to. Have you ever asked me anything without me answering you?" (*Sanhedrin* 10b, *Megilla* 23a).

Another Advantage of Brevity: Honing the Mind

Teaching through brevity also sharpens the minds of the listeners by forcing them to utilize all their mental acumen. Indeed, the goal of developing the mental abilities of their students was one of the reasons some lecturers kept their ideas as cryptic as possible. The correct understanding of a teaching could become a challenge and a matter of competition to the listening scholars, and the one who would succeed in "cracking" the puzzle was praised:

יתיב רב יוסף קמיה דרב המנונא ויתיב רב המנונא וקאמר, „כשם שאין הבנים יורשין
אלא מן הקרקע, כך אין הבנות ניזונית אלא מן הקרקע."

אוש עליה כולי עלמא (דסבורים שסתם ירושה קאמר, שאין הבנים יורשין
מטלטלין—ע"פ פרש"י) [וסבורין דקאמר דמי] דשביק ארעא הוא דירתי ליה
בָּנֵיהּ; דלא שביק אראע לא ירתי ליה בָּנֵיהּ.

א"ל ר' יוסף, „ודלמא כתובת בנין דכרין קאמר מר."

אמר ליה: „מר דגברא רבא [אולי צ"ל רבה] הוא ידע מאי קאמינא!" (כתובות נ:).

Rav Yosef was seated before Rav Homnuna, and Rav Homnuna stated: "Just as sons inherit only real estate, likewise unmarried daughters receive support only from the sale of real estate."

All those present shouted at him [for they thought he was referring to a standard inheritance and was saying that male children clearly do not inherit movables and] that . . . one without land cannot bequeath anything to his sons.

Rav Yosef said to him, "Perhaps the teacher is referring to the portion the sons get of their widowed or divorced mother's bestowal?"[3]

Rav Homnuna replied to him, "[That is precisely what I was referring to!] He who is a great man understands what I mean!" (*Kesubos* 50b).

Taking Pains to Avoid False Teaching

Despite the mind-honing value of being cryptic, however, when the Sages recognized that their words or actions had a good chance of permanently misleading others, they took pains to avoid misunderstandings. A number of passages relate how Sages considered desisting from actions above and beyond the requirements of the law if there was a fear that onlookers would think that such practices were mandatory. One example is the following incident related in *Pesachim* (100a):

„מפסיקין לשבתות"—דברי רבי יהודה.

רבי יוסי אומר, „אין מפסיקין."

ומעשה ברשב״ג ורבי יוסי שהיו מסובין בעכו וקדש עליהם היום. א״ל רשב״ג לר' יוסי, „נפסיק וניחוש לדברי יהודה חבירנו?" . . . „לא נפסוק, שמא יראו התלמידים ויקבעו הלכה לדורות."

אמרו, „לא זזו משם עד שקבעו הלכה כר' יוסי."

"[Even those in the midst of a meal on Friday evening before *Shabbos*, and *Shabbos* is approaching], should terminate the meal and recite *Kiddush*."—The words of Rebbi Yehuda.

Rebbi Yosay says, "They must not terminate."

Once, in Acco, Rabban Shimmon ben Gamliel and Rebbi Yosay were having a meal and Shabbos was approaching. Rabban Shimmon ben Gamliel said to Rebbi Yosay: "Shall we terminate in deference to the opinion of Yehuda, our colleague?"

---

[3] That is, the monetary gains the mother was promised in her marriage contract in the event of her becoming widowed or divorced.

"... We must not terminate the meal, lest the disciples seeing this establish it as the *halacha* for posterity!"

They did not move from there until they established it [clearly] that the *halacha* follows Rebbi Yosay's opinion.

Despite the proper desire to honor a colleague's opinion, the overriding concern is to refrain from misleading posterity regarding the *halacha*.[4]

Keeping Disciples "on Their Toes:" Providing Intentionally False Information

Nevertheless, some Sages' methods of presentation were particularly challenging for their students. They intentionally said or did things *incorrectly* to see if their *talmidim* would catch them in their "mistake."[5] The phrase the *Gemora* uses for this approach is: "לחדד בו את התלמידים, to sharpen with it the [wits of the] students."[6] Of course, this method is valuable only for advanced scholars.

ההוא דנחית קמיה דרבה ואמר, "אתה חסת על קן צפור, אתה חוס ורחם עלינו." אמר רבה, "כמה ידע האי צורבא מרבנן לרצויי למריה!"

א"ל אביי, "והא, ,משתקין אותו' תנן!" ורבה נמי לחדודי לאביי הוא דבעי (ברכות ל"ג: ומגילה כה.).

Someone was praying and said, "You had mercy upon the bird [by commanding that she be chased away before one takes her egg or chick from the nest (*D'varim* 22:6)]. May you have mercy and pity on us!" Rabbah said, "How [well] this scholar knows to pray to his Master!"

---

[4] See also *Kesubos* 50b, *Brachos* 11a, *Yerushalmi Brachos* 10:1.

[5] See *Ohr Yisroel*, a collection of Reb Yisroel Salanter's teachings, p. 37 in the Vilna, תר"ס edition: "וכבר התירו חז"ל לומר לפעמים דבר שאינו לפי האמת, כדי לחדד את התלמידים שיתנו לב להשיב, Our Sages have gone so far as to permit, at times, saying something untrue, to sharpen the [wits of the] students [by encouraging them] to be prepared to challenge."

[6] "לחדד בו את התלמידים" appears in eight locations: The two in which the passage to be quoted in the text appears (*Brachos* 33b and *Megilla* 25a), *Eruvin* 13a (concerning Rabbi Akiva), *Nazir* 59b (where Rabbi Yehoshua is speaking to his disciples), *Zevachim* 13a (Rav Huna to his disciples), *Ḥullin* 43b (Rabbah to Abbaye), *Needa* 4b (again, Rabbah to Abbaye) and *ibid.* 45a (concerning Rabbi Akiva).

Abbaye said to him, "But the *Mishna* states, 'Silence anyone who prays thus!'"

And indeed Rabbah meant only to sharpen Abbaye (*Brachos* 33b, *Megilla* 29a).

In another case (*Ḥullin* 43b), Rabbah "tested" Abbaye by an *action* he performed:

ההוא ספק דרוסה דאתאי לקמיה דרבה, הוה קא בדיק ליה רבה לוושט מאבראי.

א"ל אביי, „והא מר הוא דאמר וושט אין לו בדיקה אלא מבפנים!"

אפכיה רבה ובדקיה, ואישתכח עליה ב' קורטי דמא וטרפה. ורבה נמי לחדודי לאביי הוא דבעי.

[There was a question whether an animal had been clawed before slaughter, a situation which would render the meat unkosher.] The perhaps-clawed animal was brought before Rabbah for examination, and he began to examine the esophagus from the outside.

Abbaye said to him, "But the teacher himself taught that the esophagus can only be examined from the *inside* in order to find a flaw!"

Rabbah examined it by turning it inside out, found two drops of blood, and declared it unkosher.

And indeed, Rabbah only meant to sharpen Abbaye.

This approach was commonly practiced by many of our Sages even when speaking in the lecture halls of their academies. It demanded, on the part of the attending scholars, a perfect mastery of the Oral Law as handed down until then.[7] In *Zevachim* 12b-13a, "לחדד בו את התלמידים, to sharpen with it [the wits of] the disciples," is said of a lecturer, Rav Huna, who first declared that a *Tanna's* source for a *halacha* was a *k'ra yesayra*.[8] Objections are raised, answers are given, but finally the assertion is refuted. "Rather" ("אלא"), the passage continues, the source was a *kal v'homer*.[9] This, too, is repudiat-

---

[7] See Additional Notes at the end of this chapter.

[8] *K'ra yesayra*: A word or phrase in Scripture superfluous for conveying the plain meaning of the verse, indicating an additional teaching.

[9] *Kal V'homer*: The rule of *kal v'homer*, weak and powerful, works with the logic that if the mandate assigned by the Torah to a subject can be attributed to a certain

ed, after a series of objections and defenses. Finally, the *Gemora* declares that the only known source for the *Tanna* was a teaching going back two centuries to the time of Yavneh. He had no scriptural verse with which to back it up.

Why then, the *Gemora* asks, did Rav Huna originally declare that there *was* a scriptural indication for this *halacha*? It answers, "To sharpen [the wits of] the disciples." Rashi explains: "So that they should raise an objection against his remark."[10] (Evidently, the *Gemora's* anonymous objectors to Rav Huna's assertion were the disciples attending his lecture.)[11]

Rebbi Mayir (in whose name was said the adage, "One must always instruct his disciple in a succinct way")[12] was a student of Rabbi Akiva, one of those who purposely reported the wrong decision for a given situation.[13] Rebbi Mayir himself became so proficient in defending the wrong side of an issue that his own colleagues found his true thoughts unfathomable (*Eruvin* 13b). As a matter of fact, his contemporaries did not establish as *halacha* the opinions expressed by Rebbi Mayir precisely for this reason. Since he used this method, most[14] could not be certain that they could identify his true thoughts (ibid).

---

property of that subject, things with a higher degree of that property should certainly be assigned that mandate. The logic is the same as the following: If a weak man can lift a certain weight, certainly (*kal v'homer*) a stronger man can. An objection that introduces another criterion ("maybe the strong man has a pain in his back") is called a פירכא, *peerḥa*.

[10] Here Rashi gives a second explanation of the phrase "לחדד בו את התלמידים," different from the explanation used everywhere else: So that they should master the science of *darshonning kal va'homers*. The *Gemora* had also given an optional answer that defends Rav Huna's *kal v'homer* against the objections that were raised.

[11] This sheds light on all similar passages where a Sage makes a statement, anonymous objections are raised, and the *Gemora* says, "אלא אמר כו׳, rather, he [really] said etc., etc." Is the *Gemora* saying that the Sage expressed himself incorrectly, or that he changed his mind? No. The Sage's original misstatement was intentionally propounded as a test for his disciples, and the conclusion was his actual opinion all along.

[12] *Pesachim* 4b, *Ḥullin* 63b.

[13] *Eruvin* 13a, *Needa* 45a. Perhaps this is why Rebbi Mayir was at first unable to follow Rabbi Akiva's lectures (*Eruvin* 13a), and changed over to Rabbi Yishmael's Academy, to return to Rabbi Akiva's Academy later (*ibid.*).

[14] I say "most" because eventually Rebbi Yehuda HaNassi (of a later generation) generally established Rebbi Mayir's version of *halacha* as the anonymously, authoritatively stated *mishnayos*. See Additional Notes at the end of this chapter.

High Expectations

If students failed to realize when to take remarks beyond their surface meaning, the lecturer sometimes voiced disapproval, as in this case in *Zevachim* (62a):

מדת ארכו [דמזבח] ומדת רחבו ומדת קומתו אין מעכבין. אמר ר׳ מני: „ובלבד שלא
יפחתנו ממזבח שעשה משה.״ וכמה? אמר רב יוסף: „אמה.״

אחיכו [מחכו] עליה, „„חמש אמות ארך וחמש אמות רוחב רבוע יהיה המזבח״״!

א״ל אביי, „דלמא מקום מערכה קאמר מר.״

א״ל, „מר דגברא רבה הוא ידע מאי קאמינא.״ קרי עלייהו בני קטורה (פרש״י: בני
אברהם אתם, אבל לא כזרע יצחק ויעקב)!

The physical dimensions given for the Altar for Offerings are only the ideal. Said R' Manni: "As long as the Altar is no smaller than the one that Moses made." And what is that size? Rav Yosef said: "One [square] *amoh.*"

They ridiculed him. "[The Torah clearly states,] 'The Altar shall be five square *ahmos*!' "

Abbaye said to him, "Perhaps the teacher is referring to the area on the Altar where the firewood is arranged?"

He replied, "[That is precisely what I was referring to!] He who is a Great Man understands what I mean." And he called the others, "Sons of Ketura." (Rashi: You are descendents of Avraham, but not like his [superior, Jewish] descendents [through Sarah], Yitzchak and Yaakov!)

"Why Not Be Clear?"

All this was meant to train the scholars in quick, deep, and profound reasoning and in mastering the sources. The goal of learning Torah is not merely to know the answers to questions, but even more important, to master the methods of arriving at them. This was accomplished through the system of honing the mind through intellectual battle. So integral is this pursuit for the perpetuation of Torah, it was intentionally employed even at the risk of *halachic* error. Similarly, even after the Talmud was put in writing, its language was kept terse so that it cannot be understood without elaboration. It is up to the students of the Talmud to supply that elaboration through their mastering its style of intimations and the sources it hints to. If the Talmud's laws were all exhaustively spelled out in all their details, relieving scholars of the necessity to apply constant effort to understand them, no doubt such an "encyclopedia" would soon find its permanent place on a dusty bookshelf, "always available" for consultation, but unused and forgotten. In the long run, the intellectual efforts that go into understanding the Torah's laws serve the purpose of preserving those laws better than would a code of hard and fast rules.

Machlokess

Thus, this pedagogic method opened the door to *machlokos*, when both the lecturer and his scholarly audience thought that the remark was understood, whereas in reality not all understood it the same way. If someone's true intention was not ascertained and recorded while he was still alive, then a *machlokess* concerning it could endure forever.

Determining the Correct Version

On the other hand, the scholars, numbering in the thousands and thoroughly preoccupied with these teachings, discussed them constantly and exhaustively, to ascertain their correct versions and meanings. Premium attention was paid to those disciples known to constantly verify their impressions with the teacher, as is demonstrated in *Brachos* 38b:

דרש רב נחמן . . . „עולא משמיה דרבי יוחנן אמר: ,שלקות—מברכין עליהן שהכל נהיה בדברו'."

. . . אמר ר' חייא בר אבא, „א"ר יוחנן: שלקות—מברכין עליהן בורא פרי האדמה."

ור' בנימין בר יפת, „א"ר יוחנן: שלקות—מברכין עליהן שהכל נהיה בדברו."

אמר רב נחמן בר יצחק: „עולא לשבשתיה כר' בנימין בר יפת."

תהי בה ר' זירא (פרש"י: במחלוקת זו שהוזכרה בבית המדרש): „וכי מה ענין ר' בנימין בר יפת אצל ר'חייא בר אבא (במחלוקת בית מדרש)?! (הרי אין ר'בנימין כדאי לחלוק עליו!) רבי חייא בר אבין דייק וגמיר שמעתא מר' יוחנן רביה, ורבי בנימין לא דייק; ועוד, רבי חייא בר אבא כל תלתין יומין מהדר תלמודיה קמיה דר' יוחנן רביה, ור' בנימין לא מהדר!"

Rav Nachman taught: ". . . Ula said in Rebbi Yoḥonon's name:

'[The formula of] the blessing said before eating boiled vegetables is *shehakol* . . .'"[15]

[Now, there is an earlier dispute over Rebbi Yoḥonon's opinion:]

Rebbi Ḥeeya bar Abba said: "Rebbi Yoḥonon said that for boiled vegetables we say *boray p'ri ha'adomma.*"

Rebbi Binyamin bar Yeffes said: "Rebbi Yoḥonon said that for boiled vegetables we say *shehakol* . . ."

Rav Nachman bar Yitzchak said: "Ula's version [of Rebbi Yoḥonon] was confused, based upon the [confused] teaching of Rebbi Binyamin bar Yeffes [cited in the above paragraph]."

Rebbi Zeyra expressed astonishment (Rashi: that this dispute was even mentioned in the Academy): "How can anyone compare Rebbi Binyamin bar Yeffes to Rebbi Ḥeeya bar Abba?! Rebbi Ḥeeya bar Abba was meticulous in learning directly from Rebbi Yoḥonon, his teacher,[16] whereas Rebbi Binyamin bar Yeffes was not so meticulous. Furthermore, Rebbi Ḥeeya bar Abba would review his learning together with his teacher, Rebbi Yoḥonon, every thirty days,[17] whereas Rebbi Binyamin bar Yeffes did not follow this practice."

The Solidity of the Oral Law

Thus, despite occasional errors by individuals, the accuracy of the Oral Law and *halachic* reports has been preserved remarkably well. Hundreds and sometimes thousands of scholars attended and analyzed the lectures, and centuries of research were spent checking for the correct versions and meanings of *halachic* teachings before they were recorded in the Talmud for posterity. Thus have we been provided with the most authentic versions and meanings of *halachic* statements that are humanly possible. This is true of teachings

---

[15] I.e., the "universal" blessing for food, blessing the One "through Whose Word everything came into being" and not specifying the food's origin. A vegetable's blessing is normally בורא פרי האדמה, blessing the One Who "creates the produce of the ground." If boiling a vegetable changes its nature enough, the blessing should no longer identify the food as something that "grew out of the earth."

[16] See *Pesachim* 52b.

[17] See *Ḥullin* 86b, *K'ressos* 27a.

whose version or meaning have suffered variant interpretations and all the more so of teachings whose interpretations enjoy unanimous agreement.

It is important to understand the solidity of the conclusions presented in the Talmud. It is often unappreciated because students compare the open-ended possibilities raised in the Talmud to the apparently hard-and-fast textbook facts presented to them in other disciplines, and conclude that the ideas in the Talmud are relatively dubious. But the firmness of the textbook presentations is illusionary. The truth is that they simply gloss over disputes among their authorities and work with unverified assumptions, whereas the Talmud openly discusses the questions that arise. The final results set down in our Talmud are undoubtedly the most rigorously analyzed and clarified representations of ideas in history. We can proudly proclaim that, more than any other body of knowledge that man has attempted to fathom: ''מצות ה' ברה מאירת עינים, The commandment of Hashem is clear, enlightening the eyes!'' (T'hillim 19:9).

Additional Notes to Chapter 8

7. This may be the thought behind the *Midrash Rabbah* on *Kohelles* 1:8 (no. 5) which states:

כל הדברים יגיעים: אפי' דברי תורה מגיעין את האדם: בתחילה אדם נכנס ללמוד תורה והן מטהרין לו את הטמא ומטמאין טת הטהור והוא אינו יודע שכל מה שהן מתישין בהן כחו סוף שהוא מוציא מוציא קלות וחמורות וגזרות שוות וטומאה וטהרה ואיסור והיתר.

"All things strain [a person]" (*Kohelless* 1:8). Even Torah matters strain a person. At first a person enters to learn Torah and they declare to him that impure things are pure and that pure things are impure, and he doesn't realize that after all their weakening him he will be able to produce laws of the pure and impure through *kal v'homers* and *gezayros shavvos*.

But this may merely mean that a novice can get confused over the הוה אמינות produced by intermediate steps of logic which show that which he knows to be *tahor* to be otherwise. Indeed, the commentators on the *Midrash Rabbah* (פי' מהרז"ו ופי' מנחת כהונה) explain the passage to be referring to the novice's wrong opinions being corrected.

14. Rebbi Yehuda HaNassi generally established Rebbi Mayir's version of *halacha* as the anonymously, authoritatively stated *mishnayos*:

סתם משנה הוא מה שהסכים עליו דעת רבים והשתוה עיונם בו ולא נפלה בו מחלוקת או
שיקבלוהו רבים מפי רבים עד משה . . . והמקבל הקרוב שנתיחס אליו המאמר הוא ר״מ. וזה
ענין שאמרו סתם משנה רבי מאיר. אלא במקצת סתומות שאפשר שהם לר״מ לבדו ועליו
מחלוקת או יהיו לאיש אחר חוץ מר״מ והתלמוד יבאר אותו (הקדמת הרמב״ם לפירושו
למשניות, בסופו, "הפרק הששי").

An anonymously authored *mishna* contains either that which the
Sages agreed to through analysis . . . or that which they received from
the preceding bodies of Sages dating from Moses. . . . The most recent
authority to Rebbi Yehuda HaNassi in possession of such a teaching
was Rebbi Mayir, and this is what is meant by "An anonymous *mishna* is by Rebbi Mayir." However, some anonymously authored *mishnas* may represent Rebbi Mayir's individual stand with which others
disagree, or it may be by someone other than Rebbi Mayir, whom the
Gemora will identify (*Maimonides' Introduction to the Talmud*, p.
200).

Chapter 9

Disciples Disagreeing With Their Mentors

W e have seen that the opinions voiced by the Sages were often only repetitions of the teachings of their mentors and mentors' mentors. But did disciples ever disagree with their teachers practically, or even academically? The answer is, yes, and this is said without ignoring the dictum (*Sanhedrin* 110a), "כל החולק על רבו כחולק על השכינה, Whoever differs with his *rebbi* is virtually differing with G-d."

Tosefos vs. Rashi

The permission to differ with one's *rebbi* is clearly demonstrated by the many times that the *Baaley Tosefos* disagreed with their grandfather and teacher, *Rashi*.[1] They constantly bombard *Rashi's*

---

[1] The *Rashbam* (ר' שמואל בן מאיר) and *Rabbeynu Tahm* (ר' יעקב בן מאיר) were the grandsons of Rashi, through his son-in-law, Rebbi Mayir ben Shmuel. The latter had become Rashi's disciple after studying with the Sages of Lorraine. After marrying Rashi's daughter he left for Germany to study under *Rabbeynu Yitzchak Ha-Levy*, who also had been one of Rashi's teachers. Together with Rashi's main teacher, *Rabbeynu Yaakov ben Yakar*, Rabbeynu Halevy had been a student of *Rabbeynu Gershon*, "Light of the Exile." Basically, then, the learning of the *Baaley Tosefos*, Rashbam and Rabbeynu Tahm, as well as Rashi's, was based on the teachings of *Rabbeynu Gershon*. The ר"י, *Rabbeynu Yitzchak of Dampierre* (דנפיר), was Rashi's great-grandson.

explanations with contradictions and offer other explanations
instead.[2] Far from forsaking their tradition, by questioning the
analysis of their teachers they were very much following the tradition of Jewish learning: One may not deny facts that are proven to
originate with Hashem and Moses. But if the assertion of one's rebbi
is based upon his *analysis* of information to which the disciple has
equal access, then the disciple may contest it.

Rashi vs. Gaonim

Rashi himself will at times disagree with his teachers, and even with
Gaonim. For example, in *Kesubos* 3a (also *Gittin* 33a and *Yevomos*
90b), Rashi finds the explanation taught by his teachers untenable
and therefore rejects it in favor of his own, original explanation:

שמעתי כל רבותי מפרשים (בגיטין: מרבותי קבלתי) דקדיש בכספא דקידושי דרבנן
נינהו. ואי אפשר לומר כן. . . . על כרחך צריך אתה לפרש כמו שפרשתי (בגיטין:
בכל מקום מלבי).

All my teachers explain that the attainment of marriage through
presenting the bride with something of value (e.g., a ring) is a
rabbinical enactment, since this procedure is not explicitly mentioned in the Torah, but is derived through a *drash*. But this is
impossible (*Gittin*: but there are strong contradictions against
such an understanding). You must explain the passage as I have
(*Gittin*: on my own).

In *Yevomos* (90b) Rashi describes the rejected explanation as a
"טעות גדול, a great mistake."

The explanation Rashi *received from his teachers* was the one
used by the Rambam and was evidently the explanation given by the
previous generations of *Gaonim*. Still, he rejects it in favor of his
own original explanation.

Sages of the Talmud Disputing Their Rebbeim

It is no different when we come to *Tannaim* or *Amoraim*. Later

---

[2] True, the differences between *Tosefos* and Rashi may hinge on points more subtle
than they appear at first. But ultimately *Tosefos* is disagreeing with Rashi over
something.

authorities regularly dispute the earlier ones of their era. A simple
fact will make this obvious: One of the rules of *p'sak* is that אזלינן בתר
בתרא, we follow the most recent of authorities when there is a dispute
among them,[3] ואפילו בתלמיד ורבו, and even if the later authority is a
disciple of the earlier one. (*Why* this is so is not pertinent to this discussion. But the fact that there is a rule about whom to follow in an
argument between a *rebbi* and a *talmid* shows the reality that disciples did not refrain from disagreeing with their rebbis' analyses.)

P'sak

What of the dictum cited above, "Whoever differs with his rebbi
is virtually differing with G-d" (*Sanhedrin* 110a)? It is speaking of
the respect due to one's mentor in particular circumstances and is
conditional. Considerations include whether one is dealing with the
same case that the *rebbi* was addressing—as opposed to even another
identical case;[4] whether one has his *rebbi's* permission to disagree;
whether one is permitting, rather than forbidding something;
whether one has formally set himself up as an authority, rather than
poskenning on an *ad hoc* basis; whether the question is academic or
practical; and if the *p'sak* may be popularly perceived as revolutionary (a חידוש).[5]

Generally, Disciples Do Not Contest Their Teachers

Of course, the *right* to disagree with earlier authorities was not to be
exercised irresponsibly. One's learning, devotion to Torah behavior
and attitudes—his fear of heaven and profound regard for Torah
teachers past and present—must have first earned him proper stature
for him to take it upon himself to seriously and publicly differ with
other authorities. And realistically, even men of such stature had to
think long and hard before finally calling to task experts of old. A
fascinating *Gemora* passage (*Shabbos* 134b) illustrates this principle

---

[3] From the time of Abbaye and on. See *Halichos Olom* 5:3, *K'lahlay HaGemora*, by
the author of the Shulchan Aruch, Rabbeynu Yosef Karo, and the *Yaavin Shamua*,
Klahl 272.
[4] *Sheeta Mikubetsess*, *Bava Bassra* 130b, in the name of the *Ra'ah* and the *Ran*.
[5] See *Mishneh Torah*, *Hilchos Talmud Torah*, 5:1-3 and *Hagahos Maimonis* there
quoting his *rebbi*, ר"י. Rashi on the passage in *Sanhedrin* 110a restricts the prohibition to one who differs with his rebbi's Yeshiva (i.e., Sanhedrin).

very well. Two early *Amoraim* explain a perplexing *mishna* in a way
with which Rava, a later *Amora*, took issue. The *Gemora* goes on to
cite a *braissa* that had said the same as Rava word-for-word. Yet
when Rava became ill, he blamed his sickness on his decision to disagree with the interpretation of the earlier *Amoraim*. "Why did I
have to get involved with the explanation given by elders!" he
exclaimed. ("אנא בהדי תרגימנא דסבי למה לי")

The rabbis pointed out to him that he did, after all, have a
braissa, a *tannaitic* source, to support his interpretation. He replied
that by looking over the *mishna* once more, he concluded that the
early *Amoraim* were correct!

We see here the interaction and tension between the right to
independent thought on one hand and the caution required when
challenging superiors on the other. Had Rava's reexamination of the
source reaffirmed his interpretation, he would not have considered
himself in the wrong. He would have been expected to maintain his
position against the earlier authorities.[6] Yet because he failed to give
enough weight to their words the first time, he felt he deserved
punishment.

Indeed, the Gemora generally assumes that a *talmid* is following
the opinion of his *rebbi* as long as there is no compelling reason to
say otherwise. Sages are always concerned with quoting their mentors, or mentor's mentors, and so on, and attempting to pinpoint
their opinions. Assertions that authorities ruled one way are challenged on the basis that their teachers are known to have ruled differently.[7] Rulings by *Amoraim* are questioned because of opposite
rulings by a past *Amora* whose authority was widely accepted, such
as Rav or Levi[8]. But there are many exceptions to this, and it is by no

---

[6] Yet paradoxically, the *Gemora* concludes that both Rava and his superiors were
disagreeing with even greater superiors—the authors of the *braissa*—over the correct
interpretation of a *mishna*!

[7] See, e.g., *Tosefos*, top of *Shavuos* 42a, which pits a ruling by Rebbi Ḥeeya against
a purported ruling by his teacher, Rebbi Yehuda HaNassi. *Shabbos* 128a, *Bava
Kamma* 115a, and *Beytsa* 40a question purported rulings by Rav Huna since they
contradict those of his teacher, Rav. Rav Nachman is expected to conform to either
Rav or Shmuel in *Bava Bassra* 35a—see פרש"י ד"ה שודא. (See also *Bava Bassra* 153a,
Tosefos ד"ה תניא כוותיה דריש לקיש, regarding an opinion of Rabbi Akiva's which is
taken as "probably" shared by his teacher, Rebbi Yoḥonon. (Sources cited by *Seder
HaDoros*.)

[8] *Bava Metsia* 46b, *Tosefos* ד"ה ופירי (to be cited in text later).

means a rule. A *talmid* was not obligated to accept all his *rebbi's* teachings or rulings.

Tosefos: Tannaim Disagree with Predecessors

Thus, *Tosefos* (ב״מ דף ד: תד״ה אין נשבעין על כפירת כו׳) upholds the version of a *mishna* that has Rebbi Shimmon ben Elazar disagreeing with his teacher, Rabbi Akiva. He states,

ואע״ג דר׳שמעון בן אלעזר היה תלמידו של ר״ע, אין לחוש מה שחולק עמו, והוזכר קודם, דכעין זו מצינו לקמן (דף ז.) גבי שנים אדוקים בשטר, דפליג רבי עם רשב״ג אביו.

And even though Rebbi Shimmon ben Elazar was a disciple of Rabbi Akiva, there is no problem with the fact that he is arguing with him. For we find the same kind of situation further on where Rebbi is arguing with his own father, Rabban Shimmon ben Gamliel!

The fact is Tosefos could have cited any one of *seventeen* places where Rebbi Yehuda HaNassi was in face-to-face disagreement with his father—the *Nassi* who preceded him.[9]

Amoraim, Too, Disagreed with Predecessors

Indeed, Tosefos considers an explanation necessary whenever the *Gemora* challenges one *Amora's* opinion because of another's, even if the two authorities are generations apart. In *Beytsa* 9a, a statement by Rav is pitted against the opinion of Rav Ḥannan bar Ammi. Tosefos comments:

אע״ג דרב היה אמורא, מ״מ פריך שפיר (ד)כיון דרב גדול היה בדורו, וראש ישיבה ל(עם) ישראל חוץ משמואל, אין סברא דרב חנן פליג עליה.

Even though Rav was [only] an *Amora* [just like Rav Ḥannan bar Ammi], nevertheless a contrary statement by Rav constitutes a valid objection. Since Rav was a great man in his generation, and the Rosh Yeshiva of Jewry, sharing that status only

[9] See Additional Notes at the end of this chapter.

with Shmuel, it is *improbable* that Rav Ḥannan would have differed with him.[10]

Clearly, a later *Amora* is not beholden to the opinions of earlier
ones unless the earlier ones bear some special distinction or status.
Tosefos' terminology in a similar situation in *Bava Metsia* 46b
makes it sound even less compelling for an *Amora* to accept a previous *Amora's* opinion:

מסתמא לא יחלוק רב נחמן על רב ולוי שהיו קדמונים.

Normally, Rav Nachman would not differ with Rav and Levi,
who were much earlier.

Here we are dealing with Rav Nachman, who was not only much
younger than Rav, but a disciple of his. Yet the best reason Tosefos
can offer for why Rav's opinion is used to question the report of Rav
Nachman's is that *normally* Rav Nachman would not disagree with
Rav because of Rav's particularly unusual status.[11]

(The *Maharats Ḥayos* points out that *Tosefos* does not even
attempt to justify the *Gemora* with the adage [from *Kesubos* 8a and
elsewhere] that Rav had the status of a *Tanna*—"רב תנא הוא ופליג." He
explains that this remark is referring only to Rav's ability to disagree
with a *Tanna*; it is not suggesting that a later *Amora* is beholden to
him. As proof, we find Rav Sheyshess disputing a statement by Rav
with the words: "אמינא כי נייס ושכיב רב אמר להא שמעתתא!"—"I say that
Rav made that statement when he was falling asleep!"[12] And Rav
Sheyshess was a disciple of Rav Huna, a disciple of Rav!)

---

[10] See Additional Notes at the end of this chapter.

[11] Tosefos and Rashi give the same kind of explanation in other *Gemoras* which
consider *Amoraim* subject to statements by Rav Kahana (*Bava Kamma* 33b) and
Rabba (*Moed Kotton* 2b).

[12] This criticism appears (at least) eight times: *Yevomos* 24b, 91a, 109b; *Bava
Kamma* 47b, 65a, 67b; *Bechoros* 23b; *Needa* 60a. (Of course, simply by understanding the criticism literally, we can avoid the implausible impression that it was
meant disrepectfully.) In every instance, the objection is based upon a *braissa* that
apparently contradicts Rav. In all these cases, the *Gemora* never counters by saying,
"רב תנא הוא ופליג, Rav has the status of a *Tanna*, entitled to his own opinion," but
conforms Rav's opinion to the *braissa*. For more examples of strongly-worded criticisms, see the chapter entitled "Errors on the Receiving End."

Rabbeynu Ḥananale's Explanation

Like Tosefos, *Rabbeynu Ḥananale* sees need to explain why any *Amora* must conform to any other *Amora's* opinion. However, his explanation (in *Bava Metsia* 7a) differs slightly:

וק"ל דלא מקשינן לא ממשנה ולא מברייתא ולא ממימרא אלא אם כן היה הלכה.

> We have a rule that we [that is, the *Gemora*] will not consider a statement to be a negation—whether it is a statement of a *mishna*, *braissa*, or *Amora*—unless it was [known to have already been established as] the *halacha*.

The passage upon which this comment was made raised an objection against Rav Ḥeeya bar Ahvin by citing an opinion of Rebbi Yoḥonon,[13] who, like Rav, was a singular figure. Yet *Rabbeynu Ḥananale* asserts that only if the Talmud knows that an *Amora's* statement had already been accepted by the Jewish nation as law could it be used to call to task another *Amora's* opinion. It has nothing to do, *per sé*, with how early in history the previous *Amora* flourished or with how prestigious he had been. The strength of the objection is based on the prestige of his *statement*, namely, its having been officially accepted as law. The reason that his name is mentioned at all is only incidental; perhaps, since the statement was declared as law in his name, the association remained.

This leaves us, the students of the *Gemora*, without a way of knowing in advance when the Talmud will use one *Amora's* statement to invalidate another's. When the statements of two *Amoraim* contradict, regardless of when the *Amoraim* lived, we can anticipate only that the Gemora will point out that the two authorities are in disagreement. If we do see the *Gemora* objecting to an *Amora's* opinion based upon another *Amora's* remark, we can thereby deduce that the remark must have been known to the Gemora to have been a final *halacha*.

This explains why the פוסקים ראשונים, the post-talmudic authorities whose role it was to ascertain and decide *halacha*, will often base their decision on the fact that the *Gemora* uses a statement as an objection: The composers and sealers of the Talmud must have known the statement to have already been established as the *hala-*

---

[13] See Additional Notes at the end of this chapter.

cha, because otherwise they wouldn't have used it to form an objection.[14]

Rabbeynu Ḥananale's rule tells us something even more intriguing: Even a *mishna*—not to mention a *braissa*—that contradicts an *Amora*, is considered a disproof only if it became the *p'sak* of the Jewish nation, and not because it was uttered by a *Tanna*. You will remember that a later Great Sanhedrin could disagree with an earlier one over the correct way to *darshon* a *posuk*. Theoretically, we reasoned, an *Amoraic* Sanhedrin therefore has the power to disagree with a Scriptural interpretation recorded in the *Mishna*. We suggested an explanation for why no such disputes are found. (The law in question may have originated with G-d.) We also noted that the superiority of the *Tannaitic* Sanhedrins kept the *Amoraim* from meddling with those *takkonos* and *gezeyros* of the Mishna known, as *Rabbeynu Ḥananale* emphasizes, to have been declared binding. Now we have learned that, regarding analyzing statements made by human authorities, the *Amoraim* had the power to criticize and contest any opinions expressed by *Tannaim*. The only obstacle was the general acceptance of the *mishnayos* as the *halacha* in the days of Rebbi Yehuda HaNassi. However, since there were issues left unresolved by the Mishna and which remained so in the days of the *Gemora*, *Amoraim* could dispute about which *Tanna* the *halacha* should follow, or could even create hybrid opinions of *Tannaim* to which no *Tanna* himself would have agreed. It is true that *Amoraim* used their power to disagree sparingly. They felt their inferiority to the *Tannaim* so strongly that they rarely dared criticize their analyses. Even in cases of unresolved issues, they limited themselves to deciding between *Tannaim*, without introducing additional positions. Yet, in exceptional cases an *Amora* did feel more certain about an issue than a *Tanna*, and in some cases an *Amora* did declare that a *Tanna* was mistaken.[15]

[14] As an example, *Tosefos Ryd* on *Kesubos* 22b: "ומדמקשינן דר"ה, ש"מ דזהו הלכתא, שאין התלמוד מקשה אלא מהלכה פסוקה. כך העמדנו נמי בגיטין בריש פרק המקבל, Since the *Gemora* challenges an opinion with the statement of Rav Huna, we see that the *halacha* follows Rav Huna. For the Talmud would only contest [an opinion] with a statement representing a settled law. This was also our approach in our commentary on *Gittin*."

[15] As explained elsewhere, this is only possible regarding a law which was definitely not a *kabballa* from Sinai and which was not a rabbinical law already passed by a *Tannaitic* Sanhedrin.

Tosefos understands a passage in *Gittin* 37b in such a light:

אע"פ שמסתפק רשב"ג בדברי רבנן, מ"מ לא מסתפק ליה לרבא כלל לומר דפליג(י)
לפני ייאוש.

[Regarding a captured slave whom Jews redeemed intending
that he go free and not be returned to his original owner—
Rabban Gamliel ruled that the original owner regains his slave.
The Sages ruled that the slave goes free.]

Tosefos: Rabban Shimmon ben-Gamliel [the *Tanna*] was unsure
whether the Sages disagreed with him only in a case of לאחר ייאוש
[where the original owner resigned himself to the loss], or also
in a case of לפני ייאוש [where the original owner did not resign
himself to the loss]. Nevertheless, Rava [the *Amora*] had no
doubt whatsoever that they disagreed in both cases.

Upon which the *Rashash* (Rav Shmuel Strasson of Vilna, talmudic commentator) remarks:

גדולה מזו מצינו לרב נחמן בר יצחק בר"ה (ל:) דקאמר, "רבי יהודה הוא דטעי"
(בדברי ת"ק שלו)!

We find [something] even more [astounding] in *Rosh Ha-
Shonna* 30b, where Rav Naḥman bar Yitzchak [an *Amora*] says,
"Rebbi Yehuda [the *Tanna*] erred [in understanding his oppo-
nent's words]"!

The Descent of the Generations

Whence, then, the popular misimpression that even within one era,
i.e., within the *Tannaitic* era, or within the *Amoraic* era, later authorities did not argue with earlier ones? Probably most responsible is a
hasty conclusion drawn from dictums to the effect that as one generation followed another, men's intellectual abilities continually
declined. From such dictums, some reach the conclusion that later
Sages were disqualified from contesting earlier ones of the same era.
However, a close analysis of the source of these dictums belies such a
conclusion.

One of the sources is a passage found in the Jerusalem Talmud,
tractate *Gittin*, at the end of the sixth *perek*:

רבי אמר: "כד הוה בעי מקשייה על דרבי יוסי, אמר אנן, 'עלובייא מקשין על
דר'יוסי.' שכשם לְבֵין קדשי הקדשים לחולי חולין (ז' מדרגות) כך בין דורינו לדורו
של ר'יוסי."

אמר ר׳ישמעאל בר׳ יוסי: „כשם שבין זהב לעפר (ז׳ מדרגות) כך בין דורינו לדורו
של אבא.״

Rebbi said, "Whenever I wished to raise a difficulty against
Rebbi Yosay, I would [first] say, 'The lowly raise the following
objection against Rebbi Yosay. . . .' The difference between
Rebbi Yosay's generation and ours is the same as that which is
between the holiest of holies and the most mundane [namely,
seven degrees difference]."

Rebbi Yosay's son, Rebbi Yishmael, said, "The difference
between our generation and Father's is the same as the difference between gold and dirt [i.e., seven degrees]."

Probably the most famous of these dictums is the one in *Eruvin*
53a:

אר׳ יוחנן: „לָבָּן של ראשונים כפתחו של אולם, ושל אחרונים כפתחו של היכל. ואנו
כמלא מחט נקב סדקית.״

ראשונים: ר״ע.

אחרונים: ר״א בן שמוע; [תלמידו, ורבי של רבנו הקדוש]

א״ד: ראשונים: ר״א בן שמוע.

אחרונים: ר׳אושעיה ברבי.

Rebbi Yoḥonon said, "The hearts of the ancients were as
[encompassing as] the doorway to the Temple's *Ulam*; [the
minds] of the later scholars—as [encompassing as] the opening
to its *Haichel*. And ours—as [encompassing as] the area of a
needle hole."

The ancients—Rabbi Akiva.

The later scholars—Rabbi Elazar ben Shamua [Rabbi Akiva's
disciple, and the teacher of Rebbi].

Others say: The ancients—Rabbi Elazar ben Shamua.

The later scholars—Rabbi Oshiah, son of Rebbi [and teacher of
this statement's author, Rebbi Yoḥonon (*Ḥulin* 54b)].

But to what quality does "narrowness of heart" refer? Rashi (*s.v.* לב
כל אחד ואחד) defines לב, *heart*, in this context, as a reference to mental

sharpness.[16] And he further defines this inferiority as being able to understand only a little of what is heard and only with difficulty.[17] One may infer, however, that after all the difficulty, whatever the later scholars did understand they mastered completely. Indeed, despite Rebbi Elazar ben Shamua's perceived inferiority to the scholars of Rabbi Akiva's generation, we do find him disagreeing with Rabbi Akiva's *rebbi*, Rabbi Eliezer ben Horkinus (*Temura* 3:3). We also find other members of Rebbi Elazar ben Shamua's generation (Generation no. 3 in the Rambam's list)[18] disagreeing with members of Rabbi Akiva's generation (Generation no. 2). Namely, Rebbi Mayer (Generation no. 3) disagrees with Ḥannina Ish Ono (Generation no. 2) in *Gittin* 67a; and in *Pesaḥim* 34a Rebbi Nosson (Generation no. 3) disagrees with Rebbi Yishmael ben Rebbi Yoḥonon ben B'roka (Generation no. 2), who is also disputed by Rebbi Shimmon (Generation no. 4) in *Eruvin* 8:2.

In *Moed Kotton* 20b and *Bava Metsia* 4b, Rabbi Akiva himself (Generation no. 2) is contested by Rebbi Shimmon ben Elazar (Generation no. 4), who lived a generation *after* that of Rebbi Elazar ben Shamua's!

In fact, the very author of the declaration we are dealing with, Rebbi Yoḥonon, who professes inferiority to his elder, Rebbi Oshiya, ("ואנו כמלא נקב מחט סידקית", and our generation is as [small] as a needle hole") nevertheless disputed two of Rebbi Oshiya's rulings (*Zevaḥim* 113a and *Ḥaggiga* 9a).

In matters of analysis, teachers encouraged their students to question them or even to disagree. *Bava Bassra* 10b even describes a discussion wherein which Rabban Yoḥonon ben Zakkai preferred a student's analysis of a *posuk* over his own.[19]

---

[16] As opposed to חכמה, *wisdom*, which refers to the amount of information one has learned, as *Rashi* explains in s.v. א"וחכמת כל או.

[17] *Rashi* s.v. כסירתא בגודא לגמרא:

כיתד שנועצין אותו בכותל בנקב צר ונכנס בדוחק. כך אין יכולין אנו להבין מה שאנו שומעים כי אם מעט ובקושי.

Just as it is hard to insert a peg into a narrow hole in a wall, we cannot understand what we hear except for a little and with difficulty.

[18] As per *Maimonides' Introduction to the Talmud*, pp. 193-196. The first chart on p. 181 depicts our text graphically.

[19] He had asked his disciples to expound on a *posuk* speaking of the Jewish people and mentioning the gentiles as well (עי' רבינו גרשום שם). Rabban Yoḥonon ben Zakkai, whose interpretation was uncritical of the gentiles, preferred the explana-

Disagreeing with One's Rebbe

And so, surprising as it may seem, it is not very unusual for a *talmid* to disagree with his *rebbi*. In fact, quite a long list can be made of instances where *Tannaim* and *Amoraim* disagreed with their mentors. We already mentioned five such cases. Here is a random selection of a few more:[20]

> *Pesachim* 6a[21]—Rav Ashi interprets a *braissa* differently from his *rebbi's rebbi*, Rava.
>
> *Bava Metsia* 5b, 6a—According to *Rashi* (ד"ה אביי אמר: טעמא דמתניתין לאו כדרבי יוחנן), Abbaye disagrees with Rebbi Yoḥonon (of two generations before).[22]
>
> *Bava Metsia* 7b—Ravina disagrees with his *rebbi*, Rav Poppa, in determining which of two versions of a *braissa* is correct (שר"פ ס"ל שלא לאיפוך, ורבינא ס"ל דלאיפוך).
>
> *Bava Bassra* 6a[23]—Rav Yosef disagrees with the ruling of his *rebbi*, Rav Nachman, and even acts upon his own opinion . . .

tion, which did disparage some of them, given by one of the disciples, Rebbi Neḥunia ben HaKanna.

[20] The second chart on p. 181 is provided to illustrate the most famous links in the *rebbi-talmid* chain.

[21] The Rabbis stated in a *braissa*: "If a non-Jew enters a Jew's courtyard (on Pesach) with bread in his hand, the Jew need not do away with it (i.e., ask the non-Jew to leave—*Rashi*) [because it is not the Jew's in any way, and only possessing bread is forbidden]. If it is given to the Jew to hold on to—he must [have the non-Jew remove it]. But if the Jew designated a room for the sole purpose of a non-Jew to deposit bread for safekeeping, he need not have it removed. As the Torah says: '*Chometz* may not be found . . .'" Now, to which case was the verse brought as a source? Said Rav Poppa: "To the second case. I.e., if the Jew was given the bread to hold onto it, it must be removed, because the verse says, 'It may not be found' (Sh'mos 12:19)]." Rav Ashi said: "To the third case. I.e., if a room is designated for the bread, it need not be removed, because the verse says, 'It may not be found *in your houses*,' [and the *braissa* quoted only the first part of the verse.]"

[22] מהקדמה למשנה תורה: „ומגדולי החכמים שקיבלו מר' יוחנן"

[23] If one claims to have been granted use of his neighbor's property (such as rights to lean boards against his neighbor's wall) and the neighbor is known to have expressed no objection to seeing it done, we may assume that rights were indeed granted. Rights to less damaging uses of that type are automatically assumed as well. Said Rav Nachman: "If one gained permission to allow the rain falling on his roof to flow onto his neighbor's property, he may not do so if he reconstructs his roof to be sloping and covered with willow branches (since the drippings thereby

Bava Bassra 6a-b— . . . and Rav Nachman himself disagrees with *his* rebbe, Rabba bar Avuha.[24]

Bava Bassra 6a-b—Rav Nachman disagrees with his *rebbi*, Shmuel.

Bava Bassra 7b—Rava disagrees with the ruling of Shmuel, who lived a century before him and was his *rebbi's rebbi*.[25]

Gittin 2a-b—Rava disagrees with his *rebbi*, Rabba, over the reason beind a *mishna's halacha*, and the *Gemora* points out practical differences resulting from each opinion. (The later authorities rule as the *talmid*, Rava.)

Gittin 38a—Ravina disagrees with Abayye, his *rebbi's rebbi*, over the intent of Rav Yehuda, the *rebbi* of Abbaye's *rebbi*).

Nedarim 8:7—Rebbi Yehuda's son disagrees with his father's ruling.[26]

In conclusion, it was usual for disciples to support their teachers' opinions. But though later Sages had infinite respect for their predecessors, when *halachic* evidence forced them to disagree, they did not refrain from doing so. Their attitude parallels the one expressed by the *Shach*, great commentator on the *Shulchan Aruch* and *posek:*

ואף שאין אני כדאי להשיג על גדולי הראשונים, מכל מקום התורה מונח בקרן זווית, וראיות ברורות יתנו עדיהן, ויצדקו. והאמת יורה דרכו (ש״ע חו״מ הל׳ טוען ונטען, סי׳ צ״א ס״ק ל״ג).

Though I am not fit to criticize the *Great Rishonim*, still, the Torah is accessible to all, and clear proofs present their evidence, and Truth points out its own course (*Shulchan Aruch, Ḥoshen Mishpaht, Hilchos To'ain V'nit'ahn*, 91:33).

---

become so close to each other that they prevent the neighbor from working in the area.)'' But Rav Yosef opined that also gained was the right to let any kind of rainfall from the roof flow onto the property, and he carried out this decision in practice.

[24] On the issue of whether [when unspecified by agreement] the tenant of a multi-dwelling building may have use of the hanging-pegs located in the resident owner's front garden, though the garden is not meant for traffic.

[25] However, the *Hagahos HaBach* substitutes Rav, a contemporary of Shmuel, for Rava, and so it would appear from 65a.

[26] According to the *Ran*. The dispute involves whether we judge a person's probable intent (rather than follow his words literally) when he declares an oath concerning rabbinical *takkannos*, such as Ezra's decree to eat garlic on Friday nights, although we do not do so regarding Scriptural imperatives, such as eating a meal the eve of *Yom Kippur*. See *loc. cit.*

Additional Notes to Chapter Nine

9. In addition to in *Bava Metsia* 4b, Rebbi Yehuda HaNassi disagrees with his father in *Maaseros* 5:5; *Eruvin* 32b; *Taanis* 14b; *Shabbos* 19a; *Pesachim* 10a; *Rosh Hashonna* 32a; *Yevomos* 64b and 90b; *Gittin* 22a, 32b, 33a; *Bava Metsia* 7a; *Bava Bassra* 169b; *Needa* 16b and 60a; *Bava Metsia* 48b. In all but the last three cases, Rebbi is cited first. The first few of these sources contain disputes over which version of a *mishna* is the correct one and over the power of enforcement with which their ancestor, the *Nassi* Rabban Gamliel the Elder, backed his decree: If someone went ahead and did something in a proscribed way, did Rabban Gamliel declare the results null and void. They also disputed, in a case where several agents were designated simultaneously, whether removal of their designations must also be done collectively, or if it may be done one person at a time?

10. The statement by Rav, raised as an objection, is: "כל מקום שאסרי חכמים מפני מראית עין, אפי' בחדרי חדרים אסור", Every permissible act that the Sages prohibited [us from doing (e.g., eating kosher food in an unkosher restaurant)] because others may be misled by it [to transgress actual prohibitions (thinking that all the restaurant's food is kosher)] is prohibited even in the most private chambers [where no one will see it]." It is interesting that even with such a seemingly fundamental maxim, it is not assumed that Rav was reporting a *kabbala*, but stating his own opinion. Perhaps this is because Rav's terminology was "אפי' בחדרי חדרים אסור," and not "אסרו."—"It is prohibited," and not "they prohibited it." At any rate, the *Gemora* goes on to answer that Rav also had *Tannaitic* basis to his opinion, because this maxim was a subject of dispute between the *Tanna* Rebbi Shimmon, who prohibited, and the *Tanna* Rebbi Eliezer, who permitted, performing misleading acts in private.

13. Apparently, Rav Ḥiyya bar Abin lived only one generation after Rebbi Yoḥonon, since he often speaks in the name of the contemporaneous Shmuel. But the works *Doros Harishonim* and *Toldos Tannaim V'Amoraim* (Hyman, 1910) present evidence that he lived much later than Rebbi Yoḥonon. Despite his citings of Shmuel, the *Gemora* mentions no face-to-face meeting of the two, there are indications that he was a mere child when Shmuel died, and we know that he was still alive in the days of Abbaye, who lived much later than Shmuel. Therefore, Shmuel could not have personally taught him, and he clearly flourished much later than Rebbi Yoḥonon.

eneration 1	Generation 2	Generation 3	Generation 4	Source
	(of Rabbi Akiva) *The Ancients*	(of R' Elazar ben Shamua) *The Later Ones*		
Eliezer		R' Elazar ben Shamua		*Temura* 3:3
	Ḥannina Ish Ono	Rebbi Mayir		*Gittin* 67a
	R' Yoḥonon ben B'roka		Rebbi Shimmon	*Eruvin* 8:2
	R' Yoḥonon ben B'roka	Rebbi Yehuda b' Elai		*Shavuous* 7:15
	Rebbi Yishmael ben R' Yoḥonon ben B'roka	Rebbi Nosson		*Pesaḥim* 34a
	Rabbi Akiva		Rebbi Yehuda HaNassi	*Shavuous* 4b
	Rabbi Akiva		Rebbi Shimon ben Elazar	*Moed Kotton* 20b *Bava Metzia* 4b

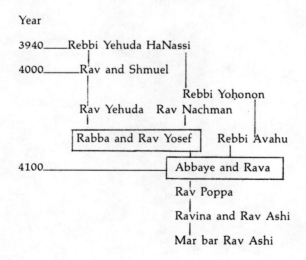

Year

3940——Rebbi Yehuda HaNassi

4000———Rav and Shmuel

Rebbi Yoḥonon

Rav Yehuda   Rav Nachman

Rabba and Rav Yosef   Rebbi Avahu

4100————Abbaye and Rava

Rav Poppa

Ravina and Rav Ashi

Mar bar Rav Ashi

Chapter 10

The Control and Proliferation of Machlokos—Keeping the Torah One

As soon as the first long-term *machlokos* appeared, the true knowledge of Torah suffered (*Sota* 47a-b):

משמת יוסי בן יועזר איש צרידה ויוסי בן יוחנן איש ירושלים בטלו האשכלות—איש
שהכל בו. פרש"י: תורה באמיתה ואין דופי ושכחה ומחלוקת.

Ever since Yosay ben Yoezer of Ts'rayda and Yosay ben Yoḥonon of Jerusalem [his contemporary] died, the *eshkollos* [אשכלות, lit., grape bunches]—[the existence of any] man (איש) who has all (שכל) [Torah mastered]—passed into oblivion. (*Rashi:* Torah in its true state, without doubt [דופי—two faces] and forgetfulness and *machlokess*.)

Machlokess Undesirable

Now, from the outset, the Torah provided for the event of *mach-*

183

lokos ("Follow the majority!"—*Sh'mos* 23:2). Nevertheless, a sustained *machlokess* was undesirable. Yes, "These and those" may be the words of the Living G-d, and increased *machlokos* brings with it increased Torah discussion and the creation of more *halachos* which even when rejected for practice are labelled by *Hashem* as "Torah;"[1] and true, the prohibition of "לא תתגודדו, You may not form diverse *halachic* cliques" applies only to dissensions within one jurisdiction (*Yevomos* 14a). All the same, the lack of a clear knowledge of the facts G-d revealed to us at Sinai is considered a tragedy:

The day that the disciples of Hillel and Shammai found themselves in dispute was "as difficult as the day the Golden Calf was made" (*Halachos Gedolos, Hilchos Tish'a B'av V'Taanios*) and occasioned the decree of an annual fast day on par with those marking deaths of Torah greats and destruction of holy works (*ibid.* and *Shulchan Aruch, Orach Chaim,* 580:2). In view of the hundreds of issues under dispute by those great bodies, the *Gemora* (*Sota* 47b) lamented that "נעשה תורה כשתי תורות, the Torah became like two Torahs," and the generations from that of Moses until that of Rebbi Yosay ben Yoezer were admired for the fact that they experienced no enduring *machlokos* (*Temura* 15a; see *Hagahos HaG'ra* no. 1).

Thus, the increase in *machlokos* in the days of *Bes Shammai* and *Bes Hillel* was an unhappy situation that could not be avoided. The following presentation will provide the principles of *halachic* decision and historical phenomena responsible for this new situation.[2]

When It Is Forbidden to Obey the Sanhedrin

Great insight can be gained by the solution to an apparent contradiction between two teachings. The first teaching is contained in the first *mishna* of *mesechta Horios:*

הורו ב״ד וידע אחד מהן שטעו, או תלמיד והוא ראוי להוראה, והלך ועשה על פיהן
. . . הרי זה חייב. . . .

If one of the members of the Sanhedrin, or a qualified scholar, feels that the Sanhedrin erred in a decision, yet [that individual

---

[1] See chapter entitled, "These and Those."

[2] Although we are calling it a "new situation," it should be born in mind that since the majority of people followed the teachings of *Bes Hillel,* the general complexion of Jewish observance remained the same.

follows its decision ... he is [acting wrongly and is] חייב, obligated to bring an offering in repentance.

This is surprising, considering the mandate that one must follow the Sages' decisions even if they seem to be calling black white, and white black, the principle by which a "rebellious elder" is executed (*D'varim* 17:11-13):

על־פי התורה אשר יורוך ועל־המשפט אשר יאמרו לך תעשה; לא תסור מן הדבר אשר יגידו לך ימין ושמאל (דברים י״ז:י״א): אפילו נראים בעיניך על שמאל שהוא ימין ועל ימין שהוא שמאל שמע להם!

"According to the Torah that they [the judges of the Sanhedrin] will teach you and according to the judgments they will tell you, you shall do; you shall not turn away from that thing that they will tell you—right or left" (*D'varim* 17:11)—Even if [their words] seem to you to be saying about right, that it is left; or about left, that it is right—listen to them! (*Sifray loc. cit.*)

A Fair Hearing

HoRav Ẓvi Hirsch Ḥayyos[3] cites The *Ramban* (*Commentary on Sefer HaMitzvos, Shoresh Rishone*)[4] to solve this contradiction:

ויש תנאי בענין שמועה לבית דין הגדול ... והוא שאם היה בזמן הסנהדרין חכם ראוי להוראה, והורו בית דין הגדול ... והוא סבור שטעו בהוראתם, אין עליו לשמוע להם, ואינו רשאי להתיר לעצמו הדבר האסור לו. אלא ינהג חומרא לעצמו. וכ״ש אם היה מכלל הסנהדרין—יושב עמהם בבית [דין] הגדול. ויש עליו לבא לפניהם ולומר טענותיו, והם ישאו ויתנו עמו ... ומ״מ היה חייב לקבל דעתם אחר ההסכמה עכ״פ.

The obligation to obey the *Great Sanhedrin* was conditional: If the *Great Sanhedrin* issued a *halacha* permitting an act, and a scholar qualified to promulgate decisions felt that they erred, he was not obligated to listen to them. And he was not permitted to allow for himself that which he felt was prohibited—especially not if he was himself a *member* of that body. It was his responsibility to come before them and state his arguments, and they were obligated to discuss and debate the issue with him.

[3] *Torahs Nevi'im* and *Atterress Tzvi*, in *Koll Sifray Maharatz Ḥayyos*, pub. *Divray Chachamim*, Jerusalem, 5718.
[4] Page 14 in our editions.

> Nevertheless, once a conclusion is reached [after due considera-
> tion, followed by a vote if necessary], he was required to accept
> their decision unequivocally.

Once a Sage presented his case, if after due consideration his arguments were rejected, he was no longer permitted to differ. But as long as his views were not represented in the forum of the *Great Sanhedrin*, and he felt that were he to defend them, the others would be convinced of his position, he was permitted, and (if he had a more stringent view) he was obligated, to continue to follow the truth as he saw it.[5]

This, of course, carries important ramifications regarding the subject of *machlokess*. If, for any reason, a qualified Sage did not attend a session of the *Great Sanhedrin*, he was not held to their conclusions if he personally disagreed. Even at the sacrifice of unity, he was obligated to follow his own opinion. But for this very reason the Sages saw to attending the sessions of *Sanhedrin* in order to bring their own opinions to the floor. The arguments were all presented, and a decision—either a unanimous one or one arrived at through a majority vote—was reached. The *machlokess* was short-lived and usually soon forgotten. For all practical purposes, *machlokess* was never sustained.

An Historical Perspective

Indeed, when life was normal within Jewry—when the Great San-hedrin held court, when things were calm and there were no perse-cutions, expulsions, or battles creating turmoil for Jewish living and learning—no *machlokess* lasted for long. Whenever a law came into doubt, if a *machlokess* was born, it was quickly aborted by the Great Sanhedrin, which enjoyed full attendance. The issue was duly dis-cussed and considered, brought to a vote, and settled. In those cases where a later Sanhedrin could reverse a decision, such reversal, too, was accomplished speedily.

However, beginning in the days of the Second Holy Temple, when the land of Israel was under Greek rule and influence (c. 3450-3700), and even among the Jews themselves there were vio-lent individuals who savagely disrupted the smooth flow of life,

---

[5] See Additional Notes at the end of this chapter.

Sages were murdered, expelled, and forced to flee from danger. This turbulence created a two-pronged threat.

Increased Disparity of Thinking

First, through its influence on the environment, the unrest threatened to weaken severely the quality of study and the incisiveness of minds. This could cause the thinking patterns of scholars to differ as never before, creating a multitude of diverse conclusions even when based upon identical information:

כל ב׳ אנשים בהיותם שוים בשכל ובעיון ובידיעת העקרים שיוציאו מהם הסברות,
לא תפול ביניהם מחלוקת בסברתם בשום פנים. ואם נפלה תהיה מעוטה...אבל
כאשר רפתה שקידת התלמידים על החכמה ... נפלה מחלוקת ביניהם בעיין על
דברים רבים. שסברת כל אחד ואחד מהם היתה לפי שכלו ומה שיש בידו מן העקרים.

Any two men will arrive at the same conclusions if they are equal in intelligence, [method of] analysis, and in their knowledge of the data. No disputes will arise between them. If any at all should arise, they will be in only a few cases. . . . But when the diligence of the disciples slackened . . . there was an increase in the number of their disputes in the analysis of many issues. For each one's analysis followed his own intellect and the data to work with that he possessed.[6]

Lost Benefits of Discussion and Vote

Secondly, since they were unable to gather together, the Sages lost the advantages inherent in mutual discussion and debate. Even where discussion may have failed to eliminate disparate viewpoints, a gathering of Sages would have provided the opportunity to arrive at a uniform law by taking a vote, officially nullifying all other opinions from law. As we have explained above, this was impossible without a normally functioning Sanhedrin, a Sanhedrin in which all the Sages' opinions were represented.

These two problems made the prospect of a factional and disorganized Judaism loom menacingly.[7] At the time of Yosay ben

---

[6] *Maimonides' Introduction to the Talmud*, p. 90.

[7] True, all this turmoil was taking place only in the land of Israel. The scholars of the Babylonian Yeshivos enjoyed tranquility. Still, since by Jewish law the Great Sanhedrin could meet only in Israel, the official elimination of variant opinions was impeded.

Yoezer and Yosay ben Yoḥonon (five generations before Hillel and Shammai, c. 3500) the pressures began to take their toll, and an irreconcilable *machlokess*[8] arose.[9] Yet the Sages were unrelenting in their efforts to keep the *halacha* clear. Incredibly, for the next two centuries this was the sole *machlokess* that split the Sages. Even when matters grew worse, *machlokess* was persistently kept to a minimum.

The Phenomenon of Bes Shammai and Bes Hillel

In 3704, while Sh'maya was the *Nassi*, the Romans banned the Jews from having any central body of law. Even when the Sanhedrin was finally legalized again (by order of Julius Caesar in 3712) the interferences by the Christians, Bysoosim, and Herod made normal Sanhedric procedure impossible. Hillel and Shammai were forced to keep their houses of learning separate, and found themselves in dispute over three new issues.[10] The scholars who studied in their *Houses* sustained even more disagreements.[11] Without an organized body to discuss and vote on the issues, *machlokess* persisted.

כשהיה בית דין הגדול קיים, לא היתה מחלוקת בישראל. . . . אם לא היה הדבר ברור

Incidentally, this turmoil was symptomatic of the attempts by the the Greeks and sympathizers "to cause them to forget Your Torah," in the words of the *Al Hanissim* passage we recite on Ḥanuka. Rav Yitzchak Hutner (*Pachad Yitzchak, Ḥanuka*) points out that while the persecutions did succeed in producing loss of information, Torah increased, taking "Torah" in the sense of the creation of multitudinous *halachic* opinions, which, even if rejected as final *halacha*, G-d Himself sanctions as "Torah." Rather than causing frustration and abandonment of Torah study, the Grecian strategy backfired.

[8] The issue was "*semicha*," the classically cited first long-standing *machlokess* (*Yerushalmi, Ḥaggiga* 2:2). See Additional Notes at the end of this chapter.

[9] And with chaotic conditions preventing a fully-constituted Sanhedrin from convening, the *machlokess* remained unsettled. See Additional Notes at the end of this chapter.

[10] See Additional Notes at the end of this chapter.

[11] HaRav Shamshon Raphael Hirsch (*Collected Writings, Volume V,* Feldheim, 1988, p. 65) approximates a total of 280 disputes between *Bes Shammai* and *Bes Hillel*: 90 concerning *gezayros*, 25 concerning *takkonos*, and 130 concerning Scriptural interpretation. Approximation is necessary, he points out (p. 66), because the points of divergence between *Bes Shammai* and *Bes Hillel* are sometimes themselves matters of debate in the *Gemora*.

אצל בית דין הגדול—דנין בו בשעתן, ונושאין ונותנין בדבר עד שיסכימו כולן, או
יעמדו למנין וילכו אחר הרוב, ויאמרו לכל השואלים: כך הלכה. והולכין להן.

משבטל בית דין הגדול, רבתה מחלוקת בישראל. זה מטמא ונותן טעם לדבריו, וזה
מטהר ונותן טעם לדבריו; זה אוסר, וזה מתיר (ממרים א:ד).

As long as the *Great Sanhedrin* stood, there was no *machlokess*
in Jewry. . . . If the solution was not already clear to the Great
Sanhedrin, then it would deliberate over the issue there and
then, until it would come to a unanimous conclusion. Or it
would take a vote and follow the majority. It would then declare
to all: "This is the *halacha!*" and go on to its other proceedings.

But from the time that the Sanhedrin ceased to operate, *machlokess* increased in Israel (*Mahmrim* 1:4).

The passage of the Talmud (*Sanhedrin* 88b) paraphrased by the
Rambam above identifies the time of increased disputes with the era
of the disciples of Hillel and Shammai:

משרבו תלמידי שמאי והלל שלא שמשו כל צרכן, רבו מחלוקת בישראל ונעשית
תורה כשתי תורות.

[But] when the disciples of Shammai and Hillel increased—who
insufficiently attended to their teachers—*machlokess* increased
within Jewry,[12] and the Torah became virtually two Torahs.

Still, even then *machlokess* was kept to a minimum. Within each
House, the disciples succeeded in reducing their own opinions to one
per issue, and therefore at most only two opinions coexisted within
Jewry on a given point of law.[13]

Even "two Torahs" were one too many in the eyes of the Sages.
But at this point, nothing could be done. Hillel's *House* attracted the

---

[12] See Additional Notes at the end of this chapter.

[13] Incredibly, the disputes that did arise concerned mere technicalities that rarely, if
ever before, touched normal life. They concerned extreme and borderline cases,
such as the very minimum amount which one must give a woman to marry her (i.e.,
must the ring be worth a quarter or just a penny?). Only one dispute pertained to a
fundamental *d'oraissa* law: the dispute about צרת הערוה, whether one should conduct *yibbum*, a levirate marriage, in the event that his deceased brother had two
wives, one of whom was the subject's blood relative (see Chapter I). Hardly a normal occurrence!

majority of scholars, but the scholars of Shammai's *House* were sincerely convinced of their own conclusions, and, in accordance with the concept developed above, they therefore could not bow to the decisions of *Bes Hillel*. The two opinions of *Bes Shammai* and *Bes Hillel* continued to exist side-by-side, until after the destruction of the Temple in 3828 (70 C.E.).

Seizing Opportunities to Vote

At sporadic moments during the Roman rule, the Sages were able to convene for discussion and vote. They took advantage of the opportunity and went to work on clarifying precisely what the past decisions had been, exactly how past statements were phrased, and creating any new *rabbinical* legislation that had become necessary. When consensus was still not reached, they sometimes agreed to taking an issue to a vote.[14]

Yavneh

Shortly after the Holy Temple and Jerusalem were destroyed, about one hundred years after Shammai and Hillel's *Houses* were established, a major opportunity arose. The Academy of Yavneh had been saved from Rome's destructive rage through the efforts of Rabban Yoḥonon ben-Zakkai, who persuaded Vespasian to spare "Yavneh and its Sages" (*Gittin* 66b).

The Academy benefited from the phenomenon of having the totality of surviving Sages in attendance. It seized this now rare opportunity to complete the task begun by Shammai and Hillel's Academies: coming to a unified practice of Jewish law. In most cases the *halachos* whose original understanding eroded into two interpretations and remained thus unresolved were decided in favor of the interpretation that Hillel's proponents understood them originally to have had, and questions of new decisions and decrees were established to follow Hillel's opinion. From then on, the old issues of debate between *Bes Shammai* and *Bes Hillel* were closed.[15]

---

[14] See Additional Notes at the end of this chapter.

[15] Unfortunately, after ten years this Sanhedrin was subject to Roman tyranny, and once again many Sages were forced to disperse. New *halachic* disputes broke out between Rabban Gamliel, Rebbi Yehoshua, and Rebbi Eliezer, the leaders of the Sanhedrin. The *Doros HaRishonim* explains that underlying these disputes was the issue of whether the new situation brought about a change in the way majority rule was to operate.

When It Was Forbidden to Be Stringent

After this decision, it was considered urgent to discourage any endeavors to follow the old decisions of *Bes Shammai*. This is illustrated in *Brachos* 10b, as explained in Rav Moshe Chaim Luzatto's *Messillass Yesharim* (end of משקל החסידות):

הבא להתחסד חסידות אמיתי צריך שישקול כל מעשיו לפי התולדות הנמשכות מהם.
. . . ומעשה דרבי טרפון (ברכות י׳) יוכיח, שהחמיר להטות כבית שמאי, ואמרו לו,
„כדאי היית לחוב בעצמך, שעברת על דברי בית הללו!" אע"פ שהחמיר היה. וזה,
שענין מחלוקת בית שמאי ובית הלל היה ענין כבד לישראל, מפני המחלוקת הגדולה
שרבתה ביניהם. וסוף סוף, נגמר שהלכה כבית הלל לעולם. הנה קיומה של תורה—
שגמר דין זה ישאר בכל תוקף לעד ולעולמי עולמים, ולא יחלש בשום פנים, שלא
תיעשה תורה חס וחלילה כשתי תורות.

ועל כן, לדעת המשנה הזאת, יותר חסידות הוא להחזיק כבית הלל אפילו לקולא,
מלהחמיר כבית שמאי.

Anyone who wishes to practice true *Ḥassidus* [—the procedure of going above and beyond the letter of the law—] must weigh all his actions according to their possible consequences.

The incident involving Rebbi Tarfone (*Brachos* 10b) demonstrates this. He followed the more demanding opinion of *Bes Shammai* and reclined [while reciting the nighttime *K'riass Sh'ma*], and the Sages reprimanded him with the words, "You would have deserved blame for your own death if your dangerous act [of delay while travelling in the robber-infested desert] would have proved fatal; for you violated the words of *Bes Hillel!*"—although he was merely acting *more* stringently than necessary. [*Bes Hillel* did not *object* to reclining while reciting the *K'riass Sh'ma*, it merely declared it unnecessary.] This is because the split between *Bes Shammai* and *Bes Hillel* had been a very serious issue affecting Jewry . . . and the *halacha* had finally been settled in favor of *Bes Hillel*. For the very sake of the Torah's future, it was imperative that this decision remain in all its strength for all time, and not be compromised one iota, so that the Torah would not, *G-d forbid*, become like two different Torahs. Therefore, according to this *mishna's* view, it would be a greater *ḥassidus* to fortify *Bes Hillel's* decisions even by following their leniencies, than to follow the stringencies of *Bes Shammai* [although in normal times one is always permitted to be more demanding on oneself if he believes that such is necessary.]

Universalizing Practices

Paradoxically, the very concern for uniformity can be a cause of *machlokess*. Sometimes a *halacha* admittedly could have been equally fulfilled in any of a number of ways; different communities adopted different options. Yet for the sake of unity, to eliminate the *appearance* of discordance, and perhaps to help make a Jew feel at home wherever he may find himself, the Sages saw fit to choose just one form of practice as the standard, universal one for all Jews. Thus, when we see Sages offering different opinions, it does not necessarily mean that they ever had been in dispute over the right interpretation of a *halacha*.

Rabbeynu Nissim, in his commentary on *Rosh HaShonna* 34a, cites *Rav Hai Gaon's* comments upon *Rosh HaShonna* 33b. This *Gemora* quotes two *Tannaitic* sources, each of which describes a different way to sound the *shofar*. Abbaye remarks that unlike a previously mentioned pair of statements, these two are definitely at variance with each other. The *Gemora* goes on to say that Rebbi Avahu had decreed that we must sound the *shofar* both ways. Apparently, this was because he was unsure which way was right, and so this measure was taken to make sure the *mitzva* would be correctly performed.

This raises the almost incredible implication that for some time an entire segment of the Jewish people had been failing to correctly fulfill the *mitzva* of blowing the *shofar*. Rav Hai Gaon is addressing this issue.

ד"ה אתקין רבי אבהו בקסרי וכו'. נשאל לרב האי גאון ז"ל וכי עד שבא רבי אבהו לא
היו ישראל יוצאין ידי תקיעת שופר?! ובל' הזה השיב:

It was asked of Rav Hai Gaon, "Is it possible that until Rebbi Avahu came, not all Jewry fulfilled the obligation to sound the *shofar*?" And he answered as follows:

אל תחשבו בלבבכם כי בימי רבי אבהו נפל ספק בדבר זה, שהרי משניות קדומות
הן—אחת אומרת תרועה ג' יבבות, ואחת אומרת תרועה שלשה שברים, והא אמרינן
בהדיא: „אמר אביי, בהא ודאי פליגי." וכך היה הדבר: מימים קדמונים, מנהג בכל
ישראל, מהן עושין תרועה יבבות קלות, ומהן עושין תרועה יבבות כבדים שהן
שברים. ואלו ואלו יוצאין ידי חובתן. שברים כבדים הן, יבבות קלות תרועות
הן. והיה הדבר נראה כחלוקה אע"פ שאינה חלוקה . . . אלו משנתם כמנהג, ואלו
משנתם כמנהגם. וקאמר אביי בהא פליגי, ולאו פלוגתא היא. ולא היו מטעים אלו את
אלו. אלא מר כי אתריה [קתני] ומר כי אתריה קתני. וחכמים של הללו מודים כי
יבבות תרועה היא, וחכמים של הללו מודים כי שברים תרועה היא. וכשבא רבי אבהו

ראה לתקן תקנה שיהיו כל ישראל עושין מעשה אחד, ולא יראה ביניהן דבר
שההדיוטות רואין אותו כחלוקה.

Do not imagine that in the days of Rebbi Avahu a new question
arose about this. For the *mishnayos* are ancient, one of which
states that the *teruah* sound is made up of three short blasts, and
another which states that it is made up of three long blasts; and
Abbaye clearly said, "These are certainly at variance with each
other." What happened is this: From the earliest days, the practice of Jewry was that some formed the *teruah* by producing
staccato-like blasts and some by producing heavier sounds.
And both groups of people fulfilled their obligation. Heavy,
sh'varim sounds are valid *teruahs*, and light, *staccato* sounds are
equally valid *teruahs*. However, the practices *appeared* to be the
result of different opinions, although there really was nothing at
issue. . . . [When it came to reporting in *mishnayos* the way to
sound the *teruah*,] each Sage merely reported his own practice.

This is [all that] Abbaye meant when he said that the *braissos*
were different—but not that they were in dispute. Neither side
attributed an error to the other. Each one merely reported the
practice of his own community. And the Sages of this community acknowledged that *staccato* sounds are valid *teruahs*,
and the Sages of the other community agreed that long sounds
are valid *teruahs*.
When Rebbi Avahu came, he saw fit to decree that all Jewry act
one way, to eliminate a situation which the uninformed might
see as a matter of discord.

This understanding lends a convenient answer to the question,
"What did they do *until* now?" Up until one or another historic
gathering of the Sages, numerous practices were all valid ways to
fulfill the law. At some point, however, it was deemed necessary to
establish a single practice for all Jewry. The different opinions we see
may merely be reports of how each Sage's community happened to
conduct itself, or how he happened to instruct them. Or each Sage
may have felt that a certain form of practice ought to be universa-
lized from then on. This practice did not necessarily have to be a
combination of the extant ways, as Rebbi Avahu's decree was. It
could parallel the practice that had been performed by that Sage's
community up until that point, or one that did not parallel a particular practice, but which was a form of performing a *mitzva* that the
Sage felt should be adopted as the universal one for all Jewry
anyhow.

Rebbi Yehuda HaNassi and the Official Mishna

Despite Yavneh's success at generally solving previous disputes, new issues came under discussion and spurred debate. And unclarities eventually surfaced regarding the opinions of *Yavneh's* Sages. Differences of opinion also again arose over how to apply these laws to new circumstances and over what new rabbinical decrees were demanded by the times.

In addition, some questions had not been resolved at Yavneh and remained controversial. The *Mishna*[16] itself, referring to its *mishnayos* of an earlier date, tells us:

ולמה מזכירין דברי היחיד בין המרובין, הואיל ואין הלכה אלא כדברי המרובין?
שאם יראה בית דין את דברי היחיד, ויסמוך עליו.

Why are minority opinions recorded if the law always follows the majority?—Because if a *Bes Din* will [eventually] agree with the minority opinion, it can rely upon it.

The presence of a minority opinion in a *mishna* normally indicated to later *Tannaim* that that opinion had not yet been officially eliminated. A consensus had not yet been reached, and an official vote had not yet been taken. It was therefore a future *Sanhedrin's* option—even concerning *gezayros* and *takkonnos*[17]—to decree that that opinion would be the accepted one. Until then, the issue remained unsettled and in dispute.[18]

The task of finalizing a uniform law therefore continued into the days of Rebbi Yehuda HaNassi. Each generation of Sages analyzed

---

[16] *Aid'yos* 1:5.

[17] Chapter Six, entitled "Disputes Over Drashos Previously Accepted by Sanhedrin," discusses the Rambam's *p'sak* that laws which a Sanhedrin determined through *drash* could be challenged by a later, even lesser Sanhedrin. Here we are speaking even of *gezayros* and *takkonnos*, which are less contestable.

[18] *Maharatz Ḥayyos*, p. 387. *Aid'yos* 1:6, the *mishna* that follows the one cited in our text, gives a reason for why minority opinions were recorded even in cases (such as *Mikva'os* 4:1, *Yadayim* 4:1, *Aid'yos* 5:6) where it was known that those opinions *had* already been officially nullified: Those opinions had formerly enjoyed such longevity and popularity that there was the danger that some scholars would still be under the impression that they represented the final law. It was therefore recorded that this view was indeed once an authoritative position, but one that ultimately had been rejected. (*Ibid.*)

and attempted to clarify the statements of the preceding ones. Finally, the *Mishna* was completed (c. 4000/200 C.E.). Most issues were finally closed, though some still remained open, to be determined by the *Amoraim*—the scholars we see in the *Gemora*-commentary on the *Mishna*.

Rav Ashi and Ravina and the Gemora

With the sealing of the *Gemora* two centuries later (c. 4200/400 C.E.) by the *Great Sanhedrin* of Rav Ashi and Ravina, a document of authorized law was completed. The official compendium of laws pertaining to all areas of life, it contains the most rigorous analysis possible of the past Sages' opinions. Subjected to centuries of scrutiny by countless scholars, it represents the most accurate record possible of the intent behind the words with which Hashem instructed His People.

Additional Notes to Chapter 10

5. Rav Ḥayyos (*Atteress Ẓvi, Mishpaht HaHora'a*, p. שפ"ז) explains, through this, the phrase, ״רב תנא הוא ופליג״, Rav (an *Amora*) is (equal to) a *Tanna* and can therefore disagree (with a *Mishna*).'' Rav, it is known, was a member of Rebbi Yehuda HaNassi's Sanhedrin. He usually participated in those sessions which decided what was to be admitted into the *Mishna* text as closed issues. However, when he was unable to attend a session and he did not agree to the Sanhedrin's conclusions at that session, he had the right and obligation to continue to maintain his own opinion. We can assume that it was in such cases that Rav maintained opinions independent of the *Mishna*.

8. The issue of ''*semicha*'' involved the requirement regarding some sacrifices (see *Menachos* 9:7) for one to lay his hands upon the animal to be offered, leaning upon it with his full body's weight (see *Vayikra* 1:4, 3:2). Under dispute was whether this סמיכה, leaning, must be done when the procedure of the offering begins (i.e., immediately preceding the *shechita*) or whether it may be done some time in advance. This became a practical issue once there was a דרבנן prohibition against supporting oneself upon animals on *Shabbos* and *Yom Tov*: If it is Biblically permissible to perform *semicha* sometime before the sacrifice is offered, then it *must* be done *before* the arrival of *Yom Tov*, and not *on* the *Yom Tov*.

Actually, there were even earlier *machlokos*, such as one in the days of King Shaul and David (*Sanhedrin* 19b). But the *Maharatz Ḥayyos* (*Mishpaht HaHora'a*, 9, see also *G'ra*, note 1 on *Temura* 16a) explains that these were settled immediately. (See *Tosefos*, *Ḥaggiga* 16a ד"ה יוסי בן יועזר כו'.)

9. In *Torahs N'vi'im, Maamar Torah Sheh-b'ahl Peh*, (כל כתבי מהר"ץ חיות, ירושלים, תר"א) HoRav Ḥayyos notes that the Talmud's remark (*Yerushalmi Ḥaggiga*, I) that the "first" *machlokess* took place in the days of Yosay ben-Yoezer, cannot be taken at face value. The Rambam, in his *Hakdama L'Payrush HaMishnayos* (*Introduction to the Talmud*, p. 38) states that *machlokess* and the procedure of voting upon different stands took place from the time of Moses. And *Tosefos* (*Ḥaggiga* 16a) points out that the Talmud (*Sanhedrin* 19b) mentions a *halachic machlokess* between David and King Shaul. We also know of a specific *machlokess* Aaron had with Moses (*Vayikra* 10:16-20) and another which Esther had with the Sanhedrin (*Megilla* 7a) over whether to include *The Book of Esther* in the Bible. *Maharatz Ḥayyos* explains that, as was pointed out, previous to the *machlokess* of Yosay ben-Yoezer's day, all disputes were quickly resolved by consensus or vote. Yosay ben-Yoezer's dispute with Yosay ben-Yoḥonon was the first to persist for generations.

10. The three new issues disputed by Hillel and Shammai are listed in *Aid'yos* 1:1-2 and *Shabbos* 14b, 15a tells us that these were the only ones:

Whether the amount of bread that must have *challah* taken from it nowadays is that containing even only one *kav* of flour, as per Shammai, or two *kavvim*, as per Hillel

Whether the physical perception of the *tum'ah* of a *needa* has a retroactive effect (דיין שעתן—as explained in the first chapter of this book)

Whether the amount of unfit water (שאובים) that renders a *mikveh* unkosher is only one *hin*, as per Hillel, or nine *kavvim*, as per Shammai.

The first issue deals with interpreting Scripture (i.e., *darshonning* the word עריסותיכם in *Bamidbar* 15:20), the last one with a rabbinical *gezayra*, and the middle one with an issue which some *Rishonim* understand to be *d'oraissa* and some understand to be rabbinical.

Another new *machlokos* between Hillel and Shammai concerned whether to decree a *gezayra* that harvested grapes be treated as susceptible to *tum'ah* even if they were not first wetted (*Hilchos Tum'as Ochlin* 11:1, but see *Rashi* on *Shabbos* 15a). (Based upon *Vayikra* 11:34, the Oral Law teaches that if certain liquids fall upon one's food products, the food products contract *tum'ah* when a dead crawling creature falls upon them; but only if one would otherwise consider the liquid beneficial.) But Hillel eventually conceded to the institution of this *gezayra* (*Shabbos* 15a, *Avoda Zorra* 39b).

12. According to the Rambam (*Hakdama L'Payrush HaMishnayos*) the "increased" disputes of these bodies occurred after the three disputes that Hillel and Shammai had as individuals (*Aid'yos* 1:1-2) took place:

לא נמצא שנחלקו שמאי והלל אלא בהלכות יחידות. ... אבל כאשר רפתה שקידת
התלמידים על החכמה ונחשלה סברתם סברתם נגד סברת הלל ושמאי רבם (ס"א ובהם—ולא
מובן) נפלה מחלוקת ביניהם בעיין על דברים רבים.

Shammai and Hillel are found in dispute in only a few *halachos*. ... But when their disciples' diligence slackened and their reasoning abilities grew weak in comparison to their teachers Hillel and Shammai, disputes arose between them in analyzing many matters.

Rav Sherira Gaon, a basic source for history, dates the occurrence of these "increased" disputes after the destruction of the Temple in 3828 and the subsequent dispersions:

וכיון דחרב בית המקדש ואזלו [ליבנה ואח"כ] לביתר (סנהדרין י"ז:) וחרב נמי ביתר
(גיטין נז.) אתבדרו רבנן לכל צד. ומשום הנך מהומות ושמדים ושבושים שהיו באותו
זמן, לא שמשו התלמידים כל צרכן ונפישו מחלוקת. ... ואע"ג דאדחו ב"ש ונקבעה
לכל הלכה כב"ה (עירובין י"ג:) היתה פלוגתא בדורו של רבן גמליאל בדברים אחרים
בין ר' אליעזר דהוה שמותי ור' יהושע דאינון תלמידי רבן יוחנן בן זכאי (תלמיד
דהלל).

Once the Holy Temple was destroyed and the Sages went [to Yavneh and then] to Betar (*Sanhedrin* 17b) and Betar too was destroyed (*Gittin* 57b), the Sages dispersed in all directions. Because of these tumultuous occurrences, the persecutions and turmoil, the disciples of those times insufficiently attended to their teachers, and disputes increased in number. ... And although the *halacha* was decided [as a rule] in favor of the opinions of *Bes Hillel*, putting aside those of *Bes Shammai* (*Eruvin* 13b), there was a split in Rabban Gamliel's generation in other matters between Rebbi Eliezer, a Shammaite, and Rebbi Yehoshua, both of whom were disciples of Rabban Yoḥonon ben Zakkai.

The *Doros HaRishonim* interprets the *Gemora* differently. He insists that the "increased" disputes were not the famous disputes of *Bes Hillel* and *Bes Shammai* but occurred more than 140 years before the destruction of the Holy Temple and *before* the Sanhedrin of Hillel and Shammai was formed. He contends that the "disciples" of Hillel and Shammai, upon forming the two *Houses* under their leaders, succeeded in *reducing* the number of disputes and narrowing down to one the position of each *House*. (It was during this same time that Hillel

and Shammai had their three disputes with each other [Aid'yos 1:1-3]
and the Sages of their Academies, agreeing with neither Hillel nor
Shammai, voted in their own opinion [ibid.].) The "increased" disputes were not these but the multitude of conflicting opinions previously sustained by the two Houses. The famous disputes of Bes Hillel
and Bes Shammai were the remaining two-sided ones narrowed down
from the originally larger number of disputes.

14. Rav Ḥayyos (Torahs Nevi'im, Maamar Lo Tasur pp. 103-104) notes
that one such moment is described in the Rambam's Mishna commentary on Shabbos 13b:

וחנניה בן חזקיה בן גרון ז"ל מבעלי החכמה וגדול בדורו . . . והיו החכמים ע"ה
מבקרין אותו תמיד . . . ופעם אחת בקרו אותו ונתקבץ שם קבוץ גדול מתלמידי
שמאי ובית הלל. ולא נשאר באותו הדור מי שהיה ראוי להוראה שלא היו באותו
מעמד ונמנו והיו בית שמאי יותר והשם אמר אחרי רבים להטות.

Hannania ben-Ḥizkiah was a Gadol Hador (a Torah great of his
day) . . . and the Sages would always visit him. . . . One time,
they visited him, and all the disciples of Shammai and Hillel
were gathered there, and not one person of that generation was
absent who was qualified to rule. They (therefore) took a vote
and Bes Shammai outnumbered Bes Hillel, and the Torah
declares, "Follow the majority!"

Chapter 11

"These and Those" . . . Or: Can Everyone Be Right?

The scene is a classroom of boys with Gemoras open before them. The rebbi is in front of the room, chalk in his hand, pointing at diagrams and charts he has drawn on the chalkboard. For the fifth time that hour, he is explaining Rabba's sequence of logic, having just finished reviewing—for an equal number of times—the logic of his opponent, Abbaye.[1] Abbaye maintains that in the situation in question, one must pay for damages; Rabba disagrees. Each one has proofs for his opinion.

Suddenly, eyes open wide as the class grasps the total picture. With their new sense of understanding, the students roll the concepts over in their minds, tasting the logic of each protagonist, the logic of Rabba and the logic of Abbaye. But then one of the students

---

[1] Abbaye was Rabba's disciple. Abbaye's usual opponent was Rava, but here we are specifically speaking of *Rabba* and Abbaye.

199

*raises his hand in quest of the rebbi's attention. A look of perplexity
is on the student's face.*

*The rebbi calls on him, and the student blurts out, "But rebbi!
Who is right? Abbaye or Rabba?"*

*The rebbi looks to the class with a knowing smile. This is an old
problem he has encountered many times with younger students. His
answer is his standard one. Some students 'get it,' and others don't.
Dramatically he exclaims, "Who is right? Who is right? There's no
such thing as, 'Who is right.' They're both right!* אלו ואלו דברי אלוקים
חיים הם—*These and those are the words of the Living G-d!"*

It's a profound statement. It has the ring of truth to it.

They're *both* right. Abbaye is right, and Rabba, who disagrees, is right.

*But one student, the one who asked the question, sits perturbed.
How can two opposite opinions both be right? And if Rabba's teaching was correct, why did his disciple, Abbaye, step in to disagree
with it?*

Especially when speaking of Torah matters, words must be carefully defined. Talmud study is, after all, the careful defining of the
words of authorities, who defined the words of the Oral Law, which
is largely G-d's explanation of the words of the Written Torah.
Words are the means through which Hashem communicated His
will. They are the precious tools which build thought. As tools,
when they are kept sharply defined, they can cut through barriers of
intellectual murkiness. Dulled, they weary the user and frustrate his
attempts at comprehension.

The question "Who is right" tenaciously resists a clear answer
because the question itself is sloppily constructed. *'Who is right'
about what?*

The Word "Right"

The word "right" signifies something that conforms to a previously
established criterion. If that criterion is a statement made by a past
authority, or his intention behind it, then only a conclusion identical
to that statement or intention can be called "right."

Our perturbed student, in the illustration above, gathered that
the goal of Rabba and Abbaye was to discern the thoughts of a previous authority. After all, their entire debate revolved around
analyzing that authority's words and actions. Rabba and Abbaye,
each one reaching an opposite conclusion as to what that authority
meant, could not both be right. The honest answer to the student's

question "Who is right" would be: "I don't know. But we *posken*, in action we follow, the conclusion of So-and-So."

Obviously, only one opinion of the law can be identical to a law that was revealed to Moses. For example, let's assume that at Sinai *Hashem* specifically declared whether or not a certain object is טמא, unfit for holy purposes, and this law was forgotten. Now one Sage says it is טמא, unfit, and another says it is טהור, fit. Obviously, the two Sages can't *both* be conforming to what had originally been decreed. At least one of them must be wrong in his conclusion.

As the *Drashos HaRan* (No. 3) declares:

אחרי שדברי המטמאים והמטהרים הפכיים בעצמם, אי אפשר ששניהם יסכימו
לאמת. . . . באמת שאחד משני הדעות הוא דעת אמיתי, והשני דעת הפכו!

Since the words of those who declare something unfit and those who declare it fit are intrinsically contradictory, it is impossible for both to be conforming to the truth. . . . Clearly, one of the two opinions is the true one, and the other is the opposite!

The *Yahm Shel Shlomo, Introduction to Bava Kamma*, puts forth a similar thought:

שלא יצא הדבר מפי משה לעולם להיות שני הפכים בנושא אחד.

Never did two opposite predicates for one subject escape the lips of Moses!

Consider also a law that was determined by a Sanhedrin or Sage for the first time *after* Moses' days, because *Hashem* had left it for the Sages to uncover by analyzing Scripture. If later authorities disagree over what the Sanhedrin or Sage had meant, they cannot both be right. This is an accepted fact in the Talmud. We have seen a case[2] in which a Sage actually reported that one of his disciples misinterpreted him. But even without a Sage explicitly saying so, if two scholars are in total disagreement over the meaning of a certain Sage's remark, we must admit that at least one of them must be at variance with the Sage's original intention. The man meant to say *something*. One of the later scholars must have interpreted the

---

[2] *Ḥulin* 133a, cited in the chapter entitled "Errors on the Receiving End."

earlier Sage's statement differently from the way he had meant it to be taken.[3]

In the words of *Rashi* (*Kesubos* 57a):[4]

‏. . . דכי פליגי תרי אליבא דחד—מר אמר הכי אמר פלוני, ומר אמר הכי אמר
‏פלוני—חד מינייהו משקר.

When two Sages argue over what someone said, one saying that the man said [or held] *this*, and one saying that he said [or held] something *else*, *then one of them is making a false statement.*

Likewise, the *Tosafists* (*Kesubos* 57a) say:

‏. . . אי פליגי רבין ורב דימי בדברי רבי יוחנן ורבי יהושע בן לוי—שזה אומר כך
‏אמר, וזה אומר כך אמר—אחד מהם טעה בשמועתו.

If . . .[5] one [Sage] says, "He said [or held] *this*," and the other says, "He said [or held] *that*"—one of them erred in [properly understanding] his lesson."[6]

The cited statements by *Rashi, Tosefos, Drashos HaRan,* and *Yahm Shel Shlomo* represent these authorities' reactions to a simplistic understanding of two adages. One is found in *Eruvin* 13b:

---

[3] Several examples were given in the chapter entitled "Errors on the Receiving End." To repeat one, in *Bava Metsia* 66a we have:
‏א״ל ריש גלותא (לרב נחמן): „רב יהודה קרע לשטרך.״ א״ל: „דרדקא קרעיה?! גברא רבה קרעיה?! חזא ביה
‏טעמיה וקרעיה!״ איכא דאמרי ... א״ל: „דרדקא קרעיה! דכ״ע לגבי דידי דרדקי נינהו!״
One version depicts Rav Nachman agreeing to Rav Yehuda's invalidation of a document, whereas the other version has him vehemently opposing it. Obviously, one version is inaccurate.

[4] The *Gemora* is dealing with a situation which can tolerate two interpretations: (1) Say that two *Amoraim*, though expressing themselves differently, agree in their descriptions of each side of some earlier authorities' dispute; or (2) say that the earlier authorities were not in dispute at all. They were both expressing one thought, but the later *Amoraim* are arguing over what that thought was. The *Gemora* states that the first choice is preferable: ‏"דפליגי תרי אמוראי אטעמא דנפשייהו, ולא
‏פליגי תרי אמוראי אליבא דחד אמורא." *[It is preferable to have] two [earlier] Amoraim argue their own issue, than to have two [later] Amoraim argue over identifying an [earlier] Amoraic consensus. Rashi* and *Tosefos,* cited here in our text, explain why.

[5] For ease of reading, the following words of translation were deleted: [If] Rabbin and Rav Dimmi argue about [the sides taken against each other by] Rebbi Yoḥonon and Rebbi Yehoshua ben Levi, in that one [Sage] says . . .

[6] See Additional Notes at the end of this chapter.

שלש שנים נחלקו בית שמאי ובית הלל. הללו אומרים הלכה כמותנו והללו אומרים
הלכה כמותנו. יצאת בת קול ואמרה: אלו ואלו דברי אלקים חיים הן, והלכה כבית
הלל.

For three years, *Bes Shammai* and *Bes Hillel* disputed: These
said, "The *halacha* is as we say," and these said, "The *halacha* is
as we say." A Heavenly Voice declared: "These and those are
the words of the Living G-d! And the *halacha* follows [the
opinions of] *Bes Hillel.*"

The second, similar adage, is found in *Ḥaggiga* 3b:

„בעלי אסופות נתנו מרועה אחד," . . . „בעלי אסופות"—אלו תלמידי חכמים
שיושבים אגודות אגודות ועוסקים בתורה, הללו מטמאין והללו מטהרין, הללו פוסלין
והללו מכשירין, הללו אוסרין והללו מתירין. שמא תאמר, „הואיל והללו וכו', היאך
אני לומד תורה מעתה?" ת"ל: „כלם נתנו מרועה אחד"—כולן פרנס אחד אמרן מפי
הגבורה ברוך הוא. שנ', „וידבר אלקים את כל הדברים האלה לאמר."

"Men of Collections Given by One Shepherd" (*Kohelles*
12:11)—this refers to the Sages who sit in different assemblies
and engross themselves with the Torah, these declaring things
tom'ay and these declaring them *tahor*, these declaring things
posul and these declaring them kosher; these prohibiting things
and these permitting them. Perhaps you will say, "How then
can I learn the Torah (i.e., How do I know which ones grasped
the Truth)?" The verse goes on to say: "They were all given
from one shepherd." All of them were said by one head (Moses)
who received them all from the mouth of the Holy One, Blessed
be He. As it says, "And G-d spoke *all* these words, saying . . ."

On the surface, these passages indicate not only that both sides
of a *machlokess* are valid logical conclusions from extant information, but also that when G-d spoke to Moses, he actually conveyed
as final halacha to him "these and those" words. But it seems hardly
conceivable that G-d would have conveyed incorrect opinions to
Moses! Thus the negation of this idea by the above-quoted authorities. To again quote the *Drashos HaRan, Drash No. 3*, this time more
completely:

„וידבר אלקים את כל הדברים האלה לאמר" (שמות כ:א): דרשו מלת „כל" לומר
שאפי' דברי מי שלא השיג האמת נאמר למשה בסיני. וזה הענין צריך עיון, איך נאמר
ששתי כתות המחלוקת נאמרו למשה מפי הגבורה? הנה שמאי אומר מקב לחלה והלל
אומר מקבים. באמת שאחד משני הדעות הוא דעת אמיתי, והשני דעת הפכו! א"כ
איך לדרוש שיצא מפי הגבורה דבר בלתי אמיתי!

They *darshonned* the word "all" [in the verse "And G-d spoke all these words, saying . . ." (*Sh'mos* 20:1)] to teach that even the words of *the one who did not attain the truth* were told to Moses at Sinai. Now, this concept requires investigation. How can we say that both sides of a *machlokess* were told to Moses by G-d? Behold, it says: "Shammai says one *kav* of dough needs *challah* to be taken from it, and Hillel says two *kavs*" (Aidyos 1:2).[7] In truth, one of the two opinions is the true one, and the other is not! How could we interpret the verse to be telling us that something untruthful came from the mouth of G-d?

The Meaning of "These and Those"

What the commentators (and common sense) unanimously tell us "These and those" does *not* mean is easy to understand. What they say it *does* mean, however, is more varied and complex;[8] and applying their explanations to specific *machlokos* in the Talmud is quite demanding. The following is an attempt to present the different interpretations. As we present each interpretation, we will try to crystalize the aspect in which it understands that disputing Sages are both "right."

Rav Yisroel Salanter and Rav Yitzchak Hutner—All Opinions Are Legitimate For Study of Torah.

In our first chapter we have cited Rav Yisroel Salanter's principle, stated in the work *Ohr Yisroel*, that Hashem created all human beings with differing sensibilities regarding judgement on the most plausible arrangement of facts and the amount of weight to be given to one proof or objection over another. Rav Yitzchak Hutner (*Pachad Yitzchak, Ḥanuka, Maamer* III) refers to this as well as to Rav Salanter's application of this principle as an explanation of "These and those." Both of these relatively recent authorities emphasize as the message of the dictum not the absolute *halachic* truth to all opinions as much as their legitimacy as subjects of Torah study. All opinions arrived at through proper analysis are subsumed

---

[7] This illustration chosen for a *machlokess* is the first of the three disputes between Hillel and Shammai themselves (as opposed to between *Bes Hillel* and *Bes Shammai*.) Incidentally, the majority of Sages voted in favor of a third opinion in each of these cases.

[8] See Additional Notes at the end of this chapter.

under the title of "Torah"—including the opinions that are ultimately nullified as *halacha*. "Torah" means not only what Hashem told
Moses and which may have been lost, but also all valid attempts to
reconstruct that information. (Perhaps this can be seen from
Hashem's Own reference to all the Sages' instructions—including
those determined through vote over unclear matters—as "Torah:"
"When you have *halachic* controversy . . . according to the Torah
they teach you . . . you shall act; you must not veer from the thing
they tell you, right or left [*D'varim* 17:8-11].) In other words,
"These and those" means that one who spends his day studying and
analyzing the opinions of *Bes Shammai* is fulfilling the commandment to study Torah, although *Bes Shammai's* opinion is not the
accepted *halacha*.

Indeed, Rav Salanter maintains, certainly such a principle was
known ever since the Torah was given, since the Torah tells us that
the conclusions reached by the Sages are to constitute for us the
word of Hashem: "And you shall perform all His commandments
. . . for it is not hidden from you nor far away; it is not [any longer]
in Heaven, but is very near to you through your mouth and through
your mind." It was re-announced by the Heavenly voice regarding
the three-year dispute between *Bes Shammai* and *Bes Hillel* only so
that—

לא יפול לב העם, (בראותם כי זה שלש שנים שב"ש מחזיקים לאמור הלכה כדבריהם
כי להם היתרון, וב"ה להיפך) פן ואולי ח"ו נטו אשורייהם מעט מטהרת המחשבה,
ובאו ח"ו לקצת נגיעת הדעת. אשר לא בכמו אלה בחר ה' למסור תורתו, להקרא
תורת ה' גם בדעה הנדחית. לזאת הודיעה הבת קול, כי לדעתם היתרון. ולזאת גם
דברי ב"ש הנדחית דברי אלקים חיים הן, וההוגה בדבריהם הוגה בתורת ה' ית"ש.

The heart of the people would not despair (by seeing that for the
past three years *Bes Shammai* persevered in saying that the
halacha should follow its opinion because it was the superior
[body] and *Bes Hillel* claimed the same for itself) in the thought
that just perhaps, G-d forbid, these authorities' feet slipped ever
so slightly from untainted, objective and pure thought, and that
their thinking contained, G-d forbid, some slight self-
interest—forming opinions which are not the kind that Hashem
chose for being handed over as His Torah, the kind which, even
if rejected as final *halacha*, are called the Torah of Hashem.
Therefore the Heavenly Voice informed the people that each
side genuinely felt objectively correct, and therefore even the
rejected words of *Bes Shammai* are the words of the Living G-d,
and one who studies them is studying the Torah of Hashem.

The Yahm Shel Shlomo—Conforming to Sound Logic

Others are more specific about the aspect that grants "learning validity" even to opinions not accepted as final *halacha*. To the understanding of the *Yahm Shel Shlomo*, too, "These and those" does not mean at all to ascribe any matching of the opinions of the Sages to the facts. Though every Sage naturally attempts to match the ruling Hashem knows to be true, the adage "These and those are the words of the Living G-d" is not at all addressing the issue of whether the Sage was successful. The adage is merely speaking of each Sage's own certainty regarding the validity and holiness of his conclusions, though they are contested by another Sage:

וכולם דברי אלקים חיים, כאילו קיבל כל אחד מפי הגבורה ומפי משה שלא יצא
הדבר מפי משה לעולם להיות שני הפכים בנושא אחד. אעפ"כ דמהו החכם לרוב
אישורו וחיזקו שאין בין דבר שהוציא משכל הפועל אשר נתעוללו לו במושכלות
שניות ושלישית, לבין דבר שבא אליו בכח חוש הדיבור בהלכה למשה מסיני, אף
שלא צריירו במופת שכלו להיותו הכרח, לולי צד הקבלה איש מפי איש (הקדמה לבבא
קמא).

They are all the words of the Living G-d, as if each of the Sages received his views from the mouth of G-d and the lips of Moses. Even though two opposite predicates for one subject never escaped the lips of Moses, a Torah-scholar's thorough corroboration of facts convinces him that *there is no difference* between [the validity of the] information that he educed from G-d's Active Intellect by means of compelling logic, and [the validity of the] information that came to him through the power of speech [i.e. his sense of hearing], which tells him what Moses said at Sinai, for the factuality of the latter information does not have the benefit of logic to support it but is only based on the fact that it came from Moses through an unbroken chain of tradition (*Introduction to Bava Kamma*).

The logical inferences drawn from preserved data by a Torah-scholar are just as valid and holy—to that scholar's mind—as the data itself. Therefore, whatever conclusions a Sage reaches are *as valid and holy* as the explicit words of Hashem. And even if another Sage reaches different conclusions, they are "[both as valid and holy—to each Sage's mind—as] the words of the Living G-d."

The Kabballists

There is a citation which seemingly explains "These and those" as

an assertion of the very idea the above commentaries rejected: that
G-d assigned more than one law to a given case. Yet our *Yahm Shel
Shlomo*, at least, so strongly presumes a non-literal interpretation of
this source, that he presents it as a *support* for his position:

> והמקובלים כתבו טעם לדבר לפי שכל הנשמות היו בהר סיני וקבלן דרך מ"ט
> צינורות . . . „וכל ישראל רואים את הקולות"—הן הדיעות המחלקות בצינור, וכל
> אחד ראה דרך צינור שלו לפי השגתו, וקבל כפי כח נשמת עליונו . . . עד שאחד יגיע
> לטהור והשני יגיע לקצה האחרון לטמא והשלישי לאמצעות רחוק מן הקציות והכל
> אמת הבן.

The *Kabballists* wrote in explanation: All the souls were present
at Mount Sinai and received [the words of Hashem][9] through
forty-nine conduits. "And all the people *saw* the sounds"
(*Sh'mos* 20:15) refers to the data channelled and distributed
through those conduits, and every individual perceived [G-d's
words] through his own conduit, according to his own grasp of
things, and [thus] received [the Torah's laws] according to the
capacity of his soul from above. This produced the result that
one would reach a law of טהור, a second would reach the opposite extreme of טמא, and a third would reach a middle ground.
Yet all is Truth. Understand this.

Far from understanding this *kabballistic* source on a superficial
level, to be saying that G-d proclaimed different laws to different
people, the *Yahm Shel Shlomo* considers this source as evidence
supporting his position. The *Kabballists* are really saying the same
thing, except that they are connecting the origin of the multiple
opinions to the time of the original Revelation. By no means are they
saying that the people physically present at Sinai were told more
than one law per case. The *Kabballists*, according to the *Yahm Shel
Shlomo*, are describing how different people interpret information in
different ways.

Forty-nine Considerations

Similar to the above *kabballistic* source—and equally demanding
of a non-literal interpretation—is the comment (already mentioned
in Chapter "Loss of Halachos") by the *Ritva* on the "These and

[9] Even though the most that the people may have heard directly from Hashem were
the עשרת הדברות, the *Decalogue*, perhaps this source is considering the fact that the
Decalogue's words can be understood to allude to all the 613 commandments.

those" passage in *Eruvin*. The *Tosefos Shantz* in his commentary on *Aid'yos* (1:5) cites the same *kabballistic* teaching:

„אלו ואלו דברי אלקים חיים" (עירובין י"ג:)—שאלו רבנן צרפת ז"ל האיך אפשר
שיהא אלו ואלו דברי אלקים חיים זה אוסר וזה מתיר, ותרצו כי כשעלה משה למרום
לקבל התורה הראו לו על כל דבר ודבר מ"ט פנים לאיסור ומ"ט פנים להיתר. ושאל
להקב"ה על זה ואמר שיהא זה מסור לחכמי ישראל שבכל דור ודור ויהיה הכרעה
כמותם ונכון הוא לפי הדרש. ובדרך האמת יש טעם סוד בדבר.

"The words of both sides of a *halachic* dispute are the words of
the Living G-d"—The Rabbis of France asked how it could be
possible that they are both the words of G-d when one sides
permits something and the other forbids it. And they answered
that when Moses ascended On High to receive the Torah, they
(the Angels) showed him forty-nine considerations to forbid
each thing and forty-nine other considerations to permit it.
When he questioned the Holy One about this, he was told that
the responsibility rested upon the Sages of Israel in each generation to determine the *halacha*.[10]

This explanation leaves one perplexed. Was Moses given no
clear-cut decisions? Surely the Torah is replete with definite laws.
Pigs are non-kosher. Murder is prohibited. The "fruit of the
glorious tree" (*Vayikra* 23:40) is an *esrog*. The basic oral *halachos*
and explanations of Scripture were certainly given to Moses in a
clear, unambiguous, and unequivocal way, and that is how he
taught them to the people. Even if we restrict the above explanation
of "forty-nine considerations to permit and forty-nine to forbid" to
only *some* details of the laws—perhaps to those that effect only post-
Mosaic situations—we remain with an insurmountable paradox:
Moses was told that the Sages will determine the laws; yet the Sages'
goal is to determine the laws Moses was told, or which Hashem
desired for us. If Moses was not told the laws and *Hashem* had no
specific laws in mind, what solutions could the Sages hope to find?
What bedrock was there on which the authorities were to anchor
themselves?

In answer, it may be noted that this source does not really claim
that G-d said that there was more than one law for a given case. It
only says that Moses was shown the *arguments* that future Sages
will present to support different conclusions. Perhaps we are being
told that though Moses knew the true law, he was concerned about

[10] See Additional Notes at the end of this chapter.

the confusion of future generations. Hashem assured him that each generation will have benefit of competent Sages to make final *halachic* decisions. But this answer is unnecessary. We should note that *Rashi* elsewhere (*Menachos* 29b) understands the phrase ''בשעה שעלה משה למרום, at the time Moses ascended to the Above,'' to be referring precisely to the period *prior* to Moses' receiving the laws of the Torah. In effect, then, *before* receiving the Torah, Moses was at a loss to assign specific decisions to many situations. That is why the Torah was needed, and Hashem told Moses that the Sages, who would have the Torah, would determine the *halacha* based upon Scripture's formulae. *Then* Hashem revealed to Moses the Torah's laws and the methods of Torah interpretation. Thus, ''these and those'' conform to human logic and even the Will of Hashem as these existed *before* Hashem prescribed the limitations and parameters of *halacha*.[11]

''These and Those''— When There Was No Previous P'sak

Let us now examine how *Rashi* (*Kesubos* 57a) contrasts those situations in which we do apply ''These and those'' to those in which we do not. Rashi states:

דכי פליגי תרי אליבא דחד—מר אמר הכי אמר פלוני, ומר אמר הכי אמר פלוני— חד מינייהו משקר. אבל כי פליגי תרי אמוראי בדין או באיסור והיתר, כל חד אמר הכי מיסתבר טעמא—אין כאן שקר. כל חד וחד סברא דידיה קאמר. מר יהיב טעמא להיתירא, ומר יהיב טעמא לאיסורא. מר מדמי מילתא למילתא הכי, ומר מדמי ליה בעניינא אחרינא. ואיכא למימר אלו ואלו דברי אלקים חיים הם.

When two Sages argue over someone's statement, one saying that the man said [or held] *this*, and one saying that he said [or held] something *else* then one of them is making a false statement. But when two *Amoraim* are arguing over whether something is permitted or forbidden, each one saying, *this* is more logical—then no falsehood is present. Each one is presenting his *own* conclusion [and not attempting to report someone else's]. This one gives the reason [the matter] should be permitted, and this one gives the reason it should be forbidden. This one likens [the matter] to this subject, and this one likens it to another. Here we can say, ''These and those are the words of the Living G-d.''

[11] See the ''Perspective,'' in this work, based on the thoughts of Rav Simon Schwab, *shlita*.

Let us analyze *Rashi's* words up to this point. What is his contrast? How does the fact that each side in a dispute makes its own comparison avoid the problem that one of them is wrong? What has been gained by substituting an attempt to correctly apply a Scriptural verse for an attempt to correctly apply a *person's* statement? Deciding whether something is being described by one verse or another ultimately involves determining what the verses originally meant. The criterion remains one of corresponding to a past thought, and so it remains that only one disputant can be correct!

Perhaps *Rashi* is not talking about likening a present reality to a past description; but rather is referring to the gauging of the present reality itself. The relevant opinions of past authorities are understood the same way by all, *but the present situation is itself not clear-cut.*

There is a saying in *Needa* 20b which expresses this thought: "אין לדיין אלא מה שעיניו רואות"—a judge can only decide by the way he perceives reality. What to one judge looks, and always would have looked, like the color of blood which establishes that a woman is טמאה, will look, and would have always looked, to another judge like the color that determines her to be טהורה. The same applies to all areas of perception. Likewise, the question of "these and those" may not be one of better understanding a previous authority's remarks, but of sensory perceptions by each generation's Sages, always a subjective matter. Sizing up the present situation requires a total grasp of innumerable factors, the slightest change in which can alter the final decision. The result is variant opinions—without encroaching upon those of former authorities.

If this is *Rashi's* meaning, then we may conclude that he holds as follows: The adage "These and those" must be restricted to those issues which are matters of subjective perceptions, issues where no attempt is made to match an original decision. There is none to match. The message of "These and those" is: Trust the perception of present reality determined by your authority, though another's perception may be different, because this reality is true to his perception.

Changing Times

However, when we continue our citation of *Rashi*, we may conclude that he means something else entirely:

ואיכא למימר „אלו ואלו דברי אלקים חיים הם": זימנין דשייך האי טעמא וזימנין
דשייך האי טעמא שהטעם מתהפך לפי שינוי הדברים בשינוי מועט.

It is feasible to say "These and those are the words of the Living
G-d" [in areas that past opinions are not at issue, since] sometimes *this* consideration appertains and sometimes *that* consideration appertains; for the [pertinent] consideration reverses
itself according to a change of things/situations, with just a
slight change.

If we are to interpret the word זימנין, *sometimes*, as actually referring to different periods of time, then we might understand *Rashi* as
follows: The concept of "These and those" is not restricted to issues
of subjective sensory perception. It encompasses objective criteria,
but is restricted to disputes between Sages of different times. The
Sages *are* attempting to match the truth as was revealed by G-d, and
they are succeeding. The rulings may seem contradictory, but that is
only when viewing them superficially. For at the time of one Sage
who followed the formulae delineated by Scripture and Sinai, the
situations surrounding an issue tipped the scales of *halacha* one
way, whereas at the time of another Sage who followed the same formulae, subtly different elements came into play, tipping the scales
the other way. The circumstances the Sages are ruling on are not
really identical, and all authorities would agree on how to rule in any
given time. The message of "These and those" is: Disputes across
generations are only apparently disputes; the later Sages are really of
one opinion with the earlier ones.

(Later we shall suggest yet another interpretation of *Rashi's*
words.)

The Ohr Gedaliahu—Different Times and Places

The explanation offered by the *Ohr Gedaliahu*[12] clearly interprets
the adage of "These and those" to be referring to the decisions of
contemporaries in different locales, if not, as in our second understanding of *Rashi*, to disputes between non-contemporaries:

וזהו סוד הדבר של „אלו ואלו" . . . ששני הדעות יש להן מקור ושורש למעלה . . .
ומצינו בגמ' שבת ק"ל. דבאתריה דר"א היו כורתין עצים בשבת, כי קודם שנפסק
ההלכה דלא כר"א היו נוהגין באתריה כמותו, כי שני הדעות יש להן שורש בתורה.
ובאותו זמן היה רצון הבורא שבאותו עיר יתנהג לפי אותו השורש בתורה שמותר

---

[12] Rav Gedaliah Schor, *Sefer Ohr Gedaliahu*, p. 40, Ḥanuka—Yom Tov shel Torah
Sheh b'ahl Peh.

לכרות עצים, עד שנפסק הלכה דלא כר"א, שאז היה רצון הבורא ית' שבכל מקום
יתנהגו לפי השורש בתורה דלא כר"א.

[T]his is the point of "These and those . . ."— namely, that both
opinions are rooted and find their source in the World Above.
For example, we find in *Shabbos* 130a that they used to chop
wood on Shabbos [in preparation for a *briss meelah* that fell out
on that day] in Rebbi Eliezer's city, because before the *halacha*
was decided against Rebbi Eliezer, they conducted themselves
according to him in his city. Both opinions [Rebbi Eliezer's and
his opponents'] have their source in the Torah. And at that time
the Will of G-d was that in that city the practice should follow
that root in the Torah which permits the chopping of wood [and
this was so] until the *halacha* was established to be not in accordance with Rebbi Eliezer. Then, the Will of G-d was that everywhere the practice should follow that root in the Torah which
was not like Rebbi Eliezer.

The *Ohr Gedaliahu* posits that there is a single unifying formula
which really produces opposite results in different circumstances. As
an analogy: Wood burns, metal melts, and water boils when exposed
to fire. The fire stays the same; it is the objects subjected to it that
change We can devise a formula to explain how fire can produce
such disparate results. Similarly, the spiritual world of *halacha* has a
unifying formula that produces seemingly inconsistent results. The
Sages, using this unifying formula, are addressing different situations and are not really in dispute. Each Sage would decide the same
as the other in the other's locale and time.

This interpretation by the *Ohr Gedaliahu* and the one we gave in
our second understanding of *Rashi* restrict the concept of "These
and those" to disputes that take place across generations, or across
geographic locations. But this is an admission that if contemporaneous fellow residents are disagreeing, then at least one of them
must not have discovered the true unifying formula, and "These and
those" would not apply. The adage would also not apply to disputes
about how the *halacha* should be established for all generations and
localities. But this restricts the adage of "These and Those" to very
few *machlokos* in the Talmud. For we cannot lose sight of the fact
that the Sages in the Talmud usually do dispute each others' decisions in absolute terms. They do not concede that if they were in
their opponents' times or places they would agree with them. Each
Sage maintains that the decision *he* made for *his* city in *his* time was
the one that Hashem had intended to be the eventual, standard law

for all times in all places. Indeed, the very source from which the expression "These and those" comes, states, "שלש שנים . . . הללו אומרים הלכה כמותנו והללו אומרים הלכה כמותנו, For three years . . . these were saying, 'The *halacha* is as we say,' and these were saying, 'The *halacha* is as we say' " (*Eruvin* 13b). Each side felt that *his* understanding of the *halacha* was the way it should be for all times and all places.

It is therefore not surprising that at least one commentator is not satisfied with the above explanation and explains "These and those" in a way that allows it to apply to the *common* type of *machlokos* found in the Talmud.

Drashos HaRan: Halacha Is as Sages Say, Despite Original Intent

The *Drashos HaRan* (*Drashos Nos. 3 and 5*) maintains that the disputants are indeed attempting to match Hashem's original Will. As we have seen in an above citation of his words (from *Drasha* 3), he insists that if Sages are in disagreement they cannot have all succeeded. The message of "These and those" is simply that each opinion arrived at through approved procedures has the *potential* to become the official *halacha*, and this *halacha* is the one we must obey—whether it is true or false.

שאחר שהש"י מסר ההכרעה אליהם, מה שיסכימו הם—הוא מה שצוה ה' בדבר
ההוא. . . .

ואי אפשר אם לא על צד שכתבנו, כי אחרי שדברי המטמאים והטהורים הפכיים
בעצמם, אי אפשר ששניהם יסכימו לאמת, [ו]איך נאמר שכלן נאמרו למשה מפי
הגבורה, ומי איכא ספיקא קמי שמיא . . . אבל הענין כך . . . שה' יתברך . . . צונו
שנמשך אחריהם . . . וגם כן נאמין שאם הסכימו הפך האמת—ונדע זה על ידי בת
קול או נביא—אין ראוי שנסור מהסכמת החכמים (דרשה ה').

Once G-d transferred the power of decision to the Sages, whatever they would come to agreement upon [based upon their greatest attempts to understand the Torah]—that is [retroactively] what Hashem commanded concerning that issue. . . .[13]

There is no other possible way to understand this matter. For since the words of those who declare something טמא and those who declare it טהור are intrinsically contradictory, it is impossi-

---

[13] Note that the *Ran* is now speaking about the consensus of Sanhedrin, and no longer about either side of a *machlokess*. But he understandably applies his concept to both areas.

ble for both sides of the dispute to be conforming to the Truth.
How then could we say that they were both told to Moses by
G-d? Does G-d have any doubts as to what the Truth is?!¹⁴ But
the answer is that G-d [Himself] commanded us to follow the
Sages. . . . [A]nd we must also believe that if the Sages should
agree to the opposite of the Truth—and we could know this
through a *Bas Kol* or a prophet—it is still improper to veer away
from their consensus (No. 5).

The *Drashos HaRan* demonstrates that even if, somehow,
Hashem's intent becomes known—such as through a בת קול—this will
not determine the *halacha*. Hashem declared that the Torah's laws
are to be determined through the Sages' application of the rules of
interpretation according to their own intellect. G-d was perfectly
willing, from the beginning, to retract His desire in favor of the conclusions the Sages would reach through their best efforts of Torah-
analysis. Therefore, though there *was* an original intent, it is
irrelevant!

אבל העניין כך הוא ... שתהיה ההכרעה כפי הסכמת חכמי הדור. וזהו עניין ר' אליעזר
הגדול ומחלוקותו, ואמרו שם בבבא מציעא: ,,עמד ר' יהושע על רגליו ואמר ,לא
בשמים היא'." . . . ,,כבר נתנה למשה על הר סיני, וכתוב בה ,אחרי רבים להטות''.
הנה ראו שר' אליעזר היה מסכים אל האמת יותר מהם . . . ואעפ"כ עשו מעשה
כהסכמתם . . . אע"פ שהיו יודעים שהיו מסכימים הפך האמת.

The criterion is the consensus of the Sages of the time. This is
the meaning behind what happened in the dispute between
Rebbi Eliezer and the Sages (*Bava Metsia* 59b). [Rebbi Eliezer
was unsuccessful in persuading the majority of Sages to accept
his position. He then called nature to his witness, and miracles
occurred to demonstrate that he was correct, and finally a *Bas
Kol*, a *Heavenly Voice*, declared that he was right. But] Rebbi
Yehoshua stood on his feet and declared, "'It is not [any longer]
in Heaven' (*D'varim* 30:12)!" [which the *Gemora* explains to
mean:] "The Torah had already been given to Moses at Mount
Sinai, and it decreed, 'You shall follow the majority [decision]'
(*Sh'mos* 23:2)!" Behold, they saw that Rebbi Eliezer conformed
to the Truth more than they . . . and yet they conducted themselves according to their own consensus . . . even though they
knew that they were agreeing to something which was the
opposite of the truth (No. 5).

¹⁴ This question is a quote from a passage in *Gittin* 6b, which will be cited later.

Yet the *Ran* himself declares that he is not answering satisfactori-
ly the problem he raised. The "retroactively approved halacha"
approach works if we view the *halachic* status we give something as
an arbitrary assignment whose sole value is its designation as the
way through which we can show our loyalty to Hashem. Granted
this assumption we can say that G-d would be perfectly willing to
abandon a legal status He originally assigned something for the
opposite status voted upon by a Sanhedrin. But if we hold that the
legal status of something is a description of the actual effect it has on
people and the world, a reflection of its intrinsic nature, then the
above thesis is very hard to accept. If the Sages err about the nature
of a thing, *why should we* follow them in opposition to a *Bas Kol*?
Why shouldn't the real truth be our criterion? Why should we say
that "These and those are the words of the Living G-d"?[15]

If ritual טומאה, ritual impurity, for example, is an actual spiritual
condition of a woman revealed by her blood's color, then the only
correct *p'sak* can be that which conforms to that reality. If something unkosher is by nature harmful to our souls, declaring it kosher
should not change things. The alternative would be unwieldy: We
would have to say that Hashem actually changes the nature of things
in response to each *p'sak* in every time and locality.[16] Can the actual
nature of things be so unstable?[17]

The *Ran* expresses these thoughts as follows:

והנה יש כאן מקום עיון, והוא כי זה ראוי שימשך על דעת מי שיחשוב שאין טעם
למצות התורה כלל, אלא כלן נמשכות אחר הרצון לבד. . . . אבל אחרי שאנחנו לא
נבחר בזה הדעת, אבל נאמין שכל מה שמנעתהו התורה ממנו מזיק אלינו, ומוליד
רושם רע בנפשותינו, ואע"פ שלא נדע סבתו, לפי זה הדעת, אם כן כשיסכימו
החכמים בדבר אחד טמא, הוא טהור,—מה יהיה?! הלא הדבר ההוא יזיק אותנו ויפעל
מה שבטבעו פעול. ואלו יסכימו הרופאים על סם אחד שהוא שוא, והוא על דרך משל
חם מעלה רביעית, שאין ספק שלא תמשך פעולת הסם בגוף כפי מה שיסכימו בו
הרופאים, אבל כפי טבעו בעצמו. כן הדבר שאסרה לנו התורה מצד שהוא מזיק

[15] We are not talking about whether a person is liable for a punishment for disobey-
ing the Sages. Of course, a person must follow the dictates of the Sages of his time
and place, and must be punished if he disobeys *that* obligation.

[16] Actually, there are other alternatives, which we will be citing. But here we are
explaining the thought-process of the *Ran*, לפי עניות דעתנו.

[17] Nevertheless, the *Chazon Ish* (see יסודות נאמנים published anonymously in B'nei
B'rak) cites proof that the *p'sak* of *Gedolim* does indeed change reality.

בנפש. איך ישתנה טבע הדבר ההוא מצד שהסכימו החכמים שהוא מותר? זה אי
אפשר רק על צד הפלא. והיה ראוי אם כן יותר שנמשך בזה על פי מה שיתבאר לנו
מצד נביא או בת קול, שעל דרך זה יתבאר לנו אמתת הדבר בעצמו.

There is room for investigation here. This approach will satisfy
the opinion of those who hold that there are no reasons behind
the *mitzvos* at all and that they all just follow the [arbitrary]
Will of G-d. . . . But we do not choose this approach. We
believe that everything the Torah warns us against is indeed
[intrinsically] harmful to us, and creates a negative imprint on
our souls, even though we may not know the mechanics behind
that process. Therefore, if the consensus of the Sages is that
something is טהור—so what?! [If it is really טמא,] won't it harm us
and produce its natural effect, whatever it is? If all the physicians in the world would agree that a drug that causes high fever
only causes a moderate body heat, the drug still will not start to
act on the body in accordance to the physicians' opinion! It is
the same thing with something the Torah forbade us from doing
because it is harmful to our souls: How could the nature of that
thing change itself just because of the Sages' consensus that it is
permitted? This is impossible short of a miracle. It would therefore seem that we preferably *should* follow the revelation of a
prophet or *Bas Kol*, which would tell us the true nature of the
thing.

Benefits Outweigh Harm

The *Ran* gives a remarkable answer. He states that it is crucial to
avoid multiple practices. Now, the *Ran* continues, the Sages rarely,
if ever, come to a wrong consensus. Therefore, the benefit of uni-
formly obeying them far outweighs the damage done by those few
instances in which we act incorrectly at their behest. Furthermore,
there is a *mitzva* (*D'varim* 17:11) to listen to the Sages even when
they are wrong ("לא תסור מן הדבר אשר יגידו אליך ימין ושמאל"). The spiritual benefit we gain by obeying this *mitzva* totally counteracts the
harmful consequences of performing the other incorrectly.

שהתורה השגיחה לתקן ההפסד שהיה אפשר שיפול תמיד, והיא פרוד הדעות
והמחלוקת, ושתעשה תורה כשתי תורות, ותקנה ההפסד התמידי הזה, כשמסרה
הכרעת הספקות לחכמי הדור, שעל הרוב ימשך מזה תקון ויהיה משפטם צודק. . . .
ועם היות שלפעמים אפשר שעל צד הפלא והזרות ישגו בדבר מה, לא חששה תורה
להפסד ההוא הנופל מעט, כי ראוי לסבול אותו מצד רוב התקון הנמשך תמיד, ואי
אפשר לתקן יותר מזה.

ואני סובר עוד שאי אפשר שימשך ממה שיכריעו הסנהדרין הפסד בנפש כלל . . .

לפי שהתקון אשר ימשך בנפש מצד ההכרעה ומצות החכמים מורי התורה, הוא הדבר
היותר אהוב אצלו יתברך. . . . המשכו אחר עצתם והיותו נמשך לדבריהם יסיר
מנפשו כל אותו רוע שהיה ראוי שיתליד מצד אכילת הדבר האסור ההוא. ולכן צותה
התורה ואמרה לא תסור מן הדבר אשר יגידו אליך ימין ושמאל.

The Torah took means to prevent a misfortune that can always
arise, and that is the divergence of opinions and the creation of
machlokess, almost creating a situation of two Torahs. The
Torah's remedy for this ever-present danger was to hand over to
each generation's Sages the right to resolve *halachic* questions.
For in the majority of cases this will result in both a remedy [of
the problem of *machlokess*] and the correct decision. . . . And
even though there is the extremely remote and practically
absurd possibility that they may make a mistake, the Torah did
not concern itself with that remote danger. The risk is worth
taking for the benefit accrued.

Furthermore, I feel that it is really impossible for any harm at all
to come to one's soul by following the Sanhedrin's decision . . .
[F]or the benefit which the soul receives through [its submis-
siveness to] the Sages' decisions and decrees—that is the thing
which is most beloved by Hashem. . . . One's following their
counsel and one's submission to their words will remove from
his soul all the harm produced by eating the forbidden thing
[which the Sages mistakenly permitted]. This is why the Torah
commanded us, "You shall not turn aside from the thing they
tell you, right or left," [upon which the Tradition comments,
even if they tell you that Right is Left].[18]

It is true that there was an Original Intention, and, yes, the disputants are attempting to identify it. But they do not all succeed. The
message of "These and those . . ." simply is that we must follow
decisions reached through *halachic* procedure, regardless of whether
those decisions actually match G-d's original intention.

Absolute Truth to Both Sides of Machlokess

Other authorities are not comfortable with this idea. They feel that
"These and those" implies that there is always *some* actual truth
both to the opinion that is practiced and to the opinion which goes
unpracticed.

[18] See Additional Notes at the end of this chapter.

The Maharal of Prague: Nothing Is Black-and-White at Any Time

The *Maharal of Prague*[19] posits that both parties to a *machlokess* "touch base" with absolute truth. There are elements even of absolute truth to each side of a *machlokess*, for reality is not black-or-white. Things simultaneously have elements of *tum'a* to them as well as elements of *tahara*. They have characteristics of being kosher, as well as characteristics of being unkosher.

כמו שהשי״ת אדון כל המעשים, וממנו ימצא עולם המורכב שיש בו דברים
מתחלפים, ויש אחד הפך השני, וכך הוא דבר זה. שכל דבר יש לו בחינות מתחלפות.
שאין העולם פשוט שלא יהיה בו חילוף בחינות . . . והש״י ברא את הכל והוא ברא
הדבר שיש בו שתי בחינות. רק לענין הלכה למעשה אין ספק שהאחד יותר עיקר מן
השני, כמעשה ה׳: אף כי הדבר הוא מורכב, מ״מ אין זה כמו זה; רק האחד יותר
עיקר. שהרי העץ שהוא מורכב מד׳ יסודות, העיקר הגובר בו הוא יסוד הרוח כמו
שידוע. וכן אף שיש לדבר אחד בחינות מתחלפות—כולם נתנו מן ה׳—רק כי אחד
מהם יותר עיקר והוא מכריע, והוא הלכה.

Hashem is the Master of all entities, and from Him comes the Composite World made of opposing properties. The world is not so simple; it is composed of disparate aspects. G-d created everything, including anything that has two aspects to it. *Halacha* is part of this world. Only, for *halacha l'maaseh*, for actual practice, one aspect is unquestionably more significant than the other. This is also true of the physical entities *Hashem* created: Even though an entity may be a composite of many disparate elements, those elements are not there equally. One is more significant than the others. The tree, for example, is composed of all four elements [earth, water, air, fire], but the principal element is air, as is well known [in philosophy]. Likewise, even though any single entity has disparate *halachic* aspects to it—all given by *Hashem*—one of them is still the most significant, and that is the deciding property, and that is the *halacha*.

To use another analogy, everyone has male and female hormones in him, or different genes from different ancestors. However, some are recessive and some are dominant. If a scientist was restricted to telling the nature of a person solely through examining his hormones and genes, whatever conclusion he comes to would have a basis in fact. Nevertheless, the nature of the person is one way or another, depending upon which genes and hormones are the dominant ones.

It must be noted that even according to the *Maharal of Prague*, this is an explanation only of ''בעלי אסופות נתנו מרועה אחד'', ''They were all given by one Shepherd,'' and not of ''אלו ואלו'', ''These and those.'' The terminology ''These and those are the words of the Living G-d'' implies that the two statuses are *actually equally present*. Neither one is recessive, neither one is dominant. The *Maharal* maintains that this was true of some *machlokos*—those of *Bes Shammai and Bes Hillel* being the first—but not of all:

... ולפעמים הבחינות שוים לגמרי בצד עצמו, ואז דניהם מן הש״י בשוה ואין מכריע. וזהו מחלוקת הלל ושמאי שיצאה בת קול, „אלו ואלו כו'" ... ולכך שואל שם ... למה אמר הלכה כב״ה. ואמר מפני שהם נוחים ועלובין וכו'.

Sometimes the disparate aspects are absolutely equal, and then their G-d-given *halachic* statuses are equally valid, *and there is no deciding factor*. And this is the nature of the disputes between *Bes Shammai* and *Bes Hillel*, concerning which a *Bas Kol* declared, ''These and those . . .'' And therefore that *Gemora* asks, ''Why then is the *halacha* [solely] according to [the decisions of] *Bes Hillel*?'' And it answers, ''Because [its members] were pleasant and patient. . . .''

Applying the ''Recessive Gene'' Approach of ''These and Those'' to Historical Events and Their Causes

The saying ''These and those are the words of the Living G-d'' appears in the Talmud only twice. The first instance, concerning that of the dispute between *Bes Shammai* and *Bes Hillel*, appears, as noted, in *Eruvin* 13b,[20] and is in the context that we have been speaking of until now:

א״ר אבא א׳שמואל, שלש שנים נחלקו ב״ש וב״ה. הללו אומרים הלכה כמותנו והללו אומרים הלכה כמותנו. יצאה בת קול ואמרה אלו ואלו דברי אלקים חיים הן והלכה כב״ה.

Said R' Abba in the name of Shmuel: Three years *Bes Shammai* and *Bes Hillel* remained in dispute. These were saying that the *halacha* is as we say, and these were saying that the *halacha* is as

---

[20] Cf. *Yerushalmi Brachos* on 4:4.

we say.[21] A *Bas Kol* (Heavenly Voice) called out and said, "These and those are the Words of the Living G-d, and the *halacha* follows *Bes Hillel.*"

The second time "These and those" appears is in reference to a dispute over the details of a past event. Now, if variant reports of someone's opinion cannot be both correct, they certainly cannot both be correct regarding actual historical events. Yet the Sages surely did not base their reports of events on thin air. Each of the reports must have had some basis to it in fact, though each can contradict the other. The *Maharal's* concept of "recessive genes" can be used to solve this paradox: One Sage's report was really describing a "recessive gene" of reality—something that *almost* happened; a strongly contributive reason for an occurrence, though not the main one; or a strongly considered action, though not one finally taken. In talmudic writings, this approach is indeed taken in the name of the adage "These and those are the words of the Living G-d." Before we proceed to illustrate this, let us examine the passage in question (*Gittin* 6b):

[ר' אביתר גברא רבה ובר סמכא היה, ד]הא ר' אביתר הוא דאסכים מריה על ידיה (לגלות לו סוד לכוין דברים הסתומים על אמיתתם—פרש"י) דכתיב „ותזנה [סרחה] עליו פילגשו" (שופטים י"ט:ב) (בפילגש בגבעה). רבי אביתר אמר: „זבוב מצא לה" (בקערה—פרש"י). ר' יונתן אמר: „נימא מצא לה" (לקמיה מפרש— פרש"י). ואשכחיה ר' אביתר לאליהו. א"ל, „מאי קא עביד הקב"ה?" א"ל: „עסיק בפילגש בגבעה." „ומאי קאמר?" א"ל: „אביתר בני—כך הוא אומר; יונתן בני—כך הוא אומר." א"ל: „ח"ו! ומי איכא ספיקא קמי שמיא?!" א"ל: „אלו ואלו דברי אלקים חיים הן.—זבוב מצא ולא הקפיד; נימא מצא והקפיד" (כדמפרש טעמא ואזיל—פרש"י).

[Rebbi Avyasar was a great man, and a trustworthy one, for he] was the one who was trusted by his teacher (to hear the secret way to know how to correctly explain vague statements—*Rashi*). For it says, "And his concubine was unfaithful to him" *Shoftim* (19:2), and Rebbi Avyasar said, "[He was angered at her because] he found a fly in his plate." Rebbi Yonoson said, "He found a hair." Rebbi Avyasar met Elijah and asked him what the Holy One, blessed be He, was doing at the moment. He replied that He was involved with the subject of the concubine of [the city of] Givea.[22]

---

[21] See Additional Notes at the end of this chapter.
[22] That is, the subject of the above dispute.

"What does He say?"

He replied, "'My son, Avyasar, says this, and my son, Yonoson, says that.'"

"Heaven forbid! Does G-d have any doubts about what the truth is?!"

Elijah replied, "These and those are the words of the Living G-d! He found a fly, but this did not anger him [to such an extent]. He found a hair and this bothered him greatly."

Obviously, there are some internal difficulties with this passage. Why is Rebbi Avyasar the one being praised when his opponent is the one who was right? Even if we say that the fly *contributed* to the anger, though it was not what triggered it, as Avyasar thought, Rebbi Yonoson was still much more correct!

The *Tosefos HaRosh* (*Gittin* 6b) addresses this problem and answers that people were not aware at all of the contribution the fly made to the man's anger. They only knew about the fact that upon seeing the hair, he became enraged at his concubine. Therefore, Rebbi Avyasar's remark was a remarkable insight, explainable only as רוח הקדש, divine inspiration.

Nevertheless, we must recognize that Rebbi Avyasar himself considered his report to be irreconcilable with his opponent's. "Heaven forbid," he exclaimed, when he first heard Elijah say that Hashem accepted both of their reports, for as he saw it, either one report was right, or the other.

The issue that Rebbi Avyasar and Rebbi Yonoson were addressing—had you asked *them* what they were arguing about—was identifying the factor that *triggered* the man's anger. And the plain, direct answer to that simple question was, according to Elijah, the hair, and not the fly. Why then did Elijah say, "These and those are the words of the Living G-d"?

Building on the *Tosefos HaRosh's* explanation that—despite the opinions of the two Sages—both a fly and a hair were involved in the event, we can conclude that one's report of the facts was really a "recessive gene" cause of the anger. True, Avyasar was not correct, according to the way he understood himself, but there *was* a fly involved, and it did contribute strongly to the final anguish, though it was not its principal cause. This is what Elijah meant when he invoked the phrase "These and those." The point of "These and those" is that Avyasar's error was not baseless. He was merely reporting a contributing cause to an emotional outburst— its "recessive gene'' cause—which he mistook for the outburst's *immediate* cause.

Tosefos[23] uses this concept to reconcile two mutually exclusive versions of an event. He says that whereas one version was reporting a tradition describing the *actual* event, the other was reporting a tradition of a strongly considered action:

ומה שיסד ר"א הקליר בגשם דשמיני עצרת כר"א דאמר בתשרי נברא העולם, ובשל פסח יסד כר' יהושע—אומר ר"ת אלו ואלו דברי אלקים חיים. ואיכא למימר דבתשרי עלה במחשבה לבראות, ולא נברא עד ניסן.

[The *Gemora* states:] Whose opinion are we following in our *Rosh HaShonna* prayers that say the world was created on *Rosh HaShonna*? —Rebbi Eliezer's, for he holds that the world was created in *Tishri* (the month in which *Rosh Hashonna* falls [*supra* 8a, 10b, *Avoda Zorra* 8a]).

Rabbi Elazar HaKalir composed the *Shemini Atserres* prayer for rain, which states that the world was created in *Tishri*, as was the opinion of Rebbi Eliezer. Yet he also composed the Passover prayer for dew, which states the world was created in *Nissan* (the month in which Passover occurs), as was the opinion of Rebbi Yehoshua! How [could he contradict himself so]?

Rabbeynu Tam answers, '''These and those are the words of the Living G-d.' We can say that in *Tishri* G-d was *thinking* of creating the World, whereas he did not [actually] create it until *Nissan*.''

We see that ''These and those'' describes the method of reconciling two opinions by admitting that only one of them is a description of the subject's action (G-d's creating the world) and taking the other as a description of his prior, considered thought. Although Rebbi Eliezer certainly meant that the world was actually created during *Tishri* (or else his exchange with Rebbi Yehoshua could not be termed a *machlokess*), it is desirable, especially when it comes to historical occurrences, to minimize the gap between opponents, even if it means interpreting someone's statement differently from the way he himself intended. To this solution, *Tosefos* appends the label ''These and those.''

---

23 *Rosh Hashonna* 27a (ד"ה כמאן מצלינן זה היום תחילת מעשך), Cf. *Ohr Hachaim* on *B'ray-shis* 1:1, *siman* 16.

Another Look At Rashi

Let us now return to *Rashi's* explanation of "These and those." We may recall that *Rashi* had stated:

כי פליגי תרי . . . כל חד אמר הכי מיסתבר טעמא—אין כאן שקר. כל חד וחד סברא
דידיה קאמר . . . ואיכא למימר „אלו ואלו דברי אלקים חיים הם:" זימנין דשייך האי
טעמא וזימנין דשייך האי טעמא שהטעם מתהפך לפי שינוי הדברים בשינוי מועט.

[W]hen two *Amoraim* are arguing . . . [e]ach one is presenting his *own* conclusion [and not attempting to report someone else's]. . . . Here we can say, "These and those are the words of the Living G-d:" Sometimes *this* consideration appertains and sometimes *that* consideration appertains; for the [pertinent] consideration reverses itself according to a change of things/ situations, with just a slight change.

Before, we interpreted *Rashi* to mean that the Sages really agree upon the *halacha* and when in seeming dispute are merely addressing different situations. However, as we argued, the specific cases of *machlokos* in the Talmud do not bear this out: Each Sage insists that he is right and the other wrong in single situations. We shall suggest a different understanding of *Rashi's* words:

The Sages do, of course, differ over the *halacha* assignable to specific cases. And, as we argued, opposite reports of what G-d meant by a Scriptural phrase or of what G-d desires the *halacha* to be cannot both be correct, any more than can opposite reports of a man's statement. But "These and those" is not speaking about the correctness of the *p'sak* given by a Sage in a given dispute. The adage is rather in reference to a separate question, that of the absolute truth, which is not technically the concern of *halacha*.

Despite the description one gives of a situation, real-life situations always take on subtle, fluctuating factors which change its true status. These changing distinctions are too subtle, too involved, and too many to be reckoned with in practical decision-making. Practical decision-making requires less cumbersome, coarser units of gauging situations that will assign a *halachic* status to a broad number of them. In other words, *halachic* determination—which is certainly quite complex with distinctions as it is—requires a relative degree of generalization that extends the assignment of status to many cases at some expense of accuracy. Now, the Sages all admitted to the relatively unstable aspect of absolute truth and the fact that the criteria (טעמים, considerations) which they use are by nature

really too blanket. They were fully aware that the criteria by which
one Sage decides all situations of a kind really pertains to only some
of them, due to the real-life situations' uniquenesses, and that the
criteria advocated by the other Sage in a dispute pertains to real-life
situations only sometimes. Yet their considerations definitely have
their place—each one has its own hour, we might say—and none are
irrelevant. This concept, and this concept alone, is the meaning
behind the adage of "These and those." But this has nothing to do
with the Sages' feelings about what the correct *halacha* is. For since
halacha must be determined by a less subtle and more stable treat-
ment of criteria, each Sage maintains that the criteria which he concluded are the proper ones to use for determining practical *halacha*
for all times and situations are the ones that *Hashem* must have
desired for that purpose, and that this is not a matter of "These and
those"—they cannot both be correct about that.

Review

The following is a brief summary of the explanations we have
quoted for the meaning of "These and those are the words of the
Living G-d."

- *Rav Yisroel Salanter:* All valid attempts to reconstruct
  what Hashem told Moses are subsumed under the title of
  "Torah," including the opinions that are ultimately nullified as *halacha.*
- *The Yahm Shel Shlomo:* Since a Sage's conclusions conform to sound logic, they are *as valid and holy* as the
  explicit words of Hashem. The *kabballistic* teaching that
  all souls were present at Mount Sinai and each perceived the Torah through one of forty-nine conduits
  supports this position.
- *Ritva (Eruvin 13a)* and *Tosefos Shantz (Aid'yos 1:5)*
  cite another *kabballistic* teaching that Moses was
  shown forty-nine arguments to each side of an issue
  (totaling ninety-eight arguments to each issue) and
  was told that the decision was entrusted to the future
  Sages. We have suggested that we may here apply
  Rashi's understanding (*Menachos* 29b) that this happened *prior* to Moses' receiving the Torah. Thus,
  "These and those" positions conform to human logic
  and even the Will of Hashem *before* He prescribed
  the limitations and parameters of *halacha.*

- *Rashi according to our first understanding:* Perceptions are subjective. Trust the perception of present reality determined by your authority, though another's perception may be different, because it is a true "reality."
- *Rashi according to our second understanding:* The situations the Sages are ruling on are not really identical, and all authorities would agree on how to rule in any given time. Disputes across generations are only apparently disputes.
- *The Ohr Gedaliahu:* There is a single unifying formula which really produces opposite results in different circumstances.
- *Drashos HaRan:* Each opinion is potentially the official *halacha*, and the decided *halacha* is the one we must obey—whether it is true or false—because chances are that the decisions *do* conform to the "original intent," and the benefits we accrue by obeying the Sages outweigh and counteract the risk of harm.
- *Tosefos:* Regarding opposite reports of past occurrences, there are elements even of Absolute Truth to each side of a *machlokess*, though one is dominant and the others recessive (the *Maharal of Prague's* concept of "בעלי אסופות נתנו מרועה אחד, They were all given by one Shepherd"). Whereas one version reports a tradition describing the *actual* event, the other reports a tradition of a strongly considered action.
- *Maharal of Prague:* Two statuses are *actually equally present*. Neither one is recessive, neither one is dominant. This was true only of some *machlokos*, the first of which were those of *Bes Shammai and Bes Hillel*.
- *Rashi according to our third understanding:* All the criteria and considerations introduced by disputing Sages play a role in determining absolute truth, although in each individual situation the applicability of these factors changes, thereby changing the situation's status in terms of absolute truth. (However, such unstable and subtle considerations are too complex and cumbersome to be allowed in practical *halachic* decision-making, and opposite reports about the proper *halacha* and the proper criteria for determining it cannot both be correct.)

Conclusion

This review of how our classical commentators understood the adage "אלו ואלו דברי אלקים חיים הם, These and those are the words of the Living G-d," showed that there are different ways in which it could be understood. But we can state unequivically that according to all, neither *Hashem* when He originally established the *halacha* nor Moses when he transmitted it, stated more than one *halacha* for a given case. So far as the *halacha l'maaseh*, the practical law that we should follow is concerned, two or more opposing Sages cannot both be stating what their teacher, or teacher's teacher, or Moses or *Hashem* originally said.

If *Hashem* told Moses that the law is one way, someone saying otherwise simply does not conform to that law. In *this* aspect, we cannot say that he is "right." "These and those" does not mean that. Nor does it mean that two Sages disagreeing over the meaning of another Sage's statements are both conforming to his actual intention. If their opinions are mutually exclusive, then that just cannot be. And we cannot imagine that two students could be both correct if they disagree over what their teacher's very words were. The opposite statements could not have issued verbally from their teacher's mouth at the same time. In all such cases, someone must be mistaken.

Additional Notes to Chapter 11

6. Even according to the Gemora's preferred choice (*ibid.*)—that both of the later *Amoraim* agree upon the sides taken by the earlier ones—the fact remains that the earlier *Amoraim* had disputed in identifying the opinions of previous *Tannaim*. *Tosefos* points this out and explains that this is a much more tolerable situation, because for *Amoraim* to identify the opinions of the *Tannaim* [of the distant past—cf. *Ḥiddushay Ritva*: "שהרי לא למדו מן התנאים ולא קבלו מהם"] may be a matter of interpretation. [Over time, confusion can develop.] Failure of *Amoraim* to agree upon identifying their own master's opinions, however, shows a more serious lack in proper learning. Nevertheless, the *Gemora* concludes that in the case under discussion the disciples were indeed in conflict over interpreting their immediate mentor's opinion.

8. Complex not only because of what they plainly say, but also because of a basic, underlying concept which some of the interpretations must presume. To explain:

   According to the forthcoming commentators, what process did the Sages of the Talmud use in analyzing and debating issues? Did the Sages generate *halachos* through original, profound, philosophical insights into the cosmic mechanics of חיוב ופטור, טומאה וטהרה, איסור והיתר? It would seem so from some of the commentators' explanations of אלו ואלו, as will be seen. But this can be so only if the *halachos* were truly generated from their start by the disputants, whereas the disputes of the *Tannaim* and especially *Amoraim* are usually based upon analyses of earlier authorities' remarks and decisions. Their own philosophies would be irrelevant in deciding, for example, which of "two rows" the earlier Sages said had to be searched for *chometz* before *Pesach*. And even if one Sage shows a pattern of leniency and another a pattern of stringency, it is because each feels that his attitude is the one that had been promulgated by the Torah and Moses' understanding of it. Therefore, if Aaron perceived Torah differently than Moses did, it would still be irrelevant in explaining why Hillel perceived Torah differently than Shammai. After all, they both sought support from *Moses'* understanding. Indeed, for disputants to disprove each other's opinions ("attitudes") by citing former authorities would be pointless if, say, whereas Moses generated *halachos* using a stringent attitude, a *Tanna* would be free to generate *halachos* using a lenient attitude.

10. Although here, too, the number forty-nine is mentioned, it is not being used in quite the same sense as in the previous citation. Here, Moses is said to have been shown a total of ninety-eight (2 × 49) ways of looking at each situation. But in the previous passage, each of the "future souls"—the souls of the future Sages who would disagree over the law in a given situation—saw each situation in only *one* of forty-nine ways. Of course, the number forty-nine may merely represent a large but indefinite number. In that case, one statement would be saying that Moses was shown *all* ways of looking at the laws, and the other statement would be telling us that the "future souls" were shown only one way, each.

18. The *Abarbanel* (פרשת שופטים, שאלה ששי) cites this *Ran* and strongly rejects the possibility that Sanhedrin could ever be wrong. He considers impossible even a rare occurrence of error. He interprets the command, "You shall not turn aside from their words right or left," as referring only to areas of הוראת שעה, temporary emergency measures where *Bes Din* intentionally overrides Torah law. In such cases, one may suppose that one could disregard the Sanhedrin's ruling against "standard" law. Therefore, the Torah instructs us to obey the Sages "even when they tell you that Right is Left."

  This is not the classical understanding of the חז"ל, however. Furthermore, there is an entire *mesechta*, *Horios*, which is devoted to the laws of sacrifices the Sanhedrin must bring if it makes a mistake, in accordance with *Vayikra* 4:13. Perhaps the *Abarbanel* understands that despite these provisions, such errors never happened and never will. In any case, he does not deal with the proofs that the *Ran* brings for his opinion, and he does not treat the issue of each opinion in a *machlokess* being correct. He treats the matter as if every decision of Sanhedrin was unanimous.

21. Although *Bes Hillel*, in Yavneh, was the acknowledged majority, *Bes Shammai* felt that in the present circumstances [i.e., the lack of a genuine Temple-Sanhedrin, according to the *Doros HaRishonim*] the standard criterion of majority rule should give way to superior dialectics, which they possessed.

   However, all the commentators cited in this chapter extend the principle of אלו ואלו to cases outside of *Bes Hillel* and *Bes Shammai's* particular three-year debate. This is because they take the principle of אלו ואלו to be referring to each of the individual decisions *Bes Shammai* and *Bes Hillel* made, and not to the "umbrella" issue, under debate for three years, of whether majority rule held forth in the new circumstances.

Chapter 12

Summary and Application

T he men are intently listening to the rabbi. Seated around his dining room table, they follow along as he guides them through the Hebrew words of the Mishna and the Aramaic of the Gemora. Most of these men are professionals: a lawyer, an intern, an accountant, a computer programmer. They have been attending the rabbi's home class for some time, and now they have reached the third mishna of Brachos:

> Bes Shammai says: "At night, each person must recline as he recites the *Sh'ma*, and in the morning, he must stand up. For it says, '[You shall recite it] ובקומך בשכבך, at your lying down and your getting up'" (*D'varim* 6:7).

> Bes Hillel says: "Each man must recite it as he is. For it says, 'ובלכתך בדרך, and in your walking along the way' (*D'varim* 6:7). Why, then, did it say, 'ובקומך בשכבך'?—[It means] at the time that people normally lie down to sleep and at the time that they normally arise."

But before the rabbi can go on, one of the listeners calls out, "Wait a minute!" Something had been disturbing him from the start, though he never before verbalized it: Bes Shammai says, say it lying down, and Bes Hillel says don't? This dispute took place cen-

*turies after Moses' time! Certainly, ever since the Torah was given,
the* mitzva *of reciting the* Sh'ma *must have been fulfilled just one of
these ways! How could there suddenly be a dispute about one's
position during* K'riass Sh'ma? *Just continue doing as it has been
done until now! "What was everybody doing until now, anyway?!"*

"What Did They Do Until Now?"

We have gathered several possible solutions to the question,
"What did they do until now." Now we will summarize them, then
see how they may be applied to a *mishna* similar to the one above,
and note the factors that help determine which solutions remain
valid.

The Summary

1. The detail under question was revealed to the people at
   Sinai, but eventually it was forgotten.

2. No law specifically covering the matter at hand was ever
   revealed to Moses. From the start, Hashem wanted a Sanhedrin to determine it by following His guidelines for
   such activity. The task of making such a determination
   may have waited until the detail became a relevant, practical issue.

3. Even after a decision was made, and even if there was no
   doubt about what that decision was, there still could have
   been room for *machlokess*: A *Bes Din Gadol* may have
   contested the *drash* a previous *Bes Din Gadol* made. The
   result was a dispute between one generation's *Great
   Sanhedrin* and another's. (This possibility can only hold
   water, however, if we see that the disputants were not
   basing themselves upon the statements of the members of
   the earlier Sanhedrin, or of intermediate Sages. If they
   were, then they obviously were not contesting the past
   decision, but were attempting to conform to it.) Of
   course, the very question of *whether* to contest the previous *drash* may have been at issue and may have produced a temporary *machlokess within* the later *Bes Din
   Gadol.*

4. Actually, several practices were valid, but the time came

when it was deemed necessary to establish one single practice as the standard for all Jewry.

5. In any of the above cases, students, when dealing with the statements of mentors or earlier authorities, may have drawn different conclusions as to what they meant, even if the information had been transmitted clearly and intact to that generation. (Sometimes the original statement was kept purposely vague to train the disciples in incisive analysis of all previous statements and available information.)[1]

We see that *machlokess* can result from one or more of the following factors: The *halacha* was (1) forgotten, (2) left for Torah analysis, (3) *darshonned* and contested, (4) standardized, (5) variantly interpreted.

Let us examine the first *mishna* presented to us in the Talmud:

מאימתי קורין את שמע בערבין?

משעה שהכהנים נכנסים לאכול בתרומתן, עד סוף האשמורה הראשונה—דברי ר' אליעזר.

וחכמים אומרים: עד חצות.

רבן גמליאל אומר: עד שיעלה עמוד השחר.

מעשה ובאו בניו מבית המשתה, אמרו לו, לא קרינו את שמע. אמר להם: אם לא עלה עמוד השחר חייבין אתם לקרות. ולא זו בלבד אמרו, אלא כל מה שאמרו חכמים "עד חצות," מצותן עד שיעלה עמוד השחר. . . . א"כ למה אמרו חכמים עד חצות?—כדי להרחיק אדם מן העבירה.

As of when can one recite the *K'riass Sh'ma* at night?

As of the time that the *Kohannim* go home to eat their *terumah*.

"Until the end of the first third of night"—the words of Rebbi Eliezer.

The Sages say: "Until midnight."

Rabban Gamliel says: "Until the coming dawn."[2]

---

[1] As we have made clear, however, care was taken to clarify which facts originated from Sinai and were therefore uncontestable.

[2] See Additional Notes at the end of this chapter.

An occurrence: Rabban Gamliel's sons came home from a
reception and told him that they neglected to recite the *Sh'ma*.
He told them, "As long as dawn has not yet arrived, you are still
obligated to recite it. Not only did the Sages say that, but *everywhere* the Sages gave midnight as a deadline, the *mitzva* can be
done until dawn. . . . Why did they say 'until midnight'?—[as a
precaution] to keep people away from sin."

Possibilities

The first thing to notice about this *mishna* is that the men quoted in
it are the Sages of Yavneh. As we mentioned in the chapter, "The
Control and Proliferation of Machlokess," the Academy of Yavneh
was the headquarters of the Great Sanhedrin following the destruction of the Second Temple and Jerusalem.[3] In this Academy, the
leading participants were personalities familiar to us: The *Nassi*,
Rabban Gamliel; the *Av Bes Din*, Rebbi Yehoshua; the *Ḥacham*
(acknowledged greatest *halachic* expert), Rebbi Eliezer; and the
active participant, Rabbi Akiva.

This sheds light on the *Mishna*. When we view the first *mishnayos* of the Talmud, with Rebbi Eliezer, Rabban Gamliel, Rebbi
Y'hoshua, and the rest of the body of the Sages differing over what
the law is, we are witnessing the major opinions, distilled from careful discussion, of what the universal law should be now that the
Jewish People were facing a long period of dispersion throughout
the world.

We can now experiment with applying each of the five ways
described above to see which may explain how the *machlokos* presented in the Talmud's first *mishnayos* came about:

The Summary

1. The deadline for reciting the *Sh'ma* was explicitly
   revealed at Sinai. However, from that time, people normally recited *Sh'ma* only at normal hours and close to the
   time of the evening prayers. It was hardly relevant to
   them how *late* they could still perform the *mitzva*.[4] They

---

[3] See Additional Notes at the end of this chapter.
[4] See Additional Notes at the end of this chapter.

performed it the earliest time possible.[5] And so this was one of the almost academic details of law that were forgotten, or confused, during the turmoils of war and persecution leading up to, and climaxed by, the Destruction of the Temple. To rediscover the deadline, the Torah's *p'sukim* and statements of early authorities were carefully analysed.

2. The deadline for reciting the *Sh'ma* was *not* revealed at Sinai. Neither did Moses' Sanhedrin define it—again because there was no need to do so: The people of his time did not wait for the last minute to recite *K'riass Sh'ma*. It was left for the Sages to determine the Torah's deadline for the reciting of the nighttime *Sh'ma* whenever it would become an issue. The project of researching the Torah's *p'sukim* for this detail of law first occurred at the time of Yavneh.[6]

3. Though the deadline already had been determined by a Sanhedrin (Moses' or a later one) *before* the time of Yavneh, the determination was based upon analysis of *p'sukim*, and the Sanhedrin of Yavneh was therefore entitled to dispute the previous analysis if it felt it had a better one. This possibility allows for the suggestion that the Sages of Yavneh indeed knew what the previous practice was, but some of them felt that the *drash* that produced it must be reconsidered.

(Since the three possibilities thus far mentioned have to do with *drash*, it is noteworthy that the *Gemora* and *Rishonim* do seem to understand the opinions in our *mishna* to be based primarily upon *drash*: To what time of day does the word "בשכבך," *with your lying down*, refer? The time that people *go* to sleep (i.e., the beginning of the night), or the time during the night that people *are* asleep (i.e., all

---

[5] כדתניא חכמים עשו סייג לדבריהם שלא יהא אדם בא מן השדה בערב ואומר אלך לביתי ואוכל קימעא ואשתה קימעא ואישן קימעא ואח"כ אקרא ק"ש ואתפלל וחוטפתו שינה ונמצא ישן כל הלילה. אבל אדם בא מן השדה בערב, נכנס לבית הכנסת . . . וקורא ק"ש ומתפלל. . . . (ברכות ד:).

[6] On a definitive level for practical, universal practice.

night until dawn)?[7] If the former, does it mean the bedtime for *most* people, or even that of people who retire exceptionally late?[8] Another logical possibility is that the time for the evening *She'ma* recitation depends upon one's definition of "nighttime."[9]

(In any case, again [as noted in our first chapter] we must be cautioned against assuming that the speakers in the *mishna* were necessarily the original proponents of the views and *drashos* presented. They may merely be repeating and/or defending views expressed by previous mentors. Or, they may be trying to determine just what the previous authorities' views *were*, which would bring us to possibility number four:)

4. The deadline, though not revealed at Sinai, already had been determined by some Sanhedrin before that of Yavneh, but for the reason described above, it became forgotten. The Sages of Yavneh wished to *conform* to the practice of previous generations wherein confusion had not yet entrenched itself. They attempted to determine what that practice was by analysing the statements of the Sages of past generations (as well as any previous analyses of those original statements.) But the Sages of Yavneh differed in their interpretations.

(Evidence for this explanation is the statement of Rabban Gamliel: "ולא זו בלבד אמרו, אלא כל מה שאמרו חכמים עד חצות מצותן עד שיעלה עמוד השחר, And not only in this case [of *K'riass Sh'ma*], but everywhere the Sages said 'until midnight,' the *mitzva* is until dawn. ... Why, then, did *the Sages say* 'until midnight'? In order, etc." It certainly sounds as if Rabban Gamliel is referring to Sages before his time, and claiming—against the Sages of his time—that their "deadline"

---

[7] עי' דף ד. פרש"י ד"ה לימרו כר' אליעזר. דאמר סוף האשמורה הראשונה דודאי כל שדעתו לישן כבר שכב וישן. ופרש"י דף ב. ד"ה עד סוף ... דלא מיקרי תו זמן ... שכיבה ולא קרינן ביה „בשכבך." ודף ד: פרש"י ד"ה ואי כר"ג סבירה להו. דמשמע ליה „בשכבך" כל זמן שבני אדם שוכבים, ויש בכלל הזה כל הלילה. In other words, does the "ב" in בשכבך mean *at* [your lying down] or *during* [your lying down].

[8] עי' פסקי הרי"ד.

[9] The צל"ח asks why Rashi does not suggest this possibility: (ד"ה אלא דאכתי קשיא מנ"ל לרש"י) ... ודלמא טעמא דידהו דלא תליא בשכיבה כלל אלא בערב ובקר וס"ל כרבנן דלקמן בפ' ת"ה דמנחה עד הערב ולכן ס"ל כל הלילה ולפ"ז ממילא לדידן דקי"ל דעביד כמר עביד יוצא ג"כ בק"ש דבה"ה. He suggests an answer.

was meant merely as a precautionary measure.[10] [*Maharatz Ḥayos* takes it this way, too.][11] The cases Rabban Gamliel gives [as examples of where the Sages' midnight deadline was only precautionary] also bear out this interpretation, for they are dealing with deadlines given the sacrificial procedures, which were not practiced at the time of Yavneh. This, too, lends credence to the possibility that the Sages' rule was previously stated while the Temple was still standing and that the Sages Rabban Gamliel is referring to are not those disputing him in the *mishna*. However, the classical commentators explain that Rabban Gamliel was referring to his opponents.)

5. Until the time of the assembly at Yavneh, there were different practices even among those who agreed that "בשכבך, at your lying down," was referring to the time of day—bedtime or nighttime. Each locality had its own idea, perhaps based upon its own lifestyle, as to what constituted "bedtime" or "nighttime." The community in which Rebbi Eliezer lived considered "bedtime" to be only up until the end of the first third of the night, and the community of Rabban Gamliel considered "bedtime" to be *all* night.[12] Each community considered the other's practice as the correct fulfillment—for that community—of the Torah's requirement to recite the *Sh'ma* at its bedtime.

   But now these communities were broken up. Further dispersion was likely. A single definition, for all Jews in all places, had to be settled upon, and fortunately the means to do so were present. Arguments were presented for the soundest definition of "nighttime" or "bedtime" for the general population.[13]

---

[10] And since he is not contesting, but *explaining* the opinion of the past majority, his opinion may be followed. (*Cf.* דף ט'. ד"ה מעשה שבאו).

[11] *M'vo HaTalmud*, p. 298 in כל כתבי מהר"ץ חיות, ירושלים, *The Student's Guide Through the Talmud*, Feldheim, 1960.

[12] The third opinion, that of the *Sages* (incidentally, a term that may be referring to a single Sage, whose opinion the מסדר המשנה prefers—see *Maimonides' Introduction to the Talmud*, p. 199), is described in the *Gemora* as actually holding, as did Rabban Gamliel, that the deadline is dawn, but that a midnight deadline should be decreed (or had been decreed) as a precautionary measure.

[13] This explanation lacks support from any of the sources on this *mishna*.

Before one settles on any one of the explanations offered here, or combination thereof, the possibilities must be thoroughly tested to see which best fit(s) the context of the discussions, historical facts, and all possible sources (other *Gemora* passages, *toseftas*, *braissos*, etc.).[14] This approach can be followed concerning all *machlokos*, including the one cited at the beginning of the chapter (*viz.*, the *machlokess* between *Bes Shammai* and *Bes Hillel* about the position in which one must recite the *Sh'ma*).

The Bottom Line

The one historically correct explanation for how any particular *machlokess* developed may not always be discernible. Again, each *machlokess* must be studied separately, all the discussions analysed carefully, and all the available relevant sources must be consulted. In this book, the possibilities have been supplied and some applications suggested. It is now the reader's task to apply them properly to each *machlokess* found in the Talmud. The reader has the כללים הגדולים, the general guidelines. Now, צא ולמד . . . go and learn!

---

[14] From *braissos* and a *tosefta* cited in the *Gemora*, we see that there must have been more ways to understand the *p'sukim* than those advocated by the Sages quoted in the *mishna*, and that the issue was not settled in the time of those Sages. Additional opinions about the proper time to recite the evening *Sh'ma* were propounded by Rebbi Mayer and Rebbi Yehuda, of a later generation; and, as alluded to in the text above, there were different versions of Rebbi Eliezer's stand. Nevertheless, Rebbi Yehuda HaNassi, deciding in favor of the Sages of Rebbi Eliezer's time, recorded only the opinions expressed then.

Additonal Notes to Chapter 12

2. Notice that the question actually verbalized in the *mishna* (about when one could *start* saying the evening *Sh'ma*) was answered anonymously ("As of the time that the *Kohanim* go home to eat their *terumah*."). As the *Gemora* points out, though, this answer may be part of "the words of Rebbi Eliezer." Accordingly, the *machlokess* began only with the unasked detail of "until" when the *Sh'ma* could be said. If so, the first question and answer (about when one can *start* reciting the *Sh'ma*) may be an old (oral) "text," onto which the Yavneh Assembly added its thoughts concerning another, related issue (*viz.*, what the *deadline* is). In modern typography, the lines discussing the deadline would be put in another paragraph, or even in the form of a footnote. But paragraphs and footnotes are devices of the written word. The *Mishna*, we must remember, was originally intended to be an orally recited document, which utilized inflections of the voice to indicate digressions.

3. The Sanhedrin of Yavneh was actually in operation before the destruction of the Temple (*Shabbos* 15a), and it is possible (though unlikely, considering the turmoil of the times) that these men were its Sages and promulgated these teachings then. In either case, however, since the Sages knew that the destruction was imminent (*Gittin* 56a, *Sotah* 47a, *Yoma* 38a, 39b), the need for standardizing *halacha* described in the following paragraph still stands as an explanation for these *machlokos*.

4. This answer would not seem to satisfy the problem for the *mishna* quotes at the beginning of this chapter regarding reclining while reciting the nighttime *K'riass Sh'ma*. It was either recited in an upright position or a reclining one since the days of Moses. However, this remains a problem only according to the meaning of *Bes Shammai's* requirement to recline (יטה) as *Rashi* understands it—e.g., placing oneself in a horizontal position. The understanding of *Rabbeynu Yona*, on the other hand, favored by the *Shulchan Aruch* (see *Tur Orach Chaim siman* 63, *Bes Yosef* s.v. ומ"ש ואפילו אינו ממש) is that by "יטה" even *Bes Shammai* does not mean to require (or permit) reciting the *Sh'ma* in such a position. *Bes Shammai's* requirement is for one to *sit* while reciting the verses. Thus we can solve our problem by suggesting that from Moses' time people normally sat at the time they recited the *Sh'ma*. In the time of Hillel and Shammai, it became an issue whether this was because one must sit while reciting it or because one should remain in the position he happens to be at the time.

Epilogue
Or:
Hillel and Shammai
Vs.
Orthodox and Anti-Orthodox

In *Yevomos* 13a, we find the following passage:

> Although Bes Shammai and Bes Hillel disagreed over the rules
> that constitute valid marriages, they did not refrain from marry-
> ing into each other's group. They thus fulfilled the ideal: "Truth
> and Harmony they loved" (*Zecharia* 8:19).

This refers to the fact that *Bes Hillel* deemed certain childre
mamzerim,[1] unmarriageable to other Jews.[2] *Bes Shammai*, on th
other hand, considered the same offspring perfectly legitimate an

---

[1] *Mamzerim* (plural of *mamzer*): offspring of an adulterous or incestuous union.
[2] *Mamzerim* are, however, permitted to marry each other.

marriageable. Despite the controversy, we are taught, members of both schools often married one another. Their love for truth and harmony overrode their differences.

Those who advocate taking liberties with *halacha* often refer to this passage to legitimize, and to demand respect for, their positions. But there is, of course, a puzzling issue that must be addressed: *Halacha*, and particularly *mamzerus*, is an extremely serious matter. In view of the grievous sin involved, how could anyone allow himself to marry someone believed to have been born a *mamzer*? Were our Sages so frivolous about Torah, G-d forbid? The *Gemora* itself asks this question, and it answers that by no means did anyone marry another whom he considered a *mamzer*, or even anyone whose lineage he merely did not know. "Intermarriages" were performed precisely because such doubts were avoided: *Bes Shammai* and *Bes Hillel* advised one another as to each other's status according to the other's rules. "Your son is a fine young man, Mr. *Bes Hillel*, and I would consider it an honor to give my daughter to him in marriage, but unfortunately, according to your *halachic* opinions, my daughter is a *mamzeress*." If no such information was supplied—nothing at all said—then *Bes Hillel*, without asking, would confidently marry into *Bes Shammai*.

Why, then, is the relationship of the two *Houses* praised so highly as an example of "וְהָאֱמֶת וְהַשָּׁלוֹם אֱהָבוּ, Truth and Harmony they loved"? If none compromised his principles, if everyone wed only those who were marriageable according to his *own* interpretations, what love of harmony and what cooperation did this show?

The answer is clear. The members of *Bes Hillel* felt confident that *Bes Shammai*, even without being prompted, would be open enough to disclose the facts whenever one of its own was a *mamzer* according to *Bes Hillel's* standards. This despite the fact that *Bes Shammai* itself deemed that boy *kosher*. Underlying this confidence was the fact that *Bes Shammai* and *Bes Hillel* took each other's word and trusted in each other's forthrightness. They respected each other's opinions because they considered each of those opinions to have been the result of an honest attempt to follow tradition and obey G-d's word.

A Double Standard

Did our Sages respect *anyone's* and *everyone's* opinions? We shall demonstrate that the Sages respected only those opinions which emerged from a sincere effort to follow tradition and obey G-d's commands. And we shall see what these terms mean.

There was another group of Jews whom both *Bes Shammai and Bes Hillel* held in contempt. This group was known as the *Sadducees*. Like the *Missyavnim (Hellenizers)* before them and the *Karaites* after them, the Sadducees were considered outside the pale of authentic Judaism. The *Tannaim, Amoraim, Gaonim* and *Rishonim* did *not* respect these groups' versions of Jewish law, did not consider them legitimate forms of Judaism, and made no secret of their antagonism towards them. Why this difference in attitude? Why did *Bes Shammai* and *Bes Hillel* and their spiritual predecessors and heirs, who were so tolerant of each other's different viewpoints, suddenly become so intolerant of these groups' beliefs? Why, when the Rambam arrived in Egypt, did he openly delegitimize the Karaites' views, even though they were in the majority there?[3]

How Judaism Felt Towards Sadducees

Before we answer these questions, let us first demonstrate Judaism's disapproving attitude towards the Sadducees:

אל תאמין בעצמך עד יום מותך, שהרי יוחנן כ״ג שמש בכהונה שמנים שנה ולבסוף נעשה צדוקי (ברכות כט.).

Do not trust yourself until the day you die, for Yoḥonon the Kohane Gadol served in the High Priesthood eighty years, yet eventually became a Sadducee! (*Brachos* 29a).

Indeed, to be suspected of privately being a Sadducee was considered a shameful tragedy. We are told (*Yoma* 18b, 19b) that the Sages made the *Kohane Gadol* swear not to secretly employ Sadducee practices when performing the Yom Kippur service. The *Kohane Gadol* would actually weep in shame at the implied suspicion that he was secretly a Sadducee (״הוא פורש ובוכה שחשדוהו צדוקי״).

The Origin of the Sadducees

Who were the Sadducees, and why were they the proverbial "end-of-the-line" as far as Judaism was concerned?

---

[3] See chapter entitled *Rambam's Attack on Loss.*

Antignos Ish Soho had two disciples, one named Tsadok and the other named Bysoos, who heard their mentor preach that one's obedience to G-d should not be based on desire for reward. Misunderstanding him, they left him and said to each other, "The Rabbi explicitly said that there is no reward or punishment, and no hope at all [to compensate for the effort of following the Torah]!" They encouraged each other, declared independence from the Sages, and put aside the Torah. Each one gained a following, and the Sages called the members of their sects Sadducees and Bysoosim.

Since their ideology was so despicable, however, they were unable to attract a large following. . . . They began to tell the followers [they did have] that they did believe in the Torah and only contested the Tradition (i.e., the Oral Law). Unable to reject all—Scripture and Tradition—they used this ploy to absolve themselves, at the very least, from following the transmitted explanations of the mitzvos, and the gezayros and takkonnos. Besides, this approach gave them great leeway in interpretation. Once the interpretation became a matter of whim, they were able to be lenient or strict in whatever matters they chose (Maimonides, Ahvos, 1:3)[4]

A Gemora in Kiddushin (66a) reveals how the Sadducee attitude towards Torah manifested itself several generations later:

There was a scandalizing, wicked-hearted and irresponsible man by the name of Eliezer ben Po'eera, who told the Hashmonean[5] King Yannai that the Pharisees[6] opposed him and should be massacred. "But what will become of the Torah?" the king asked. "The Torah is rolled up and resting in the corner! Anyone who wants to study it is free to go and do so!" . . . At that moment Yannai was shot through with apikorsis (heresy), for he should have replied, "That might take care of the Written Torah, but what will become of the Oral Law?!"

Thus, the factor that separated Sadduceeism from Judaism was denial of the validity of the Oral Law. Josephus (circa 70 C.E.), a

---

[4] See Additional Notes at the end of this chapter.

[5] The Hashmoneans were the Jewish kings following the Maccabees' victory over the Syrian-Greeks.

[6] The followers of the Sages were called Pharisees, a name signifying either "separatists" or "explainers (of Scripture)."

contemporary of the Sadducees and Rabban Shimmon ben Gamliel, defines the difference between the Pharisees and Sadducees similarly:

> The Pharisees have delivered to the people a great many observances by tradition from their fathers. . . . The Sadducees reject them and say that . . . we are not to observe what is derived from the tradition of our forefathers. The Sadducees do not wish to obey [the oral laws] because they say that only the written laws are obligatory, whereas the traditions from the forefathers are optional (*Antiquities*, xiii, 10:6).

Respect for Anarchists?

It is because the Sadducees denied the validity of the Oral Law, that the Sages considered them an anti-Torah force and did not mince words in denouncing them.[7] The Sages even declared holidays to celebrate religious victories that they gained over the sect.[8] The *Gemora* passage reporting the origin of one of these holidays incidentally reveals the Bysoosim's shallow approach towards Torah and the kind of language to which the Sages subjected these heretics:

> Rabban Yohonon ben Zakkai (the leading member of *Bes Hillel*) debated with them: "*Sho'tim (Fools)!* Where did you get *this* from?"

> One of their old men rejoined, "Moses, who loved the Jewish people, knew that *Shavuos* is but one day, and he therefore decreed that it should immediately follow *Shabbos* so that we could enjoy ourselves two days in succession."[9]

[7] Likewise, the *Raavad* "attributes the destruction of the Temple and Jerusalem to the fact that 'the spirit of brotherly love within the Jewish people [prevalent in the time of Hillel and Shammai—ZL] had been disrupted through Maccabean defection to the Sadducean heresy'" (*Sefer Ha-Qabbalah, The Book of Tradition*, translated and analyzed by G.D. Cohen [J.T.S.], 1967-5728, Introduction, p. xxxix).

[8] The Sages declared the first fourteen days of *Nissan* a period of annual celebration. The first of Nissan to the eighth commemorated their confuting the Sadducees' interpretation of the law (an interpretation which allowed individuals to bring daily offerings [*Menahos* 65a]); the ninth of the month until *Passover* commemorated their defeating the Bysoosim regarding their erroneous opinion that *Shavuos* must always be on a Sunday [*ibid*.]).

[9] One wonders how this Sadducee would react to his modern-day counterparts' desire to abolish the two-day Yom Tovim instituted for the Diaspora.

"If Moses was such a 'lover of the Jewish people,' why did he
detain them in the wilderness for 40 years? . . . *Fool!* Our complete and perfect Torah shall not be treated to your group's
worthless talk!"

The Bysoosim's readiness to attribute the Torah's *mitzvos* to
Moses' genius and his love for the Jewish people was not the only
attitude to occasion Rabban Yoḥonon ben Zakkai's choice epithets.
He also ridiculed their colleagues, the Sadducees, in another episode
(*Bava Bassra* 115b) where they "interpreted" the Torah in line with
their own leanings—leanings which have a familiar ring today:

According to the Torah's rules, the sons of a deceased take priority over his daughters in receiving his inheritance. As long as there
are sons, they alone, not the daughters, receive a share of the father's
property. (If there are no sons, the daughters take priority over other
relatives.) The Sadducees readily accepted this. They disputed the
following law: Even one's grandchildren—male or female—*through*
his sons, take sole priority over his own daughters. The Sadducees
claimed that if one's granddaughter received a share of the inheritance, one's daughter should also receive a share.

> The Sadducees said: A daughter should get a share in the in-
> heritance together with one's granddaughter.
>
> "And where did you get *this* from?" Rabban Yoḥonon ben
> Zakkai challenged them.
>
> "Well, if my *son's* daughter inherits my property, it only fol-
> lows that my *own* daughter should have a share!"
>
> "World's greatest fool! Our complete and perfect Torah shall
> not be treated to your worthless talk! The only reason the
> granddaughter herself is getting a share is that since she is in the
> line of a dead son, she represents *him* in sharing the inheritance
> with the other, surviving sons."

Rabban Gamliel, another *Tanna*, was not to be outdone in dis-
paraging the Sadducees. Whereas, as we have seen, Rabban Yoḥonon ben Zakkai used the epithet of "שוטים," fools, for the Sadducees, Rabban Gamliel called his neighborhood Sadducee a תועב, a
loathsome being (*Eruvin* 68b)!

About Sincerity

Why did the Sages of *Bes Shammai* and *Bes Hillel* consider the Sadducees, *et al*, insincere in their interpretations? Why didn't they extend the respect they had for each other, despite conflicting opinions, to the Sadducees as well?[10] The obvious answer is that the respect the two *Houses* had for each other was earned. The Sadducees, *Missyavnim-Hellenizers*, and Karaites did not earn respect for their "Judaism," because they were not sincerely involved in an attempt to follow Judaism's principles. On the contrary, they openly denied one of its most basic concepts: the historical revelation of the Torah—*Oral* as well as *Written*. They did not deserve the respect due interpreters of Judaism, because they did not respect Judaism according to its own definition. Once they denied the *Oral Law's* divine origin, their "interpretations" of the Torah were not "Jewish."

Seeing that this deviationist group denied the authenticity of the Rabbis' traditions, it is not surprising that their external practice of rabbinically promulgated procedures—though in accordance with *halacha*—was sometimes recognized as qualitatively empty. The Sadducees could not unqualifiedly act as legal agents to perform *halachic* procedures while denying those procedures' true validity:[11]

השולח עירובו ביד . . . מי שאינו מודה בעירוב—אינו עירוב.

If a man designates . . . someone who does not agree to [the necessity of] the *eruv* procedure[12] to station the *eruv* somewhere, it is not a valid *eruv* (*Eruvin* 31b).

Re-forming History

We see that history and Jewish writings clearly delineate which ideology may and which may not claim to be a form of Judaism. How, then, can contemporary movements which are so patently un-Jewish,[13] rationalize their claim to Judaism? By banking on their fol-

---

[10] Incidentally, the Sadducees practiced many laws. Their wives obeyed the Sages and performed ritual immersion in a *mikva* (*Needa* 33b).

[11] See Additional Notes at the end of this chapter.

[12] See Additional Notes at the end of this chapter.

[13] *Commentary*, vol. 42, no. 2, August 1966; republished in book form, under the title, *The Condition of Jewish Belief: A Symposium Compiled by the Editors of* Commentary, Macmillan Books: New York, 1967; Quoted in *Who is a Jew?* by Rabbi Jacob Immanuel Schochet, Shofar Association of America, Inc., pp. 66 ff.:

lowers' lack of knowledge, keeping them uninformed of the primary sources of Judaism, and by rewriting history.

For example, we have seen that the sources clearly pinpoint the issue of contention between the Pharisees and Sadducees as being the acceptance of the Oral Law. Yet, around the beginning of the 19th century, with the rise of the Reform and Conservative sects of Jews, writers began to describe the differences between traditional Judaism and its past heretical sects in new terms, terms that would allow the new breakoffs to identify with the followers of historic Judaism. The new version of history had it that the heroes of Judaism really denied the traditions, yet craftily distorted Scripture's meanings to serve their ends. Thus we have such inverted depictions of history as follows:

> [T]he fixed and permanent law of the Pentateuch . . . was geared primarily to tillers of the soil, and . . . foreclosed change. . . . [A] new orientation toward G-d, man, religion and destiny . . . declared the revolutionary concepts of the two-fold law (Oral and Written), of personal salvation in the world to come, and of the resurrection from (sic) the dead.

"In what sense do you believe the Torah to be divine revelation? Are all 613 commandments equally binding on the believing Jew? . . ."
"The Bible is not infallible. "—Dr. Seymour Siegel, a senior professor at the Jewish Theological Seminary (Conservative).
"[We] reject . . . those commandments in which [w]e cannot discern any divine purpose . . . G-d no longer speaks to (us) through these commandments . . . [w]e may well replace them with new rites and rituals which are in harmony with (our) spiritual needs"—Max J. Routtenberg, President of (Conservative) Rabbinical Assembly.
"The origin of Torah lies not in an extra-mundane source which has cast down absolute truths upon a receiving people . . . Torah is rooted in . . . a people which discovers out of its experience with failure and fortune the powers of godliness residing within it . . .. Torah as revelation is the product of Israel's creative transaction with history . . . Should the ritual . . . run counter to our contemporary moral judgment . . . then the convinced religious leadership should allow the commandment to be abandoned"—Harold M. Schulweis, Conservative spokesman.
In contrast, all the replies of the Orthodox respondents showed unqualified affirmation of the Divine origin of the entire Torah, Written and Oral, and of the immutable nature of the mitzvos. In fact, it was the only group which showed any affirmative unanimity on the principles of Judaism. Judaism has always viewed itself in contrast to the nations who would not accept G-d's Torah unless they approved of what was written in it (Sifray on Deuteronomy 33:2, cited by Rashi, and the introduction to Sefer HaChinuch).

The Pharisees, a revolutionary scholar class, daringly formulated these novel and crucial doctrines. . . . [T]his movement modified the laws of the Pentateuch. . . . For example, although
previously it was not permissible to walk outdoors on the Sabbath,[14] the Pharisees or sages permitted people to walk anywhere on that day.[15] When the law was unyielding and unbend-
ing, the Pharisees made it pliable and subject to change.[16]

The popular author, Max I. Dimont,[17] bluntly propogates this
insulting absurdity. Praising the "brilliance" of the author of the
above lines, he smugly decrees that "After the fall of Jerusalem . . .
the Pharisees [i.e., Rabbi Akiva, etc.—Z.L.] saw their chance to wrest
power from the Sadducees, toppling the supremacy of the priests
with a machiavellian gambit." Despite his creative imagination,
Dimont fails to supply the names of the priests who supposedly acted as the religious leaders up until the usurpation of power "after the
fall of Jerusalem." And he also neglects to mention that this two-
century period was uninterruptedly graced by leaders such as Antignos Ish Soho and Hillel and Shammai.

Dimont had perpetuated this canard in a previous very popular
history as well:[18]

[W]hereas the Sadducees were . . . conservative in their religious
thinking, the Pharisees were . . . liberal in their religion. . . .

[14] In other words, the writer of these lines would have it that the Karaites, who
introduced this prohibition in the Middle Ages, were the real bearers of the authentic tradition. He evidently considers the Pharisees' teaching that this prohibition
never existed as a bending of the truth; the Sages were in willing disregard of what
they knew to be the Written Torah's commandment! And of course, the contemporary movement the writer promotes feels quite comfortable associating itself with
such company.

[15] The author is apparently unaware of the "liberal" Pharisees' prohibition of walking beyond 2,000 cubits of one's "place" (תחום שבת).

[16] Professor Ellis Rivkin, teacher of theology at the (Conservative) Jewish Theological Seminary, later (understandably) associated with the Reform, Hebrew Union
College, and co-author of The Jewish Dietary Laws, in Face to Face: A Primer in
Dialogue, page 34, published by Bnai Brith as the Spring 1967 issue of Jewish Heri-
tage, Vol. 9, No. 4.

[17] The Jews of America (Simon and Schuster, 1980, p. 113).

[18] Jews, G-d, and History, Simon and Schuster, Inc., 1962; paperback edition: Sig-
net Books (New American Library), no date. In several passages, Dimont contradicts himself.

They believed in the principle of religious evolution. The Pharisees stressed the new [sic] Oral Law, a series of reinterpretations
of Mosaic law. They were responsible for introducing the elasti-
city into Judaism which made possible its survival in the times
of stress ahead.

Judaism: A Definition

The need to align oneself with the Pharisees is obvious. The Pharisees were the acknowledged heroes of Jewish tradition. They included men such as Hillel, the original Maccabees, and Rabbi Akiva. The
Sadducee sect is universally recognized as having been outside the
mainstream of Judaism. Today, to be considered part of the mainstream, one has only two choices: either follow the principles of the
Pharisees, or invent a distorted definition of what those principles
were.[19] But as we have seen, mainstream Judaism stands and falls on
the issue of G-d's Revelation of both the Written and Oral Law to
Moses at Sinai.

Hillel and Shammai, despite their disputes, agreed to this principle, as did Rebbi Yoḥonon and Resh Lakish, and Abbaye and Rava.
All of these Sages, however, rejected the Sadducees and Karaites,
who denied this principle.

That is why the Rambam, in *Hilchos Mahmrim*, 3:1-3, wrote the
following lines:

מי שאינו מודה בתורה שבעל פה . . . הרי זה בכלל האפיקורוסין . . . מאחר
שנתפרנס שהוא כופר בתורה שבעל פה . . . הרי הוא כשאר כל האפיקורוסין
והאומרים אין תורה מן השמים והמוסרין והמומרין. שכל אלו אינם בכלל ישראל.

One who does not admit to the [truth of] the Oral Law . . . is
part of the group known as *apikorsim* . . . Once the fact that he
denies the Oral Law becomes known . . . he is like all other *apikorsim*, those who declare that [even] the [Written] Torah was
not revealed by G-d, informers, and those who deny that any

---

[19] Or distort the meaning of belief in "Divine Revelation." One may "reinterpret" it
to mean that the Torah is the result of "the divine spark" within all of us. But again,
all the classical sources are emphatic and clear enough about this to show that the
poetic platitudes of heterodox heresies are not the kind of things for the sake of
which our forefathers gave their lives. The Sadducees *professed*, at least, the same
belief as the Pharisees regarding the historically real, literal, revelation of the
Written Law!

part of the Torah was not given by G-d: All these are not part of *klal Yisroel.*[20]

On the other hand, for us today his following words are critical:

However, this is speaking solely of those who . . . initiate such denial, such as Tsadok and Bysoos. But the children and grand-children of these kinds of men, who were misled by their fathers, that is, those who were born into and bred by the Karaites, are like people who while still young had been taken into captivity and raised in another religion. Such captives are not quick to take hold of the *mitzvos*, for their situation is prac-tically beyond their control: Even if they later hear that they are Jewish and are exposed to Jews and Judaism, they still are consi-dered people who practice another religion only by force, since they were raised and educated erroneously. The same is true with those who keep the ways of their erroneous Karaite fathers.

What, then, should be the relationship of religiously educated Jews with those bred or schooled in Torah ignorance or hostility? The Rambam concludes:

It is therefore proper to reach out to them and bring them to repentance with peaceful words until they return to the Torah way.[21]

While not ignoring the spurious beginnings of these move-ments—on the contrary, emphasizing them—the Rambam recog-

[20] One must be wary of quick judgments about how to apply *halachic* decisions of the past to today. But considering the attitude expressed by the Rambam (and all other authorities of his time) as well as by the *Tannaim* cited above, what is one to make of statements such as the following by Conservative Rabbi Seymour Siegel of the Jewish Theological Seminary (*Time Magazine*, June 24, 1966, as reported in *The Jewish Observer*, March 1967):
"A necessary first step towards unity . . . is a recovery of Judaism's ancient toler-ance. In the 1st century B.C., for example, the Sadducees and Pharisees and the rab-binical schools of Hillel and Shammai differed bitterly in their interpretation of the law; yet they did not seek to exile opponents from the ranks of accepted Judaism. . . . [I]n today's Judaism there can be no single interpretation—which means that Orthodoxy in particular must surrender its exclusive claim to represent true Jewry."
   I suggest that the first step be honesty.
[21] See Additional Notes at the end of this chapter.

nized that those raised and educated in the Karaite system may be
innocent of the maliciousness of its founders' distortions. Though
aware that the Karaite scholars' structures may be sincere attempts
to understand the Torah, the Rambam did not gloss over, but
emphasized, the false foundation upon which those structures were
built. The Rambam's approach was to point out the insincere origin
of the Karaite movement, while trying to win over its adherents
through amiability and reason.

The only way to bring all sincere Jews back to the truth is to
teach it to them. Through exposure to historic Judaism, our people
will no longer tolerate twisted renditions, renditions offered by heirs
of sects long divorced from the religion of our Forefathers and
Prophets. They will come to realize that our leaders have to this day
preserved the Judaism of Moses and Sinai in all its essential form
and characteristics, that Jewish thought and law can be authentically
taught only by those who totally accept its Sinaitic origin, who totally accept the definitiveness of the Talmud,[22] and who are determined
not to pursue their personal preferences, noble or otherwise, in
determining the Will of G-d. With this educational process accomplished, we may look forward to greeting *Moshiach* as a people
banded under the last words of prophecy in our possession: "זכרו
תורת משה עבדי . . .!, Remember the Torah of Moses My servant . . .!"
(*Malachi* 3:22).

[22] See Additional Notes at the end of this chapter.

Additional Notes to Epilogue

4. Rashi's version (*Bava Bassra* 115b) differs slightly. Based upon *Ahvos
D'Rebbi Nosson*, Rashi writes that it was not Tsadok and Bysoos themselves who misunderstood the dictum of Antignos Ish Soho, but rather
their disciples. These took the adage to mean that one must refuse
reward for his good deeds. "Just as this teaching is ridiculous," they reasoned, "so must all the Sages' teachings be baseless." They therefore
denied all the teachings of the Sages.

Scholars differ over whether the Sadducees originally rejected the
entire Oral Law, or only the *gezayros and takkonnos* (and perhaps the
contemporary *drashos*), or just those laws which "got in their way"
politically.

11. In *Hilchos Shechita* 4:16, the Rambam specifies the rationale:

אלו הצדוקין והבייתוסין ותלמידיהן וכל הטועים אחריהן שאינן מאמינים בתורה שבעל פה שחיטתן אסורה. ואם שחטו בפנינו הרי זה מותרת. שאין איסור שחיטתן אלא שמא יקלקלו והם אינן מאמינין בתורת השחיטה, לפיכך אינן נאמנין לומר לא קלקלנו.

[Regarding] those Sadducees and Bysoosim and their students, and all those who err after them and do not believe in the *Oral Law*: the animals they slaughter are forbidden food. [However,] if they perform the slaughtering in front of our eyes, the meat is permitted. For the prohibition against their meat is only based on the fear that the slaughtering will be done in a faulty manner, since they do not believe in the rules of kosher slaughter. They are therefore not trusted to claim that they did a faultless kosher slaughter.

12. The Torah prohibits one from walking farther than 2,000 *ahmos* from his "station" (מקום) on Shabbos. However, one can redefine his "station" (in order to facilitate performing a *mitzva*). Since one's "station" is defined as any area previously designated for one's eating, one may, before the onset of Shabbos, change his permitted walking distance by safely placing food within 2,000 *ahmos* of his original "station," thereby creating a new one. This is the *eruv procedure*, the piece of food being the *eruv*, the vehicle which *combines* or extends the original walking area with the new.

21. Cf. the following *Responsa* by the Rambam (הוצאת פרייצן, ירושלים, תרצ"ד, עמוד 339):

אלה הקראים השוכנים פה . . . וזולתם, ראויים הם לחלקם מחלקי הכבוד, להתקרב אצלם במעשה יושר ולהתנהג עמהם במדת הענוה ובדרך האמת והשלום כל זמן שגם הם ינהגו עמנו בתמימות ויסירו מהם עקשות פה ולזות שפה מלדבר תועה על חכמי הרבנים שבדור, וכ"ש כשישמרו לשונם מלהתהלוצץ ומלהלעיג בדברי רבותינו ע"ה הקדושים, התנאים חכמי המשנה והתלמוד שבדבריהם והמנהגים הקבועים לנו מפיהם ומפי משה מפי הגבורה אנו הולכים. ובזאת יכוין לנו לכבדם וללכת לשאול בשלומם אפילו בבתיהם, ולמול את בניהם ואפילו בשבת, ולקבור מתיהם ולנחם אבליהם.

בודאי שאינם מצטרפים לא למנין, לקדיש, לתפילה, ולא לזמון ולא לשום דבר . . . דהם אינן משגחין בדברי רז"ל כלל כי אם מה שיראה להם מהכתובים . . . איכה נוכל להצטרף עמהם בדבר אשר הם [חז"ל] תקנו ואלו אינם מודים—ובודאי אסור הוא.

[Concerning t]hose Karaites who live here . . . : It is proper to treat them respectfully, to become close with them in honest dealings, and to conduct ourselves humbly with them in the way of truth and harmony, as long as they, too, behave nicely with us and remove from themselves slanderous speech against the wise rabbis of this generation; and certainly when they guard their tongues from ridiculing the words of our holy masters, the *Tannaim*, the Sages of the *Mishna* and Talmud, by whose words and established practices, which came from their lips and from Moses' lips and from G-d's lips, we conduct ourselves. With this [condition] it would be right for us to respect them, inquire of their welfare—even entering their houses, to circumcise their sons—even on Shabbos—and to bury their dead and comfort their mourners.

[However,] they definitely cannot [be used to] comprise part of a quorum for *Kaddish* or *Sh'moneh Essray*, nor for Grace after meals or for anything. . . . For they pay absolutely no attention to the words of the Sages, except for that which they see from Scripture. . . . How could we possibly unite with them [to form such quorums] for a matter which the Sages decreed, if they do not concede its validity?! It is certainly prohibited.

22. The principle that the *Gemora's* conclusions were final and that the Talmud, no less than the *Mishna*, was recognized as being completed by a specific time is made clear in our classical sources, of which we shall quote the following:

● שמואל ירחינאי . . . אמר . . . לדידי חזי לי ספרא דאדם הראשון וכתיב ביה:
"רבי ור' נתן סוף משנה, רב אשי ורבינא סוף הוראה" (בבא מציעא פ"ה:-פ"ו.).

Shmuel Yarchinai . . . said . . . the *Book of Adam* (see *Maharal MiPrague*) was shown to me, and in it was written: "Rebbi and Rebbi Nosson—the end of *Mishna*; Rav Ashi and Ravina—the end of *hora'a* (decision-making)" (Bava Metsia 85b-86a).

● ובתראי שחברו התלמוד הם רב אשי ורבינא וסיעתם, ובימיהם מחתם התלמוד (מבוא התלמוד לרבינו שמואל הנגיד).

The last ones to collate the Talmud were Rav Ashi and Ravina and their assemblage, in whose days the Talmud was sealed (*M'vo HaTalmud* by Rabbeynu Shmuel HaNaggid).

● וכשמתו כל החכמים ע"ה שאחרון מהם היה רבינא ורב אשי, והתלמוד כבר נגמר וכל אשר קם קם אחריו היתה תכלית כונתו וכל מאודו להבין דבריהם שכתבו בלבד ועליו אין להוסיף וממנו אין לגרוע (הקדמת הרמב"ם לפירושו למשניות).

When all the Sages passed away, peace be upon them, the last of whom were Ravina and Rav Ashi, and the Talmud had already been completed, the aim of everyone who arose after it, to which he devoted his full strength, was solely to understand their words. Upon it there is nothing to add and from it there is nothing to subtract (*Maimonides' Introduction to the Talmud*, Heb. p. 29, Eng. p. 177).

● . . . רבינא ורב אשי וחבריהם סוף גדולי חכמי ישראל המעתיקים תורה שבעל-פה
ואחר בית-דין של רב אשי שחיבר התלמוד וגמרו בימי בנו, נתפזרו ישראל בכל הארצות. . . . כל הדברים שבתלמוד הבבלי, חייבין כל ישראל ללכת בהם, וכופין כל עיר ועיר וכל מדינה ומדינה לנהוג בכל המנהגות שנהגו חכמי התלמוד ולגזור גזירותם וללכת בתקנותם, הואיל וכל אותם הדברים שבתלמוד הסכימו עליהם כל ישראל, ואותם החכמים . . . הם כל חכמי ישראל או רובם, והם ששמעו הקבלה בעיקרי התורה כולה דור אחר דור עד משה רבנו ע"ה (הקדמת הרמב"ם למשנה תורה).

Ravina and Rav Ashi and their colleagues constituted the consummation of the great Sages of Israel who transcribed the Oral Law. . . . And after the *Bes Din* of Rav Ashi, which collated the

Talmud and completed it in the days of his son, Israel was dispersed throughout all the lands. . . . All the words in the Babylonian Talmud, all Jewry is obligated to follow, and we compel every city and country to conduct itself in all the practices which the Sages of the Talmud established and to obey their *gezayros* and follow their *takkonnos*, because all the words of the Talmud were consented upon by all Israel . . . and those Sages . . . were the entirety of the Sages of Israel or the majority of them, and they are the ones who heard the *kabballa* about the basics of the entire Torah, generation after generation, [going back] until Moses our teacher, may he rest in peace. (*Introduction to Mishneh Torah*).

• איתוספא הוראה דרא בתר דרא עד רבינא ובתר רבינא איפסיקא כדחזא שמואל
ירחינאה בספריה דאדם הראשון דהוה כתוב ביה: „אשי ואבינא סוף הוראה... ובתר
הכי אע"ג דודאי הוראה לא הות, הוו סבוראי דמפרשי דמקרבי להוראה (אגרת רב
סעדיה גאון).

Hora'a [the promulgation of law for the Jewish nation] continued generation after generation until Ravina. After Ravina *hora'a* ceased, as had been foretold in the passage, from the *Book of Adam* seen by Shmuel Yarchinai, which stated: "[Rav] Ashi and [R]avina: End of *Hora'a*" . . . After this, even though there was no longer any *hora'a*, there were the *Saboraim* who were explainers, closely similar to [excercising] *hora'a* (*Iggeress Rav Sherira Gaon*).

The *Doros Harishonim* (see also *Exalted People* by Rabbi Avigdor Miller pp. 301-302 and *History of the Jewish People from Yavneh to Pumbedisa*, Mesorah/Hillel, pp. 207-215) explains that the generation of Sages who took part in Rav Ashi's assemblage but lived on after him (such as Ravina II, who outlived Rav Ashi by 48 years) were the last of those providing *hora'a*, decision-making. They continued to add to the Talmud's text a small number of rulings that had not yet been recorded and closed the Talmud in the year of Ravina II's death (500 CE). The following assembly, too, the first generation of *Saborai*, elucidators, added unreported opinions of Rav Ashi's assemblage and inserted some explanations of the text. The next three generations of *Saborai* (514-589 CE)—there were a total of four—added to the text only some literary improvements: brief words of clarification and the short quotations from the *mishna* to show what part of it the *Gemora* is analyzing. Though these insertions added no new *halachic* material, they formed a significant contribution. The latter device alone makes the Babylonian Talmud much easier than the Talmud *Yerushalmi* for commentators to understand. All the additions to Rav Ashi's Talmudic text are, however, quite few, equivalent in quantity to less than one third of a single *mesechta* of the Talmud. The *Rishonim* devoted themselves to correcting any deviances from the original text that crept in, basing themselves on reliable manuscripts or evidence from the Talmudic text itself.

ADDENDA

ADDENDUM I

Interaction of Drash and Extant Laws
(Referred to in Chapter One)

Bava Metsia 54b

אמר רבא, "גבי גזל כתיב, 'וחמישיתיו יוסף עליו', ותנן, 'נתן לו את הקרן ונשבע לו
על החומש—הרי זה מוסיף חומש על חומש (פי' חומש יותר על החומש שכפר) עד
שיתמעט הקרן (חומש שהוא מחוייב כבר וחוזר וכופרו קרוי קרן) פחות משוה
פרוטה.'

"גבי תרומה כתיב, 'איש כי יאכל קדש בשגגה ויסף חמישיתו עליו,' ותנן, 'האוכל
תרומה בשוגג—משלם קרן וחומש ... חומשא דחומשא.'

"ואילו גבי מעשר, לא מכתב כתיב, ולא מיתנא תנא, ולא איבעויי איבעיא לן
(פירש"י: דפשיטא לן דלא מוסיף, דלא אשכחן ביה רמז בקרא, כדאשכחן בתרומה
רמז פורתא ... :; 'ויסף חמישתו' ... משמע שתי תוספות: יוסיף וחוזר ויוסיף. אבל
'יסף'—חדא משמע).

"גבי הקדש כתיב, 'ואם המקדיש יגאל את ביתו ויסף חמישית כסף ערכך.' ותנן,
'הפודה את הקדשו—מוסיף חומש.' 'חומשא' תנן; 'חומשא דחומשא' לא תנן. מאי?
גבי תרומא כתיב, 'ויסף,' גבי קדש נמי הא כתיב, 'ויסף;' או דלמא גבי תרומה כתיב,
'ויסף,' אי שקלת ליה לוי"ו ד,ויסף' ושדית ליה על 'חמישיתו'—הוה ליה
'חמישיתיו.' "[אבל] גבי הקדש כתיב, 'ויסף חמישית;' אע"ג דכי שקלת ליה לוי"ו
ד,ויסף' ושדית ליה על 'חמישית,'—סוף סוף הוה ליה 'חמישיתו.' "

מאי הוי עלה? אמר רב טביומי משמיה דאביי [חברותא דרבא]: "אמר קרא, 'ויסף
חמישית כסף ערכך' (ויקרא ז:ט"ו)—מקיש חומשו לכסף ערכו; מה כסף ערכו—
מוסיף חומש, אף כסף חומשו—נמי מוסיף חומש."

Rava said: "Concerning thievery, when a thief returns the
stolen money, the Torah says, 'He shall add onto the money its
fifths.' Now, the *Mishna* says, 'If he swore that he had already
paid the victim the extra fifth [and then it turns out to be a false
oath], he must pay the victim, in addition to that extra fifth,
another fifth of *that.* And should he later falsely swear that he
had already paid *this* extra fifth, this procedure is repeated and
continues until a fraction of money remains which is less than a
p'ruta.' [We therefore learn the Torah's intent in writing, 'He
shall add onto the money its *fifths.*']

"Concerning *teruma*, the Torah states, 'If a man mistakenly eats
teruma, [which properly belongs to the *kohane*] he should

257

[reimburse the kohane its value] **plus** add onto it a fifth of its value].' And the Mishna says, 'Someone who mistakenly eats *teruma* should pay for it and add on a fifth of it . . . another fifth of that and still another fifth of that.' [In this verse, too, we can see an indication for the *halacha* recorded in the Mishna: Though only the singular form of 'fifth' is used, the verse still contains an extra word, 'plus.']

"Concerning *maaser [shayni]* food,* whose sanctity may be transferred onto coins, there is *no* indication in the Torah, no statement in any Mishna, and [indeed] there is no notion of any requirement for [the money to be worth] a fifth [more than the original value of the food].

"However, concerning *hekdesh* [property that one donated to the Temple] there is a problem: The Torah says, 'If someone who donated his house to the Temple fund decides to take the house back, he must pay its actual value [to the Temple fund] **plus a fifth** of that value.' And the Mishna [simply] says, 'The one who redeems his *hekdesh* adds a fifth.' The Mishna, too, only mentions 'a fifth' and does not specify additional fifths of that fifth in the event that one proceeds to re-donate the house and then again redeem it. But what does the Mishna mean? [Does it mean to negate the requirement of 'extra fifths' or not?]

"True, the word 'fifth' in the Torah appears only in the singular. But perhaps since the Torah uses the words '**plus** a fifth,' just as it did with *teruma*, *hekdesh* is meant to be treated as *teruma* and the accumulative 'fifths' *are* added?

"Or perhaps there was a special reason that the 'ו,' the word for 'plus' in the verse about *teruma*, indicated additional fifths: If it (the extra 'ו') would be transposed to the end of the word חמישיתו, its fifth,' it would come out sounding like the word, חמישיתיו, its fifths,' in the plural. Perhaps *that* is why the Oral Law reported in the Mishna required extra 'fifths'—not because of the extra 'ו,' per sé. If so, *hekdesh* would *not* bear the requirement of extra 'fifths.' For in the verse about *hekdesh*, though the word ו, plus,' is there (ויסף), it might *not* indicate that we add additional 'fifths' to the first one. For there the word for 'fifth' is spelled חמישית.' Even transposing the extra 'ו' from 'ויסף'

---

* On the first, second, fourth and fifth years of a six-year cycle, one was obligated to travel to Jerusalem with a tenth of his remaining produce (remaining, that is, after he separated from it *teruma* and *maaser rishon*—donations to the *Leviim* and *Kohanim*) and eat the produce there. There was an option of convenience to transfer the sanctity of the food onto coins and to buy the equivalent amount of food in Jerusalem (*D'varim* 14:22).

would not result in a word indicating multiple 'fifths.' [It would merely change it from the meaning of 'a fifth' to 'its fifth.']"

The Talmud goes on to solve the *halachic* question by recourse to the *gezeyra shavva* rule of interpretation:

So what is the solution? Rav Tavyumi said in the name of Abbaye (Rava's colleague): "The verse about *hekdesh* says, 'ויסף חמישית כסף ערכך, Add on a fifth to your **value**,' which creates a *gezeyra shavva* to the phrase 'כסף ערכו' stated regarding *teruma*. On this basis, *hekdesh*, like *teruma*, *should* involve accumulative 'fifths.'"

Incidentally, all the participants in this discussion lived more than two centuries after the destruction of the Second Temple when the rules of *hekdesh* could not be practiced. (Perhaps as long as the Temple had been standing the solution to this problem had been clear.) Still, the issue is directly relevant to the future redemption, may it come soon.

ADDENDUM II

Machlokess Based upon Drash
(Referred to in Chapter One)

In *Temura* 6b there is a clear example of a *machlokess* based upon *darshonning p'sukim* and specifically not based upon *s'vara*. The passage appears at the end of a discussion (*Temura* 4b-6b) concerning a fundamental issue: If one commits a *halachic* procedure in a way that is forbidden, does the procedure nevertheless produce its normal *halachic* results? This is a dispute between Rava and Abbaye. But every case brought to support the opinion of either Abbaye or Rava is demonstrated to have exceptional properties that remove it from the realm of this issue. The *Gemora* thereupon asks:

והשתא דמשנינן כל הני שינויי (דאיכא דמהני ואיכא דלא מהני ובכולהו מודו אביי ורבא)—במאי פליגי?—בריבית קצוצה קמיפלגי, ובר"א. דאר"א, "רבית קצוצה יוצאה בדיינין, אבק רבית אינה יוצאה בדיינין." ור' יוחנן אמר: "אפילו רבית קצוצה אינה יוצאה בדיינין." (אביי דאמר מהני—כר' יוחנן, דס"ל דאינה יוצאה בדיינין; ורבא—כר"א, דס"ל דלא תעשה מהני. דהכא ליכא קרא לא הכי ולא הכי.)

And now that exceptions were made in all these cases, so that in some both Rava and Abbaye agree that transgressing a prohibition thwarted normal *halachic* results and in some it did not—in which case do they argue? [The answer is:] in the same case that [the *Tannaim*] Rebbi Elazar and Rebbi Yoḥonon argue: a case wherein someone pays interest on a loan. Since the demanding and paying of interest is forbidden, does the court extract the money from the lender and return it to the borrower, or does the transaction remain in effect?

The *Gemora* continues:

א"ל: "התם בסברא פליגי?! התם בקרא פליגי! דא"ר יצחק: ,מ"ט דרבי יוחנן—אמר קרא כו',". . .מ"ט דר"א—דא"ק כו'.

ואלא במאי קמפלגי אביי ורבא—בשינוי קונה (בר מהיכא דכתיבי קרא).

But this dispute does not involve the *s'vara* (in question: a general principle about transgressing prohibitions); it is a dispute about this particular issue, based upon interpreting Scriptural verses! For Rebbi Yitzchak said, "What is Rebbi

Yoḥonon's reason for his opinion?—The verse in *Y'chezkiel*
18:13.* . . . What is Rebbi Elazar's reason for his opinion?—The
verse in *Vayikra* 25:36.

Based on this objection, the *Gemora* concludes that it is elsewhere that
Rava and Abbaye's conflicting principles produce a difference in practical
halacha. Clearly the *Gemora* considered the *drashic* interpretation of the
verses cited to be the sole criterion in this *machlokos,* independent of and
contradistinctive to any issues of *s'vara,* analysis based upon precedents
and non-*drashic halachic* principles.

---

* Other verses and attendant methods of *drash* are suggested by Rav Acha bar Adda and
Rava.

ADDENDUM III

"The First Mishna and the Later Mishna"
(Referred to in Chapter Six)

Cases described as those involving a "first *mishna*" and a "second *mishna*" that concern biblical law do not always refer to *halachos* that were originally decided (in the "first *mishna*") by a Great Sanhedrin. Thus, *Pesachim* 8:1 states,

מי שחציו עבד וחציו בן חורין לא יאכל משל רבו

A half-freed slave should not eat from his master's *Pesach* lamb,

which implies that he is, however, entitled to his own. The *Gemora* (*Pesachim* 88a) cites a *braissa* that states otherwise:

והא תניא לא יאכל משלו ולא משל רבו

[A half freed slave] may nor eat either his master's *Pesach* lamb nor his own.

The *Gemora* explains:

כאן כמשנה ראשונה, כאן כמשנה אחרונה, דתנן מי שחציו עבד וחציו בן חורין עובד את רבו יום אחד ואת עצמו יום אחד—דברי בית הלל.

בית שמאי אומרים תקנתם את רבו ואת עצמו לא תקנתם. לישא שפחה אינו יכול, שכבר חציו בן חורין. לישא בת חורין אינו יכול שעדיין חציו עבד. יבטל? והלא לא נברא העולם אלא לפריה ורביה, שנאמר, "לא בן חורין". . . .

וחזרו בית הילל להורות כבית שמאי.

[The *braissa* was reporting the original law] as [stated in] the First *Mishna*. [Our *mishna* reports the law] as [stated in] the Later Mishna. For another *mishna* states:

" 'A half-free slave should work for his master one day and for himself the next'—the words of *Bes Hillel*.

"*Bes Shammai* said: 'You have rectified matters for the master but not for the slave! He cannot marry a maidservant, since you have left him half free; he cannot marry a free woman, since you have left him half slave! What is he to do, remain single? But the

262

world was created for nothing but procreation, as it says *He did not create it empty; for inhabitation He created it* (Isaiah 45:18). Rather, for the good of the world, we must force the master to free the slave totally.'

"And *Bes Hillel* retracted its opinion in favor of *Bes Shammai's*," (and since the slave is bound to be free, he is presently entitled to his own *Pesach* lamb [as stated in the *mishna* and unlike the *braissa*]—*Rashi*).

Here, a "Later Mishna" was able to change the law taught a by a "First Mishna," because the "First Mishna" law was stated by *Bes Hillel* alone, in a dispute with *Bes Shammai*. *Bes Hillel*, without the participation of *Bes Shammai*, lacked the authority of a *Great Sanhedrin*: A *Great Sanhedrin* must represent all authoritative opinions for its rulings to be binding. As long as *Bes Shammai* and *Bes Hillel* could not sit together,* they were merely two separate courts—not *Great Sanhedrins*. There is no connection to the Rambam's scenario.

---

* Because of a Roman ban. See chapter entitled "The Control and Proliferation of *Machlokess*."

ADDENDUM IV

Missing Part of the Lecture
(Related to Chapter Seven)

The different sides of a dispute are due to different results of analysis, not error. Thus, an authority's opinion may seem to be erroneous, stemming from a lack of crucial information, but it really may not have been so. This is not to deny that Sages could have missed lectures or at least parts of them—

א"ר כהנא הוה יתיבנא בשלהי פירקין דרב (פרש"י כשסיים לדרוש באתי ולא שמעתי ולא ידענא מאי קאמר. בתר דקם רב, אמרי להו, מאי „קרי, קרי" דקאמר רב?

Rav Kahana said, "I was sitting in at the tail-end of the lecture and I heard Rav constantly refer to *melons*, and I didn't know what case he was describing. After Rav left, I asked those present, 'What is this case of *melons* that Rav was constantly referring to?'" (*Bava Metsia* 64a).

—but their disputes may still be based purely on analysis, the absence from the lecture being irrelevant, as in the following case:

משנה: מצודות חיה ועוף ודגים [ספק] שעשאן מערב יו"ט . . . [רבן גמליאל מתיר].

גמ': מותרין למאי? רב אמר מותרין לקבל. ולוי אמר מותרין [אפי'] באכילה.

אמר רב: לעולם אל ימנע אדם עצמו מבית המדרש אפילו שעה אחת. דאנא ולוי הוינן קמיה דרבי כי אמרה להא שמעתתא. באורתא אמר מותרין [דגים ממצודות שעשאן מערב יו"ט] [אפי'] באכילה. בצפרא אמר מותרין (רק) לקבל. אנא דהואי בי מדרשא—הדרי בי. לוי דלא הוה בי מדרשא—לא הדר ביה.

Mishna (*Beytsa* 3:2): [Rabban Gamliel permitted to us] animals, birds, and fish that were caught in traps which were set before *Yom Tov* began [though we are unsure whether they were caught before *Yom Tov* began].

Gemora (*Beytsa* 24b): Permitted to us for what? Rav said, permitted only for handling. Levy said, permitted even for eating.

Rav said: "A man must never keep himself from the *Bes Medrash* even for one hour. For Levy and I were both in front of Rebbi [Yehuda HaNassi] when he spoke on this subject. In the evening he said that they are permitted even to be eaten. In the morning he said that they are permitted only to be handled [but not to be eaten]. Since I was in the *Bes Medrash* [also in the morning], I retracted. But Levy, who was not there, did not retract."

Superficially it may seem that Levy's opinion was due simply to failure to possess the most current information and that he could be expected to retract upon being updated. But here again we are really dealing with the correct *analysis* of a statement. If the whole issue were the correct quoting of the *words* of *Rebbi*, then Levy certainly would have accepted Rav's report of Rebbi's retraction and there never would have been any disagreement. However, the issue at hand was not what *Rebbi's* opinion was, but what Rebbi's teacher, Rabban Gamliel, held.

Examining the text closely we see that in his lecture, Rebbi had been attempting to pinpoint Rabban Gamliel's stand on an issue. In the evening he concluded with one opinion and the next morning with another. From the very fact that Rebbi changed his mind as to what Rabban Gamliel meant by "מותר, permitted," we can see that he did not have the information through *kabballa*, a transmitted teaching, and he had to resort to analysis. Naturally, then, the fact that Rebbi concluded one way did not obligate Levy to agree.[1]

The issue between Rav and Levy was not one of identifying the opinion of Rebbi, but of identifying the opinion of Rabban Gamliel.[2] That is why, as we see further on in the passage, the *Gemora* itself did not consider the issue settled, even after Rav's disclosure of Rebbi's new opinion. Instead, the *Gemora* goes on to test which position conforms best with the authoritative sources. This is not a matter of a Sage declaring, "כך קבלתי, So have I received," the pronouncement which terminates a dispute.[3]

---

[1] Indeed, Levy is found to disagree with Rebbi's analyses on a number of issues, leading to the remark, "כמדומה לי שאין לו מוח בקדקדו, It seems to me as if he has no brains in his skull." (עי' יבמות ט., ומנחות פ:).

[2] What, then, is the criticism that Rav insinuated against Levy for being absent in the morning? After all, even *had* Levy been in the *Bes Medrash* when Rebbi changed his mind, he would not have been obligated to accept the new understanding. We can only conjecture. Perhaps Rav was convinced that if Levy had been in the *Bes Medrash* and heard Rebbi's impressive proofs for his second opinion and the discussions among the participants in the lecture, Levy, too, would have abandoned his original opinion.

[3] "Once a Sage reports, 'I have this explanation as a *kabballa* originating with Moses,' then there is no more to talk about. . . . Thus, they say, 'If what you are telling me is a *halacha* [that G-d told to Moses], then we will have to accept it. But if it is based upon analysis, we can refute it' (*Yevomos* 8:3)"—Maimonides' *Introduction to the Talmud*, p. 88.

Sources and Authorities Cited

The following are short biographical sketches of the authorities quoted in this work and descriptions of the works cited. Each of the authorities was a giant of his time and a master of many facets of the Torah. The facts presented here have been culled from several works: Rabbi Hirsch Goldwurm's *The Rishonim*, published by Artscroll/Mesorah, Rabbi Aryeh Kaplan zt"l's *The Living Torah*, and Rabbi Zecharia Fendel's *Anvil of Sinai*.

Ayn Yaakov: A collection of and commentary on all the passages of the Talmud that do not have direct bearing on *halacha*, by Rabbeynu Yaakov ben Sh'lomo Ibn Habib (1433-1516) of Portugal and Salonica, a *posek* and head of the largest yeshiva in Spain.

Chazon Ish: See **Karelitz, Rabbi Avraham Yeshaya.**

Doros Harishonim: See **Rabinowitz, Rav Yitschak Isaac Halevy.**

Drashos HaRan: See **Ran**

Epstein, Rav Yechiel Michel Halevy (1929-1908): Author of *Aruch HaShulchan*, a multi-volume elaboration on the entire *Shulchan Aruch* plus laws from the Rambam that have to do with Messianic times.

Gershon, Rabbeynu (960-1028): Talmudic commentator and world leader.

Hagahos Maimonis, "Glosses on Maimonides": A commentary on the Rambam's *Mishneh Torah* which traces the Rambam's rulings to their talmudic sources, noting when they are based upon one opinion of a *machlokes*. It was written by Rav Mayir HaKohane of Rottenberg (1237-1299).

Hai Gaon, Rav (939-1038): Son of Rav Sherira Gaon, he was head of the yeshiva of Pumbedissa, Babylonia, and the most prominent figure of his time.

Hakdama L'Payrush Hamishnayos: The Rambam's introduction to his Mishna commentary. Translated from the Arabic into Hebrew by the Rambam's contemporary, Rav Yehuda AlHarizi (1170-1233) and in 1964 by Kapach. Two translations into English appeared in 1975, one by Dr. Fred Rosner (Feldheim) and the other by Zvi Lampel (Judaica Press).

Halevy Rabinowitz, Rav Yitschak Isaac: See **Rabinowitz.**

Hanaggid, Rabbeynu Shmuel (993-1055 C.E.) of Spain: Founder of a *kollel*, he was a Talmudist and *posek*.

Hannanel ben Huskiel, Rabbeynu (circa 1056): North African talmudic commentator, rebbi of the Rif.

Havos Ya'ir, Shaalos U'Tshuvos: Responsa by Rav Ya'ir Chaim (ben Moshe Shamshon Bacharach) of Germany (1638-1702).

266

Josephus (38-100 C.E.): Jewish historian who witnessed the events of the Destruction of the Second Temple (70 C.E.).

Kalir, Rav Eliezer: Author of a large part of our prayerbook, he is identified as either the son of Rebbi Shimmon bar Yoḥai (*Tosefos on Ḥaggigga* 13a ד"ה ורגלי), Rebbi Elazar ben Aruch (*Teshuvos Rashba* 449), or Rav Eliezer of Tiberius, circa 600 C.E.

Kapach or **Kapich:** A contemporary Yemenite scholar (b. 1917) who retranslated the Rambam's Arabic works into Hebrew, including the *Hakdama l'Payrush Hamishnayos*, first published in Jerusalem, 1964 (*Mosaad Harav Kook*).

Karelitz, Rabbi Avraham Yeshaya: (1878-1953), known by the name of his collection of novellae on Talmud and *halacha* (*Chazon Ish*), he was the eminent leader of world Jewry in post-holocaust Israel.

Karo, Rabbeynu Yosef (1488-1575): Author of the *Kessef Mishna* and *Shulchan Aruch*. Originally of Spain but exiled with the Jews in 1492 to Portugal, then lived in Turkey and finally Israel.

Kessef Mishna: A commentary by Rav Yosef Karo (see under Karo) on the Rambam's *Mishneh Torah*, tracing talmudic sources of the Rambam's decisions.

Lehem Mishneh: A commentary on the Rambam's *Mishneh Torah* by Rabbeynu Avraham ben Moshe D'Buton (1545-1588) of Solnika.

Maharal of Prague: Moreynu HaRav Yehuda ben Betzallel Loew (1525-1609). Foremost Talmudist and thinker of his time.

Maimonides: See **Rambam.**

Malbim: Mayir Leib ben Yechiel Michel Weiser (1809-1879). Chief Rabbi of Rumania, fighter of *Maskillim*, grammarian, and author of Biblical commentaries.

Meharsha: Moreynu HoRav Shmuel (Eliezer ben Yehuda Halevy) Aidels. Poland (1555-1631). Commentator on Talmud, Rashi and Tosefos and author of *Mizrachi*, on Rashi's commentary to the Chumash.

Messillas Yesharim: A classical guide to spiritual growth written by Rav Moshe Chaim Lutzatto (1707-1746), who is known by the acronym *Ramchal*.

Midrash Rabba: A *tannaitic* commentary on Torah compiled in early Gaonic period. It is also referred to by each of the books of the Torah it comments upon: *B'rayshis Rabba, Sh'mos Rabba,* etc.

Mishneh L'Melech: A commentary on the Rambam's *Mishneh Torah*, edited from writings of Rav Yehuda Rosanes (1658-1727), by Rav Yaakov Culi (1689-1732), Constantinople leader of world Jewry.

Ohr HaḤayyim: A commentary on the Chumash by Rav Chaim ben Moshe Ibn Attar (1696-1743) of Morocco and Israel.

Ohr Somayach: A commentary on the Rambam's *Mishneh Torah* by Rav May'ir Simcha HaKohane of Dvinsk (1843-1926).

Ohr Yisroel: A work containing the *mussar* teachings of Rav Yisroel (Livkin) Salanter (1810-1883) culled by Rav Yitzchak Blazer

(1836-1907), Vilna, 5450/Bnei Brak 5729. Rav Yisroel Salanter was the founder of the *Mussar* Movement and Rav Blazer, Rav of Petersburg and one of his closest disciples, was the head of the Kovno Kollel, forerunner of the *mussar*-type Yeshivos of Lithuania.

Onkelos: A convert to Judasim, he was a greatly respected Sage in the time of Rabban Gamliel the Elder, circa 3780 (*Tosefta* to *Shabbos* 8:9). He is famous for his translation of the *Chumash* into Aramaic.

Pachad Yitzchak: Writings of Rav Yitzchak Hutner (1904-1980), *Rosh Yeshiva* of Mesivta Rabbi Chaim Berlin and founder of Kollel Gur Aryeh.

Pinto: (1556-1648) Damascus and Israel. Talmudist and Kabballist. Previously printed under the title *Meor Aynayim*, his commentary on the Jerusalem Talmud has been printed in the 1885 Vilna edition under the acronym רי"ף, but he must not be confused with the *Ryf* of the Gaonic era.

Piskay HaRyd: By Rabbeynu Yeshaya Datroni HaZaken, known as the *Tosefos HaRyd*, of Terrani, Italy, a 13th century (1180-1260) Tosafist and Posek. The *Piskay HaRyd* cited in our work is a commentary on *Brachos* and *Shabbos* on the Talmud, published in 1964 by *Yad Harav Herzog*, Jerusalem.

Raavad I: Rabbeynu Avraham ben David Ibn Daud Halevy (1110-1180) of Spain, author of the historical work, *Sefer Hakabballa*. (He should not be confused with his French contemporary *Raavad* III, the Rambam's admiring critic.)

Rabinowitz, Rav Yitschak Isaac Halevy: 19th century Talmud scholar and historian. Author of *Doros Harishonim*, he combatted misrepresentations of history by the *Maskillim*.

Rambam: Acronym for Rabbeynu Moshe ben Maimon, known in English as Maimonides (1135-1204), of Egypt and Syria. He is among Judaism's leading authorities and thinkers in all fields, one of the greatest minds of his time, and physician to Sultan Saladin.

Ramban: Acronym for Rabbeynu Moshe ben Nachman (1194-1270) of Spain (Nachmanides in English). He was a prolific author, leader of world Jewry, master of *Tanach*, Talmud, Halacha, philosophy, *Kabballa*, and medicine. His *Milchemmess Hashem* defended the *halachic* decisions of the Rif against the criticisms of Rabbeynu Zerachia's *Meor*.

Ran: Rabbeynu Nissim ben Reuvain Gerodni (1308-1376), author of *Hiddushay HaRan*, a talmudic commentary, and *Drashos Haran*, lectures on fundamentals of Judaism. He is one of the most important *Rishonim* of Spain. Not to be confused with Rabbeynu Nissim Gaon of 11th century Kairwan.

Rashbam: Rabbeynu Shmuel ben May'ir (1080-1174). Grandson of Rashi, older brother of Rabbeynu Tahm. Commentator on Torah and Talmud.

Rash: Rabbeynu Shimshon ben Avraham of Sens (d. c. 1220). Brother-in-law of Rabbeynu Tahm, he wrote a commentary on part of the Mishna.

Rashi: Rabbeynu Shlomo ben Yitzchak Yarchi (1040-1105) of France. "Father of Commentators," famous for his Chumash and Talmud commentaries, he wrote commentaries on every Jewish classic. He was also a *posek* and wrote responsa.

Ridvaz: Commentary on Jerusalem Talmud by Rav Yaakov David (ben Zev) Willowsky, 20th century scholar (1845-1914) of Vilna. Came to Chicago in 1901, left for Israel in 1905.

Rif or **Ryf:** Acronym for Rabbeynu Yitzchak ben Yaakov Al-Fasi (1013-1103). Ending the Gaonic period, he compiled all *halachic* passages of the Talmud, noting the decisions to be followed. Not to be confused with the 17th century Pinto, commentator on the Jerusalem Talmud.

Rishon (Plural: *Rishonim*) Any authority of the Middle Ages (11th-15th centuries—4800-5200) between the age of the Gaonim (7th-11th centuries—4400-4800) and the Acharonim 16th century (4800) to the present.

Ritva: Rabbeynu Yom Tov ben Avraham Ishbilli (1248-1330). Commentator on Talmud and *Ayn Yaakov*, leader of all Spanish Jewry.

Rosh: Rabbeynu Asher ben Yechiel (1250-1327) of Germany and Spain. He was a posek, and commentator on Chumash and Talmud.

Ryf or **Rif:** See **Rif**

Rabbeynu Saadia Gaon: (882-942 C.E.) Greatest scholar of the Gaonic period (7th-11th centuries—4400-4800) and world leader.

Tosefos: Work compiled by the *Tosafists (Appenders)*, members of the yeshiva academies of France and Germany, 1100-1300. The work was begun by Rashi's students and grandsons, most notably Rabbeynu Tam (1100-1171).

Tosefos Rishon L'tzion: A supercommentary on the commentary *Tosefos Yom Tov*.

Tosefos Yeshonim: The first commentary to cover most of the Talmud, by Rabbeynu Betzallel Ashkenazi, disciple of the Ridvaz and rebbi of the Ari. The work is also called *Tosafos Hitzonios (Outside Tosefos)* because it is not the more famous *Tosefos Shantz*.

Tosefos Yom Tov: A commentary on the Mishna by Rav Yom Tov Lipman (ben Nosson Halevy) Heller (1579-1654), of Prague and Poland, student of Maharal of Prague.

Yerushalmi or **Talmud Yerushalmi:** The *Jerusalem Talmud*, compiled in the second century CE—a century before the (Babylonian) Talmud—by Rebbi Yohonon (ben Naphchah) and his disciples. The Babylonian Talmud is more authoritative in areas of conflict.

Zerachia Halevy, Rav of Maine (4885-4946): Young author of *Sefer HaMaor*, challenging the Rif's *halachic* decisions (later to be defended by the Ramban in his *Milchemmesss Hashem*), disciple of Moshe HaDarshon. Also a Liturgist.

Zohar: The classic *Kabballa* text from the school of Rebbi Shimmon (Bar Yochai, c. 120 C.E.).

Index